THE *SENSUS PLENIOR* OF SACRED SCRIPTURE

PONTIFICAL THEOLOGICAL FACULTY OF ST. MARY'S UNIVERSITY

THE *SENSUS PLENIOR* OF SACRED SCRIPTURE

A DISSERTATION

SUBMITTED TO THE FACULTY OF ST. MARY'S UNIVERSITY, BALTIMORE, MARYLAND, IN PARTIAL FULFILLMENT OF THE REQUIREMENTS FOR THE DEGREE OF DOCTOR OF SACRED THEOLOGY

BY

RAYMOND EDWARD BROWN, S. S., M. A., S. T. L.

WIPF & STOCK · Eugene, Oregon

Nihil Obstat:

EDUARDUS A. CERNY, S. S., S. T. D.

Censor Librorum

Imprimatur:

✠ FRANCISCUS P. KEOUGH, D. D.,

Archiepiscopus Baltimorensis

Nov. 24, 1954

The *nihil obstat* and *imprimatur* are official declarations that a book or pamphlet is free of doctrinal and moral error. No implication is contained therein that those who granted the *nihil obstat* and *imprimatur* agree with the opinions expressed.

Wipf and Stock Publishers
199 W 8th Ave, Suite 3
Eugene, OR 97401

The Sensus Plenior of Sacred Scripture
By Brown, Raymond E.

ISBN 13: 978-1-60608-070-2
Publication date 6/30/2008
Previously published by St. Mary's University, 1955

To

THE PRIESTS

WHO WERE MY TEACHERS

IN THE SEMINARY

PREFACE

The writer wishes to take this occasion to express his gratitude to all those who have made this dissertation possible. He is especially grateful to the Very Reverend Lloyd P. McDonald, S. S., Provincial of the Sulpicians in the United States, for having allowed him to complete his studies and to publish this work. Also he is thankful to the Very Reverend James A. Laubacher, S. S., Rector of St. Mary's Seminary, for having accepted him as a graduate student and for many personal kindnesses.

This dissertation profited greatly by the wise direction of the Reverend William F. Hill, S. S., who encouraged the writer's initial investigations, and of the Reverend Edward A. Cerny, S. S., under whose guidance the doctoral dissertation was written.

And, of course, he must not close without thanking those who offered advice and encouragement, those who made books available, and the very kind seminarians who aided in typing and proof-reading.

R. E. B.

TABLE OF CONTENTS

INTRODUCTION

Just some thirty years ago, in the late 1920's, Fr. Andrés Fernández, S. J., in an article on Hermeneutics, listed among the senses of Scripture a new classification called the *sensus plenior.* For nearly fifty years previously there had been evidence that scholars were not satisfied with the usual division of scriptural senses into literal (in a very narrow sense) and typical. Men like Cornely, Lagrange, Pesch, and Prat had mentioned in passing a deeper meaning of the Scriptures—called variously *accuratiorem, supralittéral, altiorem*—which they felt was involved in the exegesis of the past and the present. Fernández summed up their ideas and gave this " deeper meaning " a place in the hermeneutical classification under the title of *sensus plenior.*

Even a cursory glance at the bibliography at the end of this work will show that his idea has aroused interest, both favorable and adverse, all over the Catholic world. Students of N. T. and patristic exegesis have found the new classification useful in categorizing certain biblical interpretations in their field. Others have approached the *sensus plenior* by way of the theological use of Scripture, particularly with regard to newly defined doctrines. And finally, some of the liturgists, ever anxious that the Church's interpretation of Scripture as expressed in the liturgy be not disregarded, have hailed in pleasant surprise this attempt to justify scientifically a more profound sense of the Bible. On the other hand, some scholars, jealously guarding the impressive advance in Scripture studies effected by rendering due attention to the literal sense, have felt that the new classification was a retrogression toward the exaggerated spiritualizing of the past. To add fuel to the fire, an appalling confusion of terminology has rendered no small part of the discussion nearly unintelligible. As a result, around the theory of the *sensus plenior* has raged one of the sharpest and most complicated disputes of present-day Scripture and theology.

The purpose of the present work is an objective study of the problem as far as possible *in its totality.* It is our prime contention that failure to set the question in its proper surroundings renders an adequate solution impossible. Since the very concept of a *sensus plenior* as a classification involves the other senses of Scripture, we shall devote a preliminary chapter to the literal, typical, consequent, and accommodated senses as employed by *modern* authors (this is particularly important because older works, not having the problem in mind, offer an insufficient basis for discussion).

Then a second chapter will be devoted to the use of Scripture in its various senses down through the ages. Those who defend the fuller sense maintain that it is only a new *classification* of a sense that has *always* been recognized and employed. To pass any judgment on this assertion, as well as to understand the historical antecedents of the movement, this chapter is most necessary.

As a third chapter we shall present in full the problems which have given rise to the renewed interest in Hermeneutics, and the various solutions offered by Scripture scholars. To one of these solutions, the *sensus plenior,* a fourth and principal chapter will be dedicated. A serious effort will be made to *clearly define* this sense, to explain its divisions and its precise relations to the other senses of Scripture, and to discuss the very serious objections raised against it. Since terminology has been such a difficulty in the whole question, we have paid special attention to establishing exact working definitions of all the senses involved, so that our thought might at least be clear. The reader is our judge; may he be kind toward our inevitable failings.

R. E. B.

Chapter One

THE SENSES OF SCRIPTURE

It seems well to begin the study of the *sensus plenior* by a very important introductory step: a brief review of the classification of the senses of Scripture generally presented in textbooks. This review does not pretend to be complete; rather it can dwell only on the elements necessary for an understanding of the *sensus plenior,* and must presuppose the reader to be familiar with the general study of Noematics.*[1] Such a review should prove useful because the theory of the *sensus plenior* has important ramifications in the whole field of Noematics, and consequently creates a need for greater precision in the usual textbook classification of Scripture senses.

I. THE LITERAL SENSE

The term "literal" is commonly employed today to denote the most basic sense of Scripture. Formerly the Greeks spoke of the "sense of the words themselves"—katà rētón [2]—and down through

* In the footnotes the standard abbreviations will be used for titles of theological and scriptural magazines, but full titles are given in the bibliography. The abbreviations O. T. and N. T. (Old and New Testaments) are used throughout. In successive references to the same work, we use (a) *op. cit.,* or *art. cit.* if we have quoted from *only* one work of the author in question, (b) an abbreviation of the title if we have quoted from more than one work. The reader will thus have no difficulty in identifying the work in the bibliography. Papal and Biblical Commission pronouncements are given in English wherever possible from the translation in *Rome and the Study of Scripture* (St. Meinrad: Grail, 1946, 4th ed.).

[1] *Hermeneutics* is the most general name for the science which gives rules for interpreting the Scriptures. It may be subdivided into:

(a) Noematics—deals with the various senses of Scripture.

(b) Heuristics—explains how to discover the sense of a passage.

(c) Prophoristics—gives the rules for expounding the sense to others.

Our subject lies in the realm of Noematics.

[2] Franciscus X. Patrizi, S. J., *Institutio de Interpretatione Bibliorum* (2nd ed., Rome: 1876), p. 1.

the ages various more descriptive terms have been adopted: carnal, historical, philological, etc.[3] Although we are fortunate today in having more uniformity in the terminology of this sense, there still remains a certain amount of confusion about its definition. The basic point of division seems to be whether it is sufficient to define the literal sense as the one intended by the divine Author, or must the intention of the human author also be considered as integral to the definition.

One current of thought tends to explain the literal sense from the viewpoint of what God intended without including in its definition the human author's awareness. This view seems to stem from the scholastics; [4] for instance, it is quite similar to St. Thomas' position.[5] Cornely proposes the following definition: The literal sense is "that truth which the words, due to the intention of the Holy Spirit, immediately express." [6] Fernández approaches this, for in his most recent article he holds that the question of the human author's cognition does not enter into the definition of the literal sense.[7]

[3] These are just a few of the many, many terms used by the various authors. For examples, see:

Angelo Penna, *Principi e Carattere dell' Esegesi di S. Gerolamo* (Rome: P. B.I., 1950), pp. 59-60.

Alexander Kerrigan, O. F. M., *St. Cyril of Alexandria, Interpreter of the Old Testament* (Rome: P. B.I., 1952), pp. 35-36.

[4] Penna, *Principi*, pp. 154-155. Patrizi, *op. cit.*, p. 14.

Also A. M. Dubarle, O. P., "Le Sens Spirituel de l'Écriture," *Rev. SR*, 31 (1947), p. 43.

[5] *Summa Theologica*, I, 1, a. 10, "Quia vero sensus litteralis est quem auctor intendit, auctor autem Sacrae Scripturae Deus est . . ."

Andréa Fernández, S. J., "Sentido plenior, literal, típico, espiritual," *Bb.*, 34 (1953), p. 308, n. 1: "Sto. Tomás parece decir que el sentido de las palabras conocido y querido por solo Dios es verdadero sentido literal escriturístico."

[6] Rudolphus Cornely, S. J., Introductio Generalis, Vol. I of the *Cursus Sacrae Scripturae* (Paris: Lethielleux, 1885), p. 518: "Sensum Scripturae litteralem diximus illam esse veritatem, quam eius verba immediate ex intentione Spiritus Sancti manifestant."

[7] Fernández' thought seems to have undergone a certain development. In the 6th ed. of the *Institutiones Biblicae* (Rome: P. B. I., 1951), p. 369, he defines the literal sense thus: "Sensus vocibus expressus, quem auctor, *tam* primarius *quam secundarius*, et hic sive distincte sive confuse, cognovit

The other outlook, which is more popular today, defines the literal sense as that which both God and *the human author* intended jointly.[8] The Fathers, while neither always clear nor always in agreement, seem to favor such a limitation. (In fact they often go to the opposite extreme and limit the literal sense to something even less than the human author fully intended, since, as we shall

et intendit." (Italics ours.) Thus he requires that the secondary author have understood and intended the sense.

Yet, in footnote 2, he mentions that St. Thomas held a "sensum *litteralem* non principalem qui non est secundum intentionem auctoris (secundarii)."

Further, in "Sentido plenior," pp. 307-308, he seems to stress that the literal sense is any immediate sense of the text intended by God, *whether or not* it was known by the human author. "En la fórmula propuesta no queda prejuzgada la cuestión si 'el autor (secundario) no ha conocido sino una parte del sentido literal,' o si éste 'se restringe precisamente al objeto que tiene claramente en vista el autor' (Gribomont). Este problema cae fuera de la definición; y ha de ser tratado aparte."

Finally, he repeats the same idea in "Nota referente a los sentidos de la S. Escritura," *Bb.*, 35 (1954), p. 79: "Para soslayarlo debiera formularse la definición en términos mas generales, incluyendo únicamente los elementos que van encerrados en la misma denominación 'sentido *literal*': estar en la letra en las palabras, y ser inspirado; v. gr. 'Sensus litteralis est id quod verba immediate significant' (Nicolau), sin especificar *si es o no conocido* por el hagiógrafo." (Italics ours.)

Thus his final opinion, if we understand correctly, is that the human author's cognition of the literal sense is not a requisite of the definition. However, as he says in the last reference, he doubts if God would put into the text a sense entirely unknown by the human author. (Also *Institutiones*, p. 369.)

[8] For example, H. Simon and J. Prado, C. Ss. R., *Praelectiones Biblicae*, (Turin: Marietti, 1949), 6th ed., Vol. I, "Propaedeutica," p. 239.

Dubarle, *art. cit.*, p. 43. The literal sense "est celui voulu par l'auteur humain d'un livre inspiré . . ."

R. C. Fuller, "The Interpretation of Holy Scripture," *A Catholic Commentary on Holy Scripture* (London: Nelson, 1953), 39c: "The literal sense of Scripture is that which arises directly from the text and is intended by the inspired writer."

H. Höpfl and B. Gut, O. S. B., *Introductio Generalis in Sacram Scripturam* (Rome: Arnodo, 1950), Ed. 5a, p. 440: "Sensus litteralis (historicus) est ille, qui ab auctore S. Scripturae primarie intentus est et a verbis eius per se inest, unde ab interprete invenitur adhibitis regulis sanae explicationis."

see, many Fathers do not regard the metaphor as a literal sense.) As Penna reminds us the question of subjective intention is a modern problem, and one not directly considered by the ancients;[9] however, "On the whole, antiquity conceived of the literal sense in a very narrow manner, limiting it really to what the moderns would call an obvious sense."[10] For an example, we might note that studies of St. Jerome and St. Cyril of Alexandria place these two influential exegetes among the ranks of those who consider the literal sense to be that intended by the human, as well as the divine Author.[11]

A choice between these two opinions is necessary, and it seems better to adopt the second view. This is the outlook which is accepted by many textbooks, and which is assumed by the encyclical *Divino Afflante Spiritu.*[12] Besides, to even attempt to classify the *sensus plenior* accurately would be almost impossible if we were to accept as literal every sense of the text intended by God. And so, for the best purpose of this work, the following definition[13] may be proposed and then examined in detail: *The literal sense is that which both the Holy Spirit and the human author directly and proximately intended, and which the words directly convey, either properly or metaphorically.*

[9] Penna, *Principi*, p. 154.

[10] *Ibid.*, p. 155: "Il senso letterale in genere era concepito in maniera molto stretta in antico. Essa si limitava al senso ovvio dei moderni."

[11] *Ibid.*, p. 156 for St. Jerome.

Kerrigan, *op. cit.*, p. 43, points out that Cyril like many of the Fathers bases his hermeneutical division on the objects written about rather than subjective intention. Yet in general, he says on p. 38: "In certain passages St. Cyril states quite categorically that the literal sense is included in the σκοπός of the hagiographer, that is to say, in his purpose or intention; this is a property that can be readily predicated of the literal sense in general."

[12] *Rome and Scripture*, p. 93: "Wherefore the exegete, just as he must search out and expound the literal meaning of the words, intended and expressed by the sacred writer, . . ."

[13] This is a modification of the definition of Patrizi, *op. cit.*, p.1. Id quod enuntiare Spiritus Sanctus directe intendit ac proxime, et verba directe praeferunt, atque etiam proxime, si propria ea sint, remote autem si sint translata, idque in quantum translata sunt.

The literal sense must be *intended by both God and the human author*. It is the meaning which the human author, inspired by God, wanted to express when he composed a passage. Therefore, not everything intended by God is included in the literal sense, but only that meaning of which the hagiographer was aware. Again this meaning must be intended by both authors *clearly* and *immediately*. By " clearly " we mean to confine the literal sense to that meaning which was in the full consciousness of the human author. Thus the various developments and ramifications of the thought of the human author which he may have vaguely anticipated are not to be included in the literal sense in its strictest definition. Perhaps some who favor the idea of a *sensus plenior* as a literal sense will object to this stringent definition; nevertheless a clear and precise concept of the literal sense seems to be a necessary step in this study. The word " immediately " differentiates the literal sense from the typical sense. The typical sense does not come immediately from the text, but through the medium of a reality which is the foreshadowing of something else. Thus what the author of Numbers, c. 21, wrote of the brazen serpent literally or immediately was directed to the historical situation of the wandering in the desert, not to any mediate or typical significance which the event might convey later on.

Our definition might seem complete if we included only the first part up to the word " intended," and omitted the part about what the words themselves convey. It seems well to add, however, that an intention does not become a sense of the Bible until it is effectively *conveyed by the words*.[14] Yet we must not go to the opposite extreme and speak of this sense of Scripture solely in terms of the meaning conveyed by the words, as if it were independent of the author's intention. This is to confuse signification with sense, grammatical analysis with meaning. In Noematics we are not interested in the meanings which detached words can have (signification); the chief concern is what the

[14] Gaston Courtade, S.J., " Le sens de l'histoire dans l'Écriture et la classification usuelle des sens scripturaires," *RSR*, 36 (1949), p. 138. ". . . c'est celui que l'hagiographe avait exprimé effectivement dans et par les mots dont il s'est servi."

author meant when he used them.[15] "For, while words may have many material significations, as dictionaries attest, their actual or formal signification is determined by the concepts which they express and the proposition in which they are found." [16]

Thus the words must convey the intention of the author *directly, i. e.,* they must enable us to attain to what was clearly in the mind of the author. Now this may be done through the proper meaning of the words, or through a metaphor. This brings us to the division of the literal sense into proper and improper (*proprius, translatus; katà léxin, katà trópon*).[17] Other terms may be used for improper, *e. g.,* metaphorical and figurative.[18] The metaphor has caused much trouble in the history of Noematics. Authors who have studied the problem remark that most of the Fathers considered the meaning behind a metaphor not a literal but a secondary sense.[19] (Noteworthy exceptions to this tendency were Theodore of Mopsuestia,[20] St. Jerome,[21] and St. Cyril of Alex-

[15] John Steinmueller, *A Companion to Scripture Studies,* I, p. 226.

Ildefonsus Ayer, O. F. M. Cap., *Compendium Introductionis Generalis in Universam S. Scripturam* (2nd ed., Rome: Ferrari, 1948), p. 96.

Simon and Prado, *op. cit.* (6th ed.), p. 238.

Rudolph Bierberg, "Does Sacred Scripture Have a Sensus Plenior?" *CBQ,* 10 (1948), p. 183: "We are not interested in what words *can* mean but what they *do* mean."

[16] Bierberg, *ibid.*

[17] Patrizi, *op. cit.*, pp. 4-5.

[18] "Figurative" we might note is actually a very poor term since historically *figura* is the usual translation of *túpos,* and should refer to the typical sense. Cf. Henri de Lubac, S. J., "'Typologie' et 'Allégorisme,'" *RSR,* 24 (1947), p. 209. He quotes Junilius: "Quid est ergo typus sive figura?"

[19] Kerrigan, *op. cit.*, pp. 51-60. Surveys the individual Fathers. Penna, *Principi,* pp. 70-73.

[20] Kerrigan, *op. cit.*, pp. 51-52.

[21] Penna, *Principi,* p. 74 and esp. p. 76: "Gerolamo riteneva che il senso metaforico fa parte di quello letterale. I testi, cui risulterebbe il contrario, sono da considerarsi eccezioni, dovute all' influsso dell' esegesi origeniana ed al fatto che talvolto Gerolamo non avvertì la portata del linguaggio iperbolico-poetico dei profeti."

For Jerome's own words, cf. *Comm. in Abacuc* III: 14 (*PL* 25, 1328 C): "Audiat non semper metaphoram historiae allegoriam consonare; quia frequenter historia ipsa metaphorice texitur . . ."

andria.[22]) And so in the general patristic interpretation, were Christ to be spoken of as "the lion of Juda," the fact that he was an animal would be the literal sense. This is what explains some of Origen's reputed denial of the literal sense.[23] Actually it was only with Albert the Great and St. Thomas that the meaning behind the metaphor was universally accepted as a literal sense.[24]

* * *

Although the literal sense, by definition, is one directly intended and directly conveyed, we must not suppose that it is always easily attainable. Even where there is no textual problem, we face the question of the literary genre in which the author has couched his idea. Fr. Coppens speaks of this factor in terms of envelopes (of poetry, of conventional prophetical language, of historical framework) which must be stripped away.[25] It does not lie within the scope of our topic to treat this matter in detail; but certainly in the past the failure to recognize the literary genre has caused a rejection of the literal sense. Sometimes it was the whole nature of a book that was not grasped (*e. g.*, taking as historical what was intended as a parable); sometimes the style (*e. g.*, failing to appreciate Oriental imagery or exaggeration). But whatever the misunderstanding, the exegete, who could not accept what he

[22] Kerrigan, *op. cit.*, p. 86. "The examples reviewed in the preceding pages demonstrate that St. Cyril not only discovers figurative language in Sacred Scripture but also attaches it at times to the literal sense."

[23] de Lubac, "Typologie," pp. 200, 203. Kerrigan, *op. cit.*, p. 56. Penna, *Principi*, p. 50.

Cf. also Dubarle, *art. cit.*, p. 50. He states that even in the Alexandrian school it is only in rare cases that the literal sense is abandoned.

In a famous passage where Origen denies that there is always a literal sense (*In Gen. Hom.* 2:6 [*PG*, 12, 173B]: "Sed quia non semper in Scripturis divinis historialis consequentia stare potest, sed nonnunquam deficit, ut verbi causa, cum dicitur . . . ," many of the examples he cites are clearly metaphors.

[24] C. Spicq, O. P., *Esquisse d'une Histoire de l'Exégèse Latine au Moyen Age* (Paris: Vrin, 1944), p. 275: "Contrairement aux hésitations de ses devanciers et en plein accord avec ses contemporains, S. Thomas définit le sens métaphorique ou figuré comme étant du sens littéral." Cf. also pp. 20, 98, 272, 340.

[25] Joseph Coppens, *Les Harmonies des deux Testaments* (Tournai-Paris: Casterman, 1949), p. 22.

thought was said, would turn to a spiritual sense of the text. Today we are fortunate because philology, history and many other sciences can be marshalled to our aid in enabling us to determine the literal sense. Yet even then, faith has its role to play. Fr. Coppens, while demanding scientific certitude in discovering the literal sense of a passage, admits the power of faith to strengthen our interpretation.[26] Fr. Charlier goes even further in stating, "Faith is the foundation and summation of all the intellectual dispositions required for reading the Bible." [27] And good sense in interpreting is the first and most indispensable fruit of faith.

Now one final problem remains to be treated: the possibility of a multiple literal sense. Can one passage have many literal senses? For a long while the manifold literal sense was accepted without murmur. The last century, however, saw a bitter reaction against it in the works of men such as Patrizi and Pesch.[28] Today there is no doubt that the majority of exegetes deny the possibility of more than one literal sense for any text.[29] Yet responsible authors like Desnoyers and Sertillanges have not hesitated to defend the theory.[30] Perhaps the solution lies in a sort of rapprochement proposed by several writers to conciliate the two views. No text

[26] *Ibid.*, pp. 27, 28.

A non-Catholic view, similar to this, is that of S. Vernon McCasland, "The Unity of the Scriptures," *JBL*, 73 (1954), pp. 8-10. Faith provides the most basic unity between O. T. and N. T., and thus deeply enriches the interpretation of Scripture.

[27] Célestin Charlier, "La lecture sapientielle de la Bible," *MD*, 12 (1947), 18: "La foi est le fondament et la résumé de toutes les dispositions intellectuelles requises pour la lecture de la Bible."

[28] Patrizi, *op. cit.*, p. 15 ff.

Christianus Pesch, S. J., *De Inspiratione Sacrae Scripturae* (Freiburg: Herder, 1925), n. 543-555.

[29] Cf. for example, Höpfl and Gut, *op. cit.*, pp. 451-462.

Fuller, *art. cit.*, 39j: ". . . it would seem to follow necessarily from the nature of inspiration that the literal sense can be only one."

Steinmueller, *op. cit.*, p. 228.

J. Renié, S. M., *Manuel d'Écriture Sainte* (Lyon: Vitte, 2 ed., 1935), I, p. 187.

[30] Denis Buzy, S. C. J., "Un problème d'herméneutique sacrée: sens plural, plénier et mystique," *An Th* (1944), pp. 387, 408.

can have two heterogeneous, independent literal senses; but it is possible for there to be a twofold, homogeneous literal sense, where the second is merely a subordinate development of the first.[31] On the historical aspects of the problem, it is still hotly disputed whether or not St. Augustine and St. Thomas held a multiplicity of literal senses. Synave and Perrella deny it; Ceuppens and Zarb affirm it.[32] Perrella states: "From an examination of the data, we conclude that in fact the two great minds, Augustine and Thomas, never suspected even the possibility, never mind the fact of the bizarre theory of a multiple literal sense." [33] However, Fr. Ceuppens in his study of St. Thomas is of an almost opposite persuasion; [34] yet the problem is a rather technical one which does not directly concern our paper.

[31] *Ibid.*, p. 388.

J. Van der Ploeg, O. P., "The Place of Holy Scripture in the Theology of St. Thomas," *The Thomist*, 10 (1947), 417.

Jean Gribomont, O. S. B., "Le lien des deux Testaments selon la théologie de S. Thomas," *ETL*, 22 (1946), p. 73.

Simon and Prado, *op. cit.*, 6th ed., p. 245, suggests that the *sensus plenior* may help to clear up the difficulty.

Ayer, *op. cit.*, p. 101: "Si afferuntur loci biblici qui duplicem sensum praebere videntur, ut verba Caiphae (Joan 11, 49-52), agitur plerumque de sensu, quem hodiernis temporibus vocant pleniorem; qui sensus olim non notus vel saltem terminis circumscriptus non erat."

[32] P. Synave, "La doctrine de S. Thomas d'Aquin sur le sens littéral des Écritures," *RB* (1926), pp. 40-65.

Gaetano Perrella, C. M., "Il pensiero di S. Agostino e S. Tommaso circa il numero del senso letterale nella S. Scrittura," *Bb.*, 26 (1945), pp. 277-302.

F. Ceuppens, O. P., "Quid S. Thomas de multiplici sensu litterali in S. Scriptura senserit," *DTP*, 1930, pp. 164-175.

S. M. Zarb, O. P., "Utrum S. Thomas unitatem an vero pluralitatem sensus litteralis in Sacra Scriptura docuerit," *DTP*, 1930, pp. 337-359.

[33] Gaetano Perrella, C. M., *art. cit.*, p. 301: "Dall' esame dei vari dati (principi, testi, scrittori) non risulta affatto che i due grandi Geni, Agostino e Tommaso, abbiano mai sospettata la possibilità, molto meno il fatto, della bizzarra teoria pluriletteralista."

[34] F. Ceuppens, O. P., *art. cit.*, p. 175.

Perhaps the conclusion of Frs. Simon and Prado (*op. cit.*, 6th ed., p. 245) is the wisest at this time: "Neutra sententia adeo firmis argumentis fulcitur ut contrariam improbabilem reddat."

II. THE TYPICAL SENSE.

The term *túpos* is found in St. Paul. Yet strangely enough, not "typology" but "allegory" was the name used by the early Fathers in referring to this division of Noematics.[35] "Tropological" was another term applied to it;[36] and also this sense was closely connected to the "mystery" and "mystical sense" so often spoken of in patristic writings.[37] "Typology" is a neologism in use for only about a century, and actually seems to be of Lutheran origin.[38] Nevertheless, since both the allegorical and the tropological senses have taken on a new meaning, the term "typical sense" is perhaps the most convenient for our use. In many authors, the spiritual sense of the Bible is equated with the typical sense.[39]

The typical sense is generally defined in the textbooks as: "... that meaning by which the things, which are signified by the words of Scripture, signify according to the intention of the Holy Spirit yet other things."[40] In other words, some "thing" about which the text of Scripture speaks literally is used by God to foreshadow something else. ("Thing" here is used in a wide sense, referring to persons, actions, events, laws, etc.) A type differs from a mere symbol or metaphor: the symbol's whole existence is directed toward the thing signified, while the type has objective value in itself;[41]

[35] de Lubac, "Typologie," pp. 185, 187.

[36] *Ibid.*, p. 210. Later, "tropological" was specified to equal "moral."

[37] Henri de Lubac, S. J., *Corpus Mysticum* (Paris: Aubier, 1944), p. 57. The O. T. could be spoken of as a sacrament and a mystery because it was a symbol.

[38] Henri de Lubac, S. J., "Sens spirituel," *RSR*, 36 (1949), 552. This article is reproduced in *Histoire et Esprit* (Paris: Aubier, 1950), pp. 374-410.

[39] Cf. Courtade, "Le sens de l'histoire," p. 137, n. 2, regrets the use of the word "spiritual" about any single sense of the Bible. All the senses, literal, typical, etc. should be spiritual.

[40] Steinmueller, *op. cit.*, p. 229. Pesch, *op. cit.*, p. 565.

[41] de Ambroggi suggests that the senses of Scripture be divided into *letterale* (expressed by the words) and *reale* (expressed by the things). The latter is subdivided into:

(a) *reale-simbolico*: This is obtained from a symbol whose whole nature and it is only mediately and secondarily that it signifies the antitype. The existence of types in the Bible is a dogma of faith.[42]

* * *

Here are very briefly a few of the generally mentioned characteristics of types:

(A) There must be similarity between type and antitype; and, at best, this similarity cannot exist solely in the petty details, but rather in the very essence of things.[43] As one author expresses it, this similarity makes a reasonable appeal to the intellect, rather than an artificial invitation to the imagination.[44]

(B) Fr. Charlier suggests that between the two levels represented by type and antitype there is a double connection: (1) Internal proportionality—the type must be united to the antitype through an organic development in revelation. The latter is the growth and evolution of the former. (2) Efficient causality—the type must effectively prepare the way for the antitype.[45]

is directed toward signifying something else. This sense was normally comprehended by the human author.

(b) *reale-tipico*: This is obtained from a type whose nature is not directed toward signifying something else, but does so only by the will of God. This sense is generally not comprehended by the human author.

Cf. Pietro de Ambroggi, "I Sensi Biblici, direttive e studi recenti," *Sc Cat*, 78 (1950), p. 449.

Also "I Sensi Biblici, proposte per chiarire la terminologia," *Sc Cat*, 80 (1952), p. 233.

[42] Anthony Cotter, "The Obscurity of Scripture," *CBQ*, 9 (1947), 459, says *Proxima Fidei*.

Pesch, *op. cit.*, p. 568. He says it is *De Fide*.

The Decree of the Biblical Commission dated Aug. 20, 1941, *Rome and Scripture*, p. 131: "Although it is a dogma of faith and a fundamental principle of interpretation, as the practice of our Lord and the Apostles proves, that there is in Holy Scripture, over and above the literal sense, a meaning that is spiritual or typical . . ."

[43] Robert C. Dentan, "Typology—Its Use and Abuse," *ATR*, 34 (1952), p. 216: ". . . it is not for the most part so much concerned with the repetition of the petty details of biblical stories and legends as with the great facts which are picturesquely embodied in these stories."

[44] Dubarle, *art. cit.*, p. 57. Allegory proceeds from the imagination.

[45] Charlier, *art. cit.*, p. 31.

(C) Yet the fact that the type and the antitype are alike is not enough. "This similarity presents to us above all only the possibility of a typical application; the concrete existence [of the typical sense] is first guaranteed through divine ordination."[46] Only God's positive will can make one object a type of another.

(D) The type is imperfect: it is a silhouette, not a portrait. Consequently, realization is bound to bring surprises.[47]

(E) The type is not similar to the antitype in every aspect.[48] Christ is the New Adam, and Mary, the New Eve; but only in certain ways. Carrying this further, Buzy says that the type and antitype cannot be of the same order. Thus, if we take one of the lovers of the Canticles to be Yahweh, it is not correct to say that the book typically refers to Christ's love for the Church; for Christ and Yahweh are in the same order.[49]

(F) A final characteristic is proposed by Delporte. Working chiefly on the typology of Melchisedech, he states that there has to be a certain lacuna in the narrative of the type, a certain abruptness, incompleteness, deficiency. God wills this lacuna in order that the

[46] Athanasius Miller, O. S. B., "Zur Typologie des Altens Testaments," *Antonianum*, 25 (1950), 427, 428: "Diese Ähnlichkeit gibt zunächst zwar nur die Möglichkeit einer typischen Verwendung, die konkret erst durch die göttliche Hinordnung garantiert ist."

[47] Lucien Delporte, "Les principes de la typologie biblique et les éléments figuratifs du Sacrifice de l'Expiation," *ETL*, 3 (1926), p. 308.

St. Jerome, *Comm. in Osee*, XI, 1 (*PL*, 25, 916A): "Typus enim partem indicat: quod si totum praecedat in typo, iam non est typus, sed historiae veritas appellanda est." It is interesting to see that almost all these characteristics of typology were already set forth in St. Jerome. Cf. Penna, *Principi*, pp. 128-134.

[48] Delporte, *art. cit.*, pp. 317, 318.

[49] Buzy, *art. cit.*, p. 398: "Le type et l'antitype doivent être premièrement distincts et n'être pas du même ordre. Jahvé ne peut être la figure de Jésus."

Ayer, *op. cit.*, pp. 105-106, lists these two characteristics of types: (a) "ut res typica nequeat praefigurare aliquid simile eiusdem ordinis." The *faith* of Esther cannot be a type of the *faith* of Mary. (b) "ut id, quod pertinet ad deitatem ipsam et ad perfectionem ordinis supernaturalis, nequeat praesignificare altiora." What is said of God or of Christ cannot be a type.

antitype may more startlingly resemble the type and explain it. Thus Melchisedech's extremely abrupt appearance without any genealogy or preparation in Genesis is used by the Epistle to the Hebrews to show that the King of Salem is a type of Christ.[50] Delporte leaves the point slightly vague, and this characteristic might be difficult to apply to all types.

* * *

The typical sense of Scripture is open to misunderstandings and creates many problems. Since we shall face these same problems later with the *sensus plenior,* it is well that we at least formulate them here:

First, is the hagiographer conscious that he is writing of a type? Most textbooks do not treat the question directly, and that is not strange since questions about the psychology of the biblical authors are of recent vintage and disturbed our forefathers but little.[51] In estimating the common opinion of the authors, one might say that normally the sacred author was not conscious of any typical sense in his narrative.[52] Several reflections, however, should be made on this point. It certainly would be against the almost unanimous opinion of authors to demand that the sacred writer had

[50] Delporte, *art. cit.*, p. 311.

[51] Lucien Cerfaux, "Simples réflexions à propos de l'exégèse apostolique," *Problèmes et Méthode d'Exégèse Théologique* (Louvain: Desclée de Brouwer, 1950), p. 33, points out that apostolic exegesis was much less psychological than ours.

Occasionally, however, from chance observations one can obtain the opinion of one of the ancient writers on this subject. Kerrigan, *op. cit.*, pp. 231-233, concludes from his investigations, "In St. Cyril's opinion the human authors of Scripture were frequently aware of the spiritual signification of their words."

[52] Alberto Colunga, O. P., "Las audacias exegético-bíblicas de la teología moderna," *C Tom,* 78 (1951), p. 454, says the typical sense is outside the cognizance of the sacred author, unless he receives a special revelation. In this way the typical sense differs from the symbolical sense. (de Ambroggi is of the same opinion—Cf. note 41 above.)

Manuel de Tuya, O. P., "El sentido típico del Antiguo Testamento es 'verdadera y estrictamente' sentido da la Biblia," *C. Tom,* 80 (1953), p. 630, says it is generally admitted that the typical sense can be unknown by the hagiographer.

to be always conscious of the typical sense, and yet there are several reasons against simply assuming that he was practically never conscious of it. The truth seems to lie in between.

Jean Gribomont observes that often the hagiographer's mentality (or that of his contemporaries) with regard to the object of which he writes affects its value as a type. The Exodus and the crossing of the Red Sea form a type of Baptism, for example. Nevertheless, this type is not so much the Exodus as a historical fact, as the Exodus colored by the religious sentiments of the Jews. The flight from Egypt became for the Israelites God's deliverance of His Chosen People from the forces of evil which were destroyed in the waters of the sea. The added coloring is what makes it a type. ". . . typology is not an attribute of brute things taken in themselves, entirely abstracted from the faith of Israel and prophetic charism."[53] Now add to this the fact that many of the sacred writers, especially the prophets, were quite conscious that Israel was the recipient of a partial revelation, and that many aspects of the Jewish kingdom and religion would attain their ideal in "that day."[54] If we reflect on these two points (that types were often the things in themselves as colored or specified by the Jewish mentality, and that there was a general expectation of a fulfillment of history in Messianic times), we might expect that a vague awareness of the typical sense may have often been present. However, as Fernández remarks, Gribomont goes too far when he asserts that the typical sense was *necessarily* foreseen by the inspired author.[55] The general awareness does not guarantee awareness on the part of any particular author, or awareness of any particular type. Guillet adds that to make the human author's

[53] Jean Gribomont, O. S. B,. "Sens plénier, sens typique, et sens littéral," *Problèmes et Méthode d'Exégèse Théologique*, pp. 23-24. ". . . la typologie n'est pas un attribut des choses brutes en elles-mêmes abstraction faite de la foi d'Israël et du charisme prophétique . . ."

[54] *Ibid.*, p. 29.

[55] Fernández, "Nota referente," pp. 76-78. "Pero de ahí no se sigue que el hagiógrafo, al describir objetos o hechos particulares, tuviera siempre conciencia ni subconciencia de que tales objetos y hechos de su mundo contemporáneo fuesen figura de determinadas realidades mesiánicas."

Gribomont, "Sens plénier," p. 27, "Le sens typique est nécessairement entrevu par l'inspiré . . ."

consciousness a necessary characteristic of typology is dangerous, since it expands prophecy without limits.[56] The problem of consciousness, then, is not a simple one, and is not capable of one over-all solution.

Second, is it correct to confine typology only to things, or is it also related to words? St. Thomas has stated clearly that the literal sense refers to words, and the typical sense to things; [57] this statement is repeated in practically every textbook.[58] But here again recent authors offer some interesting suggestions. If typism is primarily based on things, it only becomes the typical sense *of the Bible* when these things or events are narrated in the words of Scripture. David was a type of Christ *in se* before a word was written about him; a typical sense in the biblical description of David came into existence only when a human author was inspired by God to compose words about David. God must inspire the verbal account itself in order that any typical sense exist. As Tuya says, " In order that it be biblical, the simple typical ordaining of extrabiblical realities on God's part is not enough." [59] This ordaining must be communicated by the Scriptures. In Coppens' words, " Biblical realities exist only by or through the words which express them." [60]

This close relation of the typical sense to words is further seen in the problem of types which enjoy only a literary existence. Here one must distinguish two classes. The first case to come to mind

[56] Jacques Guillet, S. J., " Les Exégèses d'Alexandrie et d'Antioche, conflit ou malentendu? " *RSR,* 34 (1947), p. 300. Yet he remarks that where down through the ages people have been conscious that a certain thing is a type, we have an excellent criterion for authenticity.

[57] *Quodlibetales,* VII, q. 6, a. 14. *Summa Theologica,* I, q. 1, a. 10.

[58] Renié, *op. cit.,* p. 189. Pesch, *op. cit.,* p. 553.

Steinmueller, *op. cit.,* p. 226. Cornely, *op. cit.,* p. 530.

Simon and Prado, *op. cit.,* 6th ed., p. 245.

[59] Tuya, " El Sentido Típico," p. 651: " Pues no basta para que sea bíblico la simple ordenación típica por parte de Dios de la realidad extrabíblica en su momento histórico."

Also, Coppens, *Harmonies,* p. 84.

[60] Joseph Coppens, " Nouvelles réflexions sur les divers sens des Saintes Écritures," *NRT,* 74 (1952), p. 5: ". . . les 'réalités bibliques' n'existent que par ou travers les ' paroles ' qui les expriment."

is that of a figure such as Jonas, who is traditionally a type of Christ. Yet many exegetes now hold that Jonas did not historically exist, but that the whole story is a parable. If this is so, the figure presented in the parable, who existed only in the words of Scripture, is a type (this in spite of a sometimes proclaimed statement that a type must have historically existed). The other case is that of Melchisedech who really existed and yet whose whole typology seems to spring solely from the cryptic biblical description, from the non-real circumstances left to be imagined. The real Melchisedech certainly had parents, yet Hebrews make him a type because his lineage is not mentioned in the Bible. In both these cases, if the historical person is not the type, neither may we jump to the conclusion that the literary description itself is the type; rather it is the person (Jonas or Melchisedech) as described. The words of Scripture themselves are not the type; the type is the "thing" conjured up by the words.[61] In summary of the remarks of these two paragraphs, it may be said that the typical sense is a sense of "things," but is biblical and known by us only through the words which describe these things.[62] To oppose the typical sense of things to the literal sense of words too categorically can be misleading.

A *third* point of discussion is whether or not the typical sense is really a sense of Scripture. There is no question that traditionally the literal sense and the typical sense have been considered as the two great senses of Scripture. Of course, it is to be recognized that they are not senses in exactly the same way. Fernández remarks that the typical sense does not seem to be properly scriptural because it is not immediately contained in the biblical text.[63]

[61] Fernández, "Nota Referente," p. 73: "El tipo es Melquisedec tal como aparece en la narración bíblica; no la narración bíblica que nos presenta a Melquisedec."

[62] *Ibid.*, p. 74: "No parece exacto de decir que el sentido típico se apoye en alguna manera 'sur les paroles sacrées.' En éstas se apoya el conocimento que nostros adquirimos del sentido típico, pero no éste."

[63] Fernández, "Sentido Plenior," p. 308: ". . . no parece que sea propriamente escriturístico. . . . lo que en el texto se halla directa e inmediatamente es là espresión del sentido típico; lo cual es muy distinto."

Coppens, *Harmonies*, p. 84: "Il n'est donc pas directement scripturaire."

(Typology remains primarily in the things; the word has a secondary role.) Yet when all is said and done, he holds that it is correct to speak of the typical sense as genuinely biblical, but in a broad application.[64] Certainly if one accepts a reasonably tolerant definition of a biblical sense, such as the one offered by de Ambroggi,[65] the typical sense should be considered as really a sense of Scripture.

The view of Muñoz that the typical sense is not strictly a sense of Scripture seems to go further than this generally accepted opinion.[66] His reasoning can be broken down into two steps: (a) types are ordered toward antitypes extrabiblically, independently of and before being consigned to writing; therefore the typical sense is not really scriptural; (b) since God's intention in ordaining types is extrabiblical, and since in the composition of the text the human author was not conscious of the typical sense, it is not inspired in the O. T. The inspiration came in the N. T. where certain truths were pointed out as having been types.[67]

[64] Fernández, "Sentido Plenior," p. 310.

[65] de Ambroggi, 1952 article, p. 231: "Senso biblico è il concetto che l'autore sacro (Dio e l'agiografo) intende manifestare (direttamente o indirettamente) mediante i segni biblici (parole e cose) in un determinato contesto."

Ayer, *op. cit.*, p. 96: "Sensus Scripturisticus est omnis notio, quam ipse [S. Sanctus] verbis a se inspiratis, vel immediate vel mediate, per hagiographum exprimere intendit."

Fuller, *art. cit.*, 39c: "When we speak of the *sense* of Scripture we mean what God intended to convey by or through his written word. This may indeed involve more than the human author was conscious of."

[66] Salvador Muñoz Iglesias, "El llamado sentido típico no es estrictamente sentido bíblico viejo-testamentario," *Est Bib*, 12 (1953), p. 161. He says that types are biblical "en un sentido amplio, *materialiter*, por cuanto están consignado en el Antiguo Testamento." However, in his reasonings, as shown above, he seems more radical.

[67] *Ibid.*, p. 162: "Es una simple intencionalidad providencial impuesta por Dios a los hechos, independientemente y con anterioridad a su consignación por escrito—al margen de la inspiración—peró extrínseca y formalmente distinta."

P. 161: "Estas verdades que forman el sentido típico están inspiradas en el Nuevo Testamento."

Gaston Courtade, S. J., "Les Écritures ont-elles un sens 'plénier'?", *RSR*, 37 (1950), p. 487, n. 1: "Le sens spirituel a été voulu de Dieu. *Il n'a pas été inspiré.*"

Muñoz' position has been rather thoroughly attacked by Tuya, and the latter's critique frankly seems justified. Muñoz' first argument concerns the problem (already mentioned) of the typical sense and its relations to words. The fact of the extrabiblical ordination of types does not change the fact that there is not a typical sense till these types are consigned to writing, and therefore the typical sense is a sense of Scripture. As to his second idea of noninspiration (conceding for the moment that the human author was unaware of the typical sense), we shall enter a detailed discussion about the lack of awareness in relation to inspiration when we treat the *sensus plenior.* For the present, one might ask isn't it more difficult to conceive of the typical sense being inspired postpositively through the N. T. rather than in the O. T. itself? The antitype can hardly inspire the typical sense of a passage consigned to writing long before.[68] This theory seems personal to Muñoz; and, as he admits, he has little support for it in the Scriptures or the Fathers or ecclesiastical documents.[69] In fact the Magisterium is quite clearly opposed. In *Divino Afflante Spiritu,* Pope Pius XII, after speaking encouragingly of the spiritual sense (which certainly includes the typical sense), asks exegetes to "refrain from proposing as the genuine meaning of Sacred Scripture other figurative senses."[70] In this he lucidly implies that the typical sense is a genuine sense of Scripture. The Biblical Commission has said that it is a proposition of faith that the Sacred Scripture contains, besides the literal sense, a spiritual or typical sense. An application of Scripture wider than the typical sense (accommodation) is permitted, but such accommodation cannot be called "truly and strictly a sense of the Bible nor was it inspired by God in the hagiographer."[71] Thus, by implication,

[68] Tuya, "El Sentido Típico," p. 653: "En el 'antitipo' *termina* la significación del 'tipo,' diciendo solo una cierta relación del *termino* al mismo. El 'tipo' no se constituye por la relación del 'antitipo' al 'tipo,' sino al revés."

[69] Muñoz, *art. cit.,* p. 166. Also p. 175: "Confesamos sinceramente que nuestra tesis no parece acomodarse a la manera de hablar de la Carta de la Comisión." He explains this by saying that the Biblical Commission did not envisage his theory of extrabiblical ordination!

[70] *Rome and Scripture,* p. 93.

[71] *AAS,* 33 (1941), pp. 466-467. ". . . ma il senso risultante anche dalle

the typical sense is a true and strict sense of the Bible and was inspired by God.

Fourth, are there types in the New Testament also? Patrizi denies this, but makes it clear that by the New Testament or Covenant he understands the period after Christ's death, or at least, after Pentecost.[72] The reason advanced is that the New Convenant brought perfection; and therefore, were there types in this period, the types could not be perfected by the antitype. Actually he seems almost alone in this opinion. Certainly there are no more Messianic types in the N. T. because the Messias has come. Yet there appears to be no difficulty in having prophetical, tropological and anagogical types.[73] For, although the New Covenant is a definitive one, we must still await the consummation of the Kingdom of God.[74] Types in the O. T. were shadows of antitypes in a new economy; but there is nothing to prevent the existence of types and antitypes within different phases of the same economy, *e. g.,* the first ages of the Church compared with the last stages; the Church militant compared with the Church triumphant.[75] As Peguy said, " Everything in Christianity happens three times: in the Old Testament, in Christ, and in His saints." [76] Coppens concedes to Patrizi, however, that the Fathers, while theoretically admitting types in the N. T., mention very few after Pentecost.[77]

Fifth, Fr. Daniélou brings up the question as to whether or not

accomodazioni più felici . . . non si può dire veramente e strettamente senso della Bibbia nè che fu da Dio inspirato all 'agiografo.' "

[72] Patrizi, *op. cit.,* p. 199.

[73] In an obiter dictum, even Patrizi seems to allow tropological types, p. 201.

[74] Yves Congar, O. P., " Que pouvons-nous trouver dans les Écritures? " *Vie Sp* (Oct., 1949), p. 230: " Nous sommes dès maintenant, dans l'ordre de la nouvelle et définitive alliance. Mais nous attendons encore la consommation de ce dont nous avons reçu les germes et, pour parler avec S. Paul, les arrhes."

[75] Delporte, *art. cit.,* p. 321.

[76] Th-G. Chifflot, O. P., " Comment lire la Bible," *Vie Sp* (Oct. 1949), p. 254: " Peguy a écrit qu'en chrétienté toute chose arrive ' trois fois,' dans l'Ancien Testament, dans le Christ, et dans ses saints."

[77] Coppens, *Harmonies,* p. 89.

all the types of the O. T. have Christ as their antitype. He answers in the affirmative, and equates the term "typical" with "christological." [78] Yet he is speaking of what he calls "the whole Christ." [79] Thus the earthly life of Christ, the spiritual aspects of his life, the Church or Mystical Body of Christ, Christ in the individual soul, and Christ in his second coming are all parts of this "whole Christ" which is the only antitype of O. T. typology.[80] While respecting Daniélou's scholarly researches on typology, Coppens fails to find in this characteristic of the typical sense the absolute criterion between legitimate typology and allegory which Daniélou seems to make it. On closer examination it is seen that the idea of "the whole Christ" is so broad that it changes but little our old division of types, *e. g.*, anagogical equals Christ in his second coming; tropological equals Christ in the individual soul. And in fact all typology is not formally christological: if something is a type of the Christian moral life, technically it is the supernatural life and not Christ that is the formal object of the typical sense.[81] But, of course, Coppens admits that the core of O. T. typology is oriented toward Christ and his Church.

Sixth, are N. T. usage, the agreement of the Fathers, and the Magisterium of the Church the only criteria for determining the existence of types? This seems to be the teaching of most

[78] This opinion is not peculiar to Daniélou. As Fr. Kerrigan points out, Cyril of Alexandria was quite definite that the objects of the spiritual sense are identical with the various realities of the Christian mystery (*op. cit.*, p. 131).

Also Jaak Seynaeve, W. F., *Cardinal Newman's Doctrine on Holy Scripture* (C. U. of Louvain Dissertation, 1953, Series II, Tome 45), p. 326, says that Card. Newman was of the same opinion. Seynaeve's comment is interesting: "Nevertheless, if we take into account that for Newman Christology embraces the whole of the Bible, one may reasonably doubt whether this legitimate preoccupation of confining the mystical sense to the Christology alone is such as to exclude all abuses."

[79] Jean Daniélou, S. J., "Les divers sens de l'Écriture dans la tradition chrétienne primitive," *ETL*, 24 (1948), 120: "Donc le sens typologique n'a pour objet que le Christ. Mais il a pour objet tout le Christ."

[80] *Ibid.*, pp. 121-125.

Cf. also Daniélou, "Qu'est-ce que la typologie?", *L'Ancien Testament et les Chrétiens* (Paris: Cerf, 1951), p. 200.

[81] Coppens, *Harmonies*, p. 88. Coppens, "Nouvelles Réflexions," p. 7.

manuals; the reasoning is that, since only God could arrange a type and antitype, divine revelation is necessary to recognize types.[82] It is true, however, that relatively few types are clearly taught in the N. T. or by the common consent of the Fathers. Are we then to draw to a close with the patristic era any new insight into the typical sense of Scripture, and confine ourselves to comment on the types established during that period? Some famous writers, including St. Jerome, have not been so confining.[83] Gribomont, with characteristic insight, complains: "It is only the recent authors, less interested than ever before by typology, who feel themselves obliged to economize by limiting typology to the cases mentioned in the N. T. or by a unanimous consent of the Fathers."[84] And indeed, it does seem strange to freeze original thought at a certain era, especially since in many cases we understand the literal sense better today and should more easily be able to detect types. True, the types revealed by God are the *only ones we are certain of,* but we are not forbidden to investigate the possibility of others. Coppens proposes some interesting examples of a new typology based on a better understanding of Jewish history.[85]

[82] Simon and Prado, *op. cit.*, 6th ed., p. 249. Renié, *op. cit.*, p. 178. Pesch, *op. cit.*, p. 565. Steinmueller, *op. cit.*, p. 231.

(Perhaps these manuals mean that such tradition is the only *certain* criterion.)

Worthy of note are the words of the Biblical Commission (Aug. 20, 1941), *Rome and Scripture,* p. 131: "The spiritual or typical sense, besides being based on the literal sense, must conform to the practice of our Lord, of the Apostles and of inspired writers, as well as to the traditional usage of the Holy Fathers of the Church, especially as they express themselves in the voice of the Sacred Liturgy . . ."

[83] Penna, *Principi,* p. 146: "Gerolamo non parla mai della necessità che un tipo autentico in senso stretto deve essere indicato come tale da Dio con la rivelazione."

Newman's opinion is similar: "It is arbitrary to say that the . . . typical . . . correspondence [between both Testaments] ends with these specimens . . . [which] are given in Scripture." Seynaeve, *op. cit.*, p. 258.

Among the moderns, Fernández, "Sentido Plenior," p. 311, says that there seem to be types which can be recognized without revelation.

[84] Gribomont, "Sens plénier," p. 23, n. 2: "Seuls des auteurs récents, peu intéressés d'ailleurs par la typologie, croient devoir l'économiser en la limitant aux cas mentionnés par le N. T., ou l'unanimité des Pères."

[85] Coppens, *Harmonies,* pp. 93-94.

Seventh, a few brief comments are in order concerning the probative value of the typical sense. The teaching of the manuals may be summed up by saying that types are useful for illustration and explanation, but have little apologetic value.[86] Yet, Delporte points out that, since the typical sense is intended by God, it has *in abstracto* the same value as any other sense of Scripture, although it may be difficult to demonstrate this to non-believers.[87] At any rate, the following oft-quoted statement of St. Thomas deserves comment: "Nothing necessary to faith is contained in the spiritual sense that Scripture does not clearly give to us elsewhere in the literal sense." [88] As we mentioned above, for St. Thomas the literal sense was broader than it is today, for it included all that was intended by God in the words of the text. More important, Thomas appears to be speaking only of what is necessary for faith. If we understand "necessary for faith" in the narrow sense given in moral theology (what must be *explicitly* believed by a necessity of means or precept), the doctrines defined since St. Thomas and for which we have difficulty finding a literal scriptural basis (*e. g.,* Immaculate Conception, Assumption) are not strictly speaking necessary for faith. Actually, if they do have a scriptural background, it is often closer to the typical than to the literal sense (Cf. fuller discussion in c. III). Perhaps this point of the probative value of the typical sense needs more reflection, as do many other aspects of typology.

III. THE CONSEQUENT SENSE

The consequent or scholastic sense of Scripture is that meaning which theologians draw from a text through a process of reasoning. This reasoning may be: (a) *explicative,* a simple explanation and application of the text, and thus an unfolding of what was implicit; (b) *illative,* proceeding in strict syllogistic fashion and discovering what was virtually contained. The latter may be subdivided

[86] Pesch, *op. cit.,* pp. 569-570. Cornely, *op. cit.,* pp. 537-538.

[87] Delporte, *art. cit.,* pp. 321-322.

[88] *Summa Theologica,* I, q. 1, a. 10, ad 1um: ". . . nihil sub spirituali sensu continetur fidei necessarium quod Scriptura per litteralem sensum alicubi manifeste non tradat."

according to whether the minor of the syllogism is a revealed truth or a principle of philosophy.[89]

Is the consequent sense really a sense of Scripture, or simply a derivation from it? The older authors, such as Pesch and Cornely, hold that where the consequent sense is a valid logical deduction from the text of Scripture, it is truly a scriptural sense. They reason that the Holy Spirit would have foreseen such a legitimate development and intended it.[90] Fr. Coppens wishes to judge the consequent sense by the criterion of the hagiographer's knowledge of the conclusion. Accordingly he admits that the explicative consequent sense may be strictly scriptural, but not the illative.[91] Elsewhere, he clearly defends the position that, while the consequent sense is not a strict scriptural sense, it is in a way a biblical sense since God foresaw it, and it is in harmony with the literal sense.[92] Fr. De Vine goes even further, stating that: "It is false to limit the word of God simply to the principles and not extend it to the conclusions." [93] Although he admits that the consequent sense is not explicitly a traditional sense of Scripture, he finds that it is

[89] Cf. Coppens, *Harmonies*, pp. 72-73. A detailed treatment.

Simon and Prado, *op. cit.*, 6th ed., p. 250, offers a slightly different division:

(a) Formaliter-implicite: derived "ex sola terminorum intelligentia"; no reasoning.

(b) Virtualiter-implicite: "non nisi per ratiocinium proprie dictum deprehenditur."

(c) Connexive-implicite: "sola instinctu quodam divino vel revelatione . . . perspici potest."

[90] Pesch, *op. cit.*, p. 572. Cornely, *op. cit.*, p. 529.

Simon and Prado, *op. cit.*, 6th ed., pp. 251-257, presents all the arguments for this view.

[91] Coppens, *Harmonies*, pp. 74-75. Referring to the illative, he says: ". . . elles ne tombent pas formellement sous l'inspiration et ne possèdent aucun titre à passer pour scripturaires au sens fort du mot." We shall treat his opinion in more detail when we come to the *sensus plenior*.

[92] Coppens, "Nouvelles réflexions," p. 5. "Cependant, puisque ce sens dérive en ligne droite de la parole inspirée, il est bien difficile, dans la mesure où il y est virtuellement inclus, dans la mesure dès lors où Dieu, l'auteur principal des Saints Livres, doit l'avoir entrevu et voulu, de lui refuser, du moins dans une acception large, la qualification de biblique."

[93] C. F. De Vine, C. Ss. R., "The Consequent Sense," *CBQ*, 2 (1940), 154.

really the idea behind the spiritual or mystical sense of the Fathers.[94]

On the other hand many authors hold that the consequent sense is not a sense of Scripture at all.[95] Perhaps the key to the dispute lies in the origin of this sense. As De Vine admits, it is not traditional; in fact the term definitely seems to be a recent innovation (practically all references to it are of the last 100 years). Nevertheless, is De Vine correct in saying that the idea, if not the term, lies behind the patristic spiritual exegesis? One thing shall become clear in the next chapter: much of the valid N. T. and patristic exegesis is truly more than strictly literal. But that this is best classified as consequent (in the sense of being derived by real syllogisms) is most questionable. Syllogistic interpretations seem to play no important role in the great writers or schools of interpretation.[96] Rather as Laberthonnière says: "The religious development of Jewish-Christian revelation ought not to be conceived precisely as a passage from the implicit to the explicit . . . but rather as a vital action." [97] If we need a new classification for the valid spiritual exegesis of the past, the consequent sense seems little suited to the role.

Where then did the consequent sense take its beginning? It is

[94] *Ibid.*, p. 147.

[95] Bierberg, *art. cit.*, p. 194.

de Ambroggi, "Il senso letterale pieno nelle divine Scritture," *Sc Cat*, 60 (1932), p. 301.

Also de Ambroggi, 1952 art., p. 239. The consequent sense which implies syllogistic reasoning is not biblical. It is to be distinguished from a simple analysis of the text.

R. de Vaux, O. P., Review of Coppens' *Harmonies*, Bulletin, *RB*, 58, (1950), p. 281.

Höpfl and Gut, *op. cit.*, p. 463: the virtual (illative) consequent sense is not a sense of Scripture *strictly* speaking.

[96] All the evidence is negative. In the large number of surveys of N. T. and patristic exegesis read in connection with Chapter II, we encountered no suggestions that the consequent sense was a possible classification for the more-than-literal sense involved.

[97] Quoted by Coppens, *Harmonies*, p. 55: "Le développement religieux de la révélation judéo-chrétienne devait être conçu non pas précisément comme un passage de l'implicite à l'explicite . . . mais plutôt comme une action vitale . . ."

interesting to note that it is spoken of chiefly in relation to problems about the development of doctrine. Theologians, seeing doctrines defined which are not literally contained in the Scriptures but are divinely revealed, feel that they must attach such truths to revelation by way of reasoning.[98] And so by building a syllogism on a scriptural text (thus making a consequent sense), they justify the doctrine as being virtually contained in the Scriptures. Such a method has given rise to the question of whether or not truths so derived can really be called senses of Scripture. But perhaps the whole basis of the procedure is open to objection. If one does not accept such a theory of the development of doctrine, if one does not believe that every new doctrine can be attached to revelation by way of strict reasoning, the whole *ratio existendi* of such syllogisms is removed. One may well wonder if the newer explanations of doctrinal development, such as those of de Lubac, Draguet, Simonin, Tayman,[99] will not render the consequent sense *dépassé*.

* * *

Be that as it may, some remarks on the consequent sense as it is presently spoken of should be made. First of all, the deeper meaning derived by an *explicative* method is preferably removed from the realm of the consequent sense altogether.[100] If we look at the examples in textbooks, many are no more than the literal sense, *e. g.*:

[98] In *Harmonies*, pp. 75-78, Coppens gives a discussion of various forms of the logical theory of the development of doctrine.

[99] Cf. John J. Galvin, "A Critical Survey of Modern Conceptions of Doctrinal Development," *Proceedings of the Catholic Theological Society*, 5th Meeting, 1950. The solutions differ in details, but are in accord on this: new doctrines are not derived or justified by syllogisms built on scriptural texts. "Implicit" or "virtual" deals more with the working of the Holy Spirit in the Church, rather than with Aristotelián reasoning.

Draguet's article ("L'Évolution des Dogmes," *Apologétique*, Paris: 1937, pp. 1166-1192) gives a detailed and rather convincing refutation of the dialectic theory of development.

[100] Coppens is of this opinion. Cf. "N. Réflexions," p. 14: "Qu'on réserve donc l'appellation de sens conséquent aux conclusions qui se déduisent des textes inspirés moyennant des raisonnements non-scripturaires . . ."

Höpfl and Gut, *op. cit.*, p. 463, says the formal or explicative consequent sense is a true sense of Scripture.

(a) Correlatives: In Scripture the Father says of Christ, "Behold my beloved son." The consequent sense is that God is Christ's Father.

(b) The whole and its essential parts: Scripture says Adam was a man; consequently he has a soul and a body.

(c) The whole and its potential parts: Scripture says all men shall rise on the last day; consequently I shall arise on the last day. Most of these are just other ways of saying the same thing.

The term "consequent sense" is best reserved to new truths derived by *illative* reasoning and to that sort of illative reasoning where the minor is purely a truth of philosophy.[101] Here we agree with Bierberg, de Ambroggi, de Vaux and others that this is not a real sense of Scripture at all. As remarked above, a sense of Scripture is any meaning that God intended to be expressed in the Bible. It is not merely a question of His foreseeing that men would build syllogisms on the Scriptures and draw conclusions from them (he also foresaw accommodations), but a question of His positive *willing* to include such conclusions in the text. On an *a posteriori* basis we must have evidence that authoritative interpreters of Scripture, *e. g.*, the N. T. writers, the Fathers, claim that God did include such conclusions (derived by pure reasoning) in His Scriptures—and this evidence is singularly lacking. And on an *a priori* basis it does seem that when we add from the outside a minor premise of philosophy, we have appended something to a text rather than drawn something out of it. The objection to the consequent sense is not so much that syllogistic reasoning is foreign to the Scriptures (for a syllogism is only the formal expression of a normal thinking process) but that an extraneous element goes to constitute a meaning which is supposed to be contained in the text itself. Exegesis is the determination of what God intended the text to mean, and not what a passage can mean when we add things to it.

Yet in thus maintaining that the illative consequent sense is

[101] If the major and minor premises are both scriptural, we see no difficulty in admitting that the conclusion is a true sense of Scripture. But we would hardly call this consequent. Cf. below in Chapter IV under the relations of the consequent sense to the *sensus plenior*.

not a sense of Scripture, we by no means reject many interpretations which are drawn from the Scriptures and are *called* consequent. As hinted, these are not obtained by syllogisms at all (for the minor premise of reason is inadequate to justify the conclusion) but by the *lumen quo* of the Church's insight into the real fullness of Scripture and the depth of God's intention. These are valid scriptural senses without a doubt, but we shall leave the question of their correct classification to Chapter IV. In summary of our remarks on the consequent sense, the problem is complicated by the intimate relation of this classification to a theory of the development of doctrine which is itself open to dispute. But in the present circumstances, it would seem that the explicative "consequent" sense is a true sense of Scripture, but more literal than consequent. The illative consequent sense, which alone is truly consequent, is not in our opinion a real sense of Scripture.

IV. ACCOMMODATION

It is perhaps better to use the word "accommodation" than "accommodated sense" since the meaning it refers to is not a sense of the Bible itself (it was not intended in the text by either God or the human author); but is given to the Scriptures by the reader.[102] Höpfl and Gut say that the possibility of accommodation is based on a certain similitude between the person or thing of which the hagiographer wrote and the person or thing to whom one now applies the text.[103] This similitude may be just in a name, *e. g.*, "Go to Joseph," which was originally applied to the Patriarch, but is accommodated to St. Joseph. Or there may be a similitude of situation and characteristics, *e. g.*, the texts of chapters 44 and 45 of Ecclesiasticus which literally refer to the Patriarchs, but are extended in the Office to refer to Confessor Pontiffs.[104] In any case, the similarity is extrinsic to the Scriptures and not intended by either author. Many writers call this sense "allegory"

[102] L. Pirot, "L'exégèse catholique," *Initiation Biblique* (Desclée, 1939), p. 335.

[103] Höpfl and Gut, *op. cit.*, p. 465.

[104] Pesch, *op. cit.*, p. 572.

(although, as has been mentioned, "allegory" was originally a name for legitimate typology); others, however, still distinguish in their terminology, praising allegory and condemning accommodation.[105] The term "spiritual sense" is sometimes identified with the accommodated sense, but rather unjustly. Pope Pius XII exhorts us to seek the spiritual sense, but to refrain from proposing accommodations as a genuine sense.[106] Cotter distinguishes between the allegorical and the mystical sense, the latter being the new meaning which texts acquire when placed in juxtaposition around a central idea, such as love, the cross, death, etc.[107] Both of these seem to be forms of accommodation.

Finally, even pure accommodation is not without value.[108] Even though it is not a scriptural sense, it may be a pleasant and useful means of spiritual progress. After all, in the Scriptures we are in our Father's house where the children are permitted to play.

[105] Louis Bouyer, "Liturgie et exégèse spirituelle," *MD*, 7 (1946), pp. 46, 48.

[106] *Rome and Scriptures*, p. 93, § 27.

[107] Cotter, *art. cit.*, p. 460.

[108] Chifflot, *art. cit.*, p. 256.

Both Pope Pius XII in *Divino Afflante Spiritu* and the Biblical Commission admit it may be useful to draw accommodations. Cf. *Rome and Scriptures*, pp. 93, 131.

Chapter Two

A BRIEF HISTORY OF EXEGESIS

Once working definitions of the various senses of Scripture have been established, there remains one other indispensable piece of background to be supplied before the *sensus plenior* can be intelligently examined—a history of the uses of the senses of Scripture in biblical exegesis of the past. Such a history can be useful on three scores: (a) by bringing to light similar movements, it makes the popularity of the *sensus plenior* movement more understandable; (b) it may supply evidence to solve the question whether a *sensus plenior* in fact, if not in name, has been presupposed in exegesis before our times; (c) it may offer suggestions useful in overcoming the difficulties encountered in dealing with a deeper sense.

Unfortunately no complete history of exegesis has ever been written,[1] and naturally any attempt to do so here would be foolhardy. And so in this chapter our scope must be greatly narrowed: while supplying all the details necessary for coherence, we shall concentrate in this history on only those aspects which could conceivably be useful in the study of the *sensus plenior*. Also, since the investigation of the noematical usages of even one author, particularly one of the Fathers, is often the work of a lifetime, no great attempt at original work nor any great number of examples is plausible here. We shall rely on the studies and conclusions of competent authors who have given many years to very small segments of the history of exegesis.

[1] There are, of course, short summaries of the history of exegesis in various Catholic works. One of the best is found at the end of A. Penna, *La Lettera di Dio* (Brescia: Morcelliana, 1952).

From a Protestant point of view, there is Robert M. Grant, *The Bible in the Church* (New York: Macmillan, 1948).

We might note that when we use the word "spiritual" in this chapter we attach to it no precise meaning; it covers all exegesis which seems to go beyond the narrow bounds of the literal sense as defined, and it ranges from strict typology to accommodation.

I. EARLY JEWISH EXEGESIS

Exegesis of the Bible is first found in the Bible itself. It is only natural that the writers of the later Hebrew Scriptures should occasionally refer to an earlier passage of the O. T. In such references there are interesting clues on how the Jews interpreted their own Scriptures. The first group of these instances is supplied by the Psalms and the Prophets. Certain Psalms, *e. g.*, 105, 106, 107, and some passages in the Prophets,[2] in recounting the events of Israelite history, reinterpret these events and give them a deeper spiritual meaning. The Exodus is no longer a simple escape from oppression, but a deliverance from evil ;[3] the Mosaic law takes on a deeper social value.[4] The sacred writers are drawing a lesson for the present by sublimating the events of the past. In fact, Bouyer considers such an insight into the past a part of the prophetic charism.[5]

This tendency becomes more pronounced with the post-exilic writers. As Fr. Gelin remarks, through their study of the Scriptures during the Exile, the Jews regained their vocation, and were able to find a sketch of their spiritual future in their previous history.[6] This is particularly true of Ezechiel and Deutero-Isaias.[7] In addition, if one agrees with Podechard's theories on the Royal Psalms, certain Psalms may have been readapted to apply more directly to the Messias during this period.[7 bis]

[2] Bouyer, *art. cit.*, p. 37, suggests Osee cc. 2 and 9, Is. c. 6 (liturgy of the Temple), and Ez. cc. 36-37 (alliances with Abraham, and with Moses at Horeb). We find difficulty with some of these.

Also cf. de Lubac, "Sens Spirituel," p. 567.

[3] Bouyer, *art cit.*, p. 35, suggests that the Exile in Egypt is colored in the Deuteronomy account by the Exile in Babylon.

Coppens, *Harmonies*, p. 93: "Le deutéro-Isaïe nous présente cette libération d'Israël, la première, comme une figure de la fin de l'exil babylonien, voire . . . comme celle de la libération finale."

[4] Bouyer, *art. cit.*, p. 36. Perhaps Osee would be the best example of this.

[5] *Ibid.*, p. 37. "L'inspiration prophétique prend d'abord la forme d'une illumination d'une histoire depuis longtemps bien connue . . ."

[6] A. Gelin, "Comment le Peuple d'Israël lisait l'Ancien Testament," *L'Ancien Testament et Les Chrétiens* (Paris: Cerf, 1951), pp. 117-118.

[7] *Ibid.*, p. 120. Coppens, *Harmonies*, p. 93.

[7 bis] For example on Psalm 2, cf. E. Podechard, S. S., *Le Psautier* (Lyon: Facultés Catholiques, 1949), Vol. I, pp. 18-19.

This movement of spiritualizing the O. T. seems to have reached a climax with the Book of Wisdom.[8] Yet in some ways the interpretations found in Wisdom represent a decline. Hitherto, the exegesis had consisted in the deepening of the literal meaning; now we find some examples of almost pure accommodation.[9] This accommodation, of course, is inspired; but, in the hands of a non-inspired commentator, as we shall see in subsequent history, the proclivity of spiritual interpretation to exaggerate has been a dangerous weakness. About the same time as Wisdom, other books of the O. T. were being translated into the Greek of the Septuagint, a version which has provided material for many spiritual interpretations (*e. g.,* Gen 3:15; 49:10; Balaam's prophecy; Psalm 110:3; Is 7:14).[10] And so we see that even in the O. T. itself the exegesis practiced by the later books is quite often more-than-literal. Such exegesis may well have been a part of the divine plan for educating the Jews. "Thanks to this pedagogy of leading the Jews to deepen the original experiences of their history and to discover therein a new meaning, God effected a smooth transition from a religion still somewhat primitive to a religion enlivened by prophetic revelation." [11]

* * *

Up to recent times, scholars have been handicapped in their knowledge of extra-biblical, pre-Christian exegesis. Written Rabbinic material bears witness to Jewish interpretation of the Torah in the early centuries after Christ, although its oral background is undoubtedly more ancient. It has only been with the discovery of the Dead Sea Scrolls (DSS) that we have written evidence of extra-biblical exegesis by certain groups among the Jews (seem-

[8] Dubarle, *art. cit.,* pp. 57-59, gives examples.

[9] de Lubac, "Sens spirituel," p. 568. As examples, he gives Wisdom 10: 17; 16: 5-7 and 17: 20. Also Ezechiel 28: 13-16; 47: 1-12.

Dubarle, *art. cit.,* pp. 58-59.

[10] Gelin, "Comment," p. 129. The Septuagint is often "une maturation, une targumisation commençante, une exégèse du texte hébreu." Yet cf. *infra,* c. IV, n. 169.

[11] Bouyer, *art. cit.,* p. 35: "Grâce à cette pédagogie, Dieu, en amenant l'Israélite à approfondir ses expériences originelles et à y découvrir un sens nouveau, l'a conduit sans heurt d'une religion encore primitive à une religion vivifiée par la révélation prophétique."

ingly dissenters from the established Judaic traditions) in the period just before Christ. (We are following the more common opinion that the DSS date from at least the first century B. C.) The above-mentioned trend toward accommodation almost completely dominates the sectaries' exposition of the Bible. For instance, the *Commentary on Habakkuk* (DSH) drastically reinterprets the prophet's words, searching all the while for a veiled eschatological meaning in the events narrated. The interpretation of the text is often forced and abnormal.[12] This exegesis is not proper to DSH but is true of the other DSS as well,[13] so that the whole exegesis may be summed up in the words of an outstanding authority: "Indeed, the author did not trouble about an objective interpretation; his exegesis is purely and entirely allegorical." [14]

When we turn from the sectaries of the Dead Sea to the Rabbinic exegesis of the Christian era, we find that the outlook is somewhat changed. There are two basic tendencies in Rabbinic exegesis:[15] (a) The first is the disinterested study of the biblical text. Here the Rabbis directed all the tools of a well-established science toward establishing a text, determining its meaning, and solving its difficulties. Since they were not trying to prove a particular point, this exegesis (seen at its best not in the commentaries [16] but in the translations such as the Targums) was

[12] These are the conclusions of Wm. H. Brownlee, "Biblical Interpretation Among the Sectaries of the Dead Sea Scrolls," *BA*, 14 (1951), pp. 54-76. Especially the first two hermeneutical principles on page 60.

[13] *Ibid.*, p. 70. Brownlee calls this exegesis "essentially midrashic in character." (p. 76). This needs qualification; for, while the sectarian interpretation is certainly more than literal, its very close similarity to later Rabbinic exegesis is questionable. Cf. Karl Elliger, *Studien zum Habakuk-Kommentar vom Toten Meer* (Tübingen: Mohr, 1953), p. 164: "HK steht in der Methode der Auslegung dem Buche Daniel näher als der rabbinischen Literatur. Essentially midrashic in character ist seine Exegese noch nicht."

[14] A. Dupont-Sommer, *The Dead Sea Scrolls*, trans. by E. M. Rowley (Oxford: Blackwell, 1952), p. 26.

[15] Joseph Bonsirven, S. J., *Exégèse Rabbinique et Exégèse Paulinienne* (Paris: Beauchesne, 1939), pp. 12-13, 252.

Also Bonsirven, "L'Exégèse Juive," *Initiation Biblique*, p. 291.

[16] The Midrashim, or Rabbinic homilies on the books of the O. T., contain

chiefly literal.[17] (b) The second type of exegesis is far from disinterested: its whole tenor was to give a scriptural basis for the oral law imposed by the Rabbis. This juridic, halachic exploitation of the O. T. (witnessed in the Mishna and the Talmud [18]), while sometimes over-literal in its strict interpretation of a law, in general by its very dialectic stretched the text beyond its original content.[19] Such over-legalization, plus the allegorical exaggeration practiced in the haggadic exegesis of the Midrashim, produced a strong non-literal vein in Rabbinic exegesis.[20]

And so we can trace a very definite development in Jewish scriptural exposition. In general the interpretation practiced in the O. T. was a legitimate deepening and spiritualization of the events in Jewish history, although toward the end this may have issued into accommodation. When we consult the DSS about the succeeding period, we find that a metamorphosis has taken place and a very definite cryptic exegesis holds sway. Accommodation has an important place in Rabbinic exegesis too, both in the Midrashim (which are *somewhat* similar to DSS exegesis) and the Talmud. The greatest of all the Jewish allegorizers, Philo, is better treated with the Christian school of Alexandria.[21]

much of the allegorical, haggadic expositions: they serve as a type of popularization of the Torah for the people.

[17] Lucien Cerfaux, "L'Exégèse de l'Ancien Testament par le Nouveau Testament," *L'Ancien Testament et Les Chrétiens* (Paris: Cerf, 1951), p. 133: "Les Juifs comprenaient ordinairement le texte 'à la lettre' . . . L'allégorie y tenait une place discrète."

[18] The oral laws or halakoth were committed to writing in the Mishna at approximately the end of the 2nd century A. D. However, generally the Mishna makes no scriptural reference for a law. The commentary on the Mishna (the Gemara, which together with the Mishna forms the Talmud) gives much more evidence of exegesis. Cf. Bonsirven, *Exégèse Rabbinique,* p. 14.

[19] *Ibid.*, p. 258: "Le ressort commun à la plupart de ces argumentations est l'analogie, voie plus ouverte que tout autre à l'arbitraire et à la fantaisie."

[20] Penna, *La Lettera,* p. 302, says of both halachic and haggadic exegesis: "È facile notare come i vari fini pratici portassero alla trascuratezza del senso letterale per affidarsi al più comodo e più libero senso allegorico."

[21] *Ibid.*, p. 301: "Tuttavia egli non si può considerare un esponente della scuola esegetica giudaica."

II. NEW TESTAMENT EXEGESIS

Granted the spiritual cast of Jewish exegesis, it would be startling if the scriptural interpretation practiced by the early Christians were to be of a purely literal character. It may well have been that the Jews of the time of Jesus, just like the ancient Greeks, were greatly troubled by the lack of perfect harmony between the ancient texts and their present religion, and consequently resorted to a spiritual interpretation of the Scriptures. At any rate, we must expect a certain amount of spiritual exposition to perdure in the Jews converted to Christianity.

To categorize the exegesis practiced by the N. T., we might recall Fr. de Ambroggi's remark that it is only rarely that a biblical citation in the N. T. corresponds with absolute fidelity to the sense of the original.[22] The basis for this statement is a study by L. Venard of the quotations from the O. T. found in the New.[23] He distinguishes three types of exegesis: (a) literal citations; (b) citations founded on the literal sense but giving to it a certain precision and extension; (c) citations which wander considerably from the original sense. His general conclusion is that, while N. T. exegesis is not at all predominantly allegorical and does not reject the literal sense, it is not always historical, but often a spiritualization of the literal meaning.[24] "The authors of the New Testament, just like the Jews of their time, believed that there existed in the Bible a spiritual sense which is more profound than the literal sense." [25]

[22] de Ambroggi, "Il senso letterale pieno," p. 308.

[23] L. Venard, "Citations de l'Ancien Testament dans le Nouveau Testament," *Supplément au Dictionaire de la Bible,* II, cols. 23-51.

[24] L. Venard, "Utilisation de l'Ancien Testament dans le Nouveau," *Initiation Biblique,* p. 287. Also p. 290, their exegesis is not exaggerated like that of the Rabbis.

Penna, *La Lettera,* p. 305: "Ma per la serietà di applicazione gli autori del Nuovo Testamento si rivelano molto più prudenti e moderati dei rabbini contemporanei."

[25] Venard, "Utilisation," p. 289: "Les auteurs du N. T. en effet, tout comme les Juifs de leur temps, croyaient à l'existence dans la Bible d'un sens spirituel plus profond que le sens littéral."

It seems that Fr. Cerfaux reaches about the same conclusion. True, in

In referring to individual authors, Bouyer points out how often Matthew is non-literal in using Scripture.[26] John and Paul use an even more spiritual exegesis in their adaptation of the O. T. to Christ, the Church and the human soul.[27] Special attention should be paid to St. Paul's case. That he cited the O. T. in a spiritual way is obvious; this could even be anticipated from his rabbinic training.[28] Yet sometimes his interpretations seem to go to the point of accommodation, especially (according to Fr. Cerfaux) in the Epistle to the Hebrews.[29] However, in his study of this Epistle, Fr. Van der Ploeg warns us to be careful of calling its exegesis pure accommodation: the Epistle's view of the harmony between the two Testaments often attains to an interpretation which, while it may seem non-literal, is really a fuller sense.[30] Fr. Spicq, in his monumental work on Hebrews,

"L'exégèse," p. 134, he says: "Notre Seigneur et les judéo-chrétiens palestiniens comprendront la Bible, d'une manière littérale, au sens obvie . . ." Yet in speaking of a literal sense, he is contrasting it to an unnatural accommodation which would deny the literal; he does not mean literal in the very narrow sense in which we have defined it. In "Simples Réflexions à propos de l'Exégèse Apostolique," *Problèmes et Méthode d'Exégèse Théologique* (Louvain: Desclée de Brouwer, 1950), p. 44, he says clearly: "La lecture ordinaire prend les textes au sens obvie et direct. Il y a dans cette manière un dépassement de notre sens littéral."

[26] Bouyer, *art. cit.*, pp. 32-33.

[27] Daniélou, "Les divers sens," pp. 121-125.

[28] Yet Bonsirven, *Exégèse Rabbinique*, pp. 348-349, warns us to avoid exaggerating Rabbinic influence. Paul's method of exegesis was affected by his training at Jerusalem, but his conversion gave an entirely different bent to his employment of the method he learned. His usage of Scripture and Rabbinic usage are specifically distinct. "St. Paul est *un rabbin, devenu évangéliste chrétien.*"

Also Peter Bläser, M. S C., "St. Paul's Use of the Old Testament," *TD*, 2 (1954—Winter), p. 51: "In examining Paul's use of Scripture in his Epistles, and comparing it with the types of rabbinical exegesis thus far considered, we note a real affinity as well as a profound difference."

[29] Cerfaux, "L'Exégèse," p. 134: "St. Paul est plus proche des règles rabbiniques. L'épître aux Hébreux allégorise à la mode alexandrine." Also p. 145.

We are making no attempt here to solve the authorship of Hebrews. Our remarks apply no matter who was author.

[30] J. Van der Ploeg, O. P., "L'Exégèse de l'Ancien Testament dans

is very much of the same opinion.[31] Perhaps it can best be summed up with Fr. Bläser: "If by typology we understand that besides the literal meaning a second meaning is connoted and intended by the divine Author of Scripture; and if allegory implies the complete loss of the literal sense, then there is in Paul very much typological exegesis and hardly a case of the allegorical." [32]

And so we see that N. T. exegesis is predominantly a sublimation of the literal sense of the O. T. Although there are occasional accommodations (perhaps more in Paul than elsewhere), in general it is much more restrained than contemporary Jewish exegesis, and runs in an entirely different vein. The Christian accusation that the Jews neglected the spirit for the letter throws light on how distinctively the Christians contemplated spiritual exegesis. For the Rabbis it was a means of justifying the oral law; for the Christians it was a key to the O. T., God's preparation for His Son.

III. PATRISTIC EXEGESIS

The field of patristic exegesis is enormous, and once more the student is handicapped by the lack of a really complete study of the whole period. Nevertheless, in the past few years there have been some very scholarly works on the most influential of the patristic exegetes (Clement of Alexandria, Origen, Theodore of Mopsuestia, Jerome, Augustine, Cyril of Alexandria), and on these we must draw heavily.

The scriptural interpretation practiced by the Fathers is the

l'Épître aux Hébreux," *RB*, 54 (1947), p. 193: "Ce sens n'est pas un sens accommodatrice pur et simple, car il présuppose l'harmonie surnaturelle des deux Testaments et se base sur cette harmonie."

[31] C. Spicq, O. P., *L'Épitre aux Hébreux* (Paris: Gabalda, 1952-53), Vol. I, p. 341: "On répète trop souvent que *Hébr.* cite les textes sans se préoccuper de leur signification initiale et telle qu'elle résulte de leur contexte. La vérité est que la grande majorité des citations et les plus décisives sont exploitées selon leur sens littéral, reconnu par l'exégèse rabbinique elle-même, c'est-à-dire, en fonction de leur application messianique." Again, p. 344: "Or l'exégèse de *Hébr.* apparaît au premier abord singulièrement sobre et raisonable, si on la compare aux allégories rabbiniques ou philoniennes et même aux accommodations de saint Paul (cf. *Rom.* x, 18; *Gal.* iv, 22-24; I *Cor.* ix, 9)."

[32] Bläser, *art. cit.*, p. 51.

product of many influences. The most potent leaven, of course, was that of the N. T. and particularly of St. Paul.[33] The apostolic exegetes had found that by a spiritual exegesis they could unlock the Christian meaning of the O. T.; the Fathers were only too anxious to use this magic key even more extensively. The exaggerations of Marcion and the gnostic heretics, who "took the Old Testament in its literal sense and rejected it as the work of a demigod," [34] solidified the belief that spiritual exegesis was the true Christian exegesis. This was further confirmed by the example of the Jews whose literalism was regarded as the reason for their failure to accept Christ. (Strangely, however, as we shall see, it was the exegesis of a Jew, Philo, with its exaggerated allegory, that was one of the greatest influences on non-literal Christian exegesis.[35]) All these currents combined in different ways among the individual Fathers to produce the much varied quality of patristic exegesis.

There is a great deal of scriptural quotation in the sub-apostolic writings.[36] In general the tendency is toward spiritual exegesis, and in Pseudo-Barnabas it reaches the point of exaggerated accommodation.[37] The Apologists, on the other hand, were rather

[33] de Lubac, "Typologie," p. 197, for Paul's influence on Origen.

Maurice Pontet, *L'Exégèse de S. Augustin Prédicateur* (Paris: Aubier, 1944), p. 150, for Paul's influence on Augustine: "Aucun des Apôtres mieux que lui n'avait montré l'unité de l'Écriture, cru à l'insuffisance de sa lettre et à la force vivante de son esprit, découvert enfin le secret accord des deux Testaments, ce qui restera pour saint Augustin le plus grave problème de la Bible."

[34] Beryl Smalley, *The Study of the Bible in the Middle Ages* (New York: Philosophical Library, 1952), p. 7.

Claude Mondésert, *Clément d'Alexandrie* (Paris: Aubier, 1944), p. 30.

[35] Dubarle, *art. cit.*, p. 50: "C'est à Philon que les Pères de l'Église, par l'intermediaire des maîtres d'Alexandrie, Clément et Origène, empruntèrent les procédés de l'allégorie . . ."

[36] Cf. G. Bardy, "L'Exégèse Patristique," *Initiation Biblique*, p. 295. Of all the Apostolic Fathers, Clement of Rome shows the greatest biblical familiarity.

[37] *Ibid.*, p. 296.

Grant, *op. cit.*, p. 40, says of Barnabas: "The author's theme is not new, but his exegetical method is characterized by a somewhat perverse typology. To him history is really meaningless. God's covenant has always been made

chary in their use of Scripture: St. Justin is almost an exception. His exegesis (as will be seen with apologetics of all times) was of a more literal trend.[38]

It is with the emergence of Alexandria as the intellectual center of Christianity that the great development of Christian exegesis came. The background of this burgeoning lies in a Jew, one of the most influential exegetes of all time, Philo of Alexandria. In him the wisdom of the Jews and the wisdom of Plato met, and through allegory the difficulties that had separated them were removed. "His purpose was to show that whatever the letter of the inspired text might say, its inner or spiritual meaning was in harmony with Platonism." [39] Allegory was able to give a universal quality to the Jewish Scriptures and fuse them into the wisdom of the world. Philo did not totally neglect the literal, but he drew "no clear distinction between passages . . . having a literal plus an allegorical meaning and those which, being superstitious or fabulous, like the anthropomorphisms in Genesis, must be interpreted as purely allegorical, that is, allegorical in their primary sense." [40] In general, for Philo, every syllable in the

with us Christians. There is here no analysis of the relation of the old covenant to the new; there is the simple assertion that the Old Testament has always been misunderstood by the Jews."

How much more balanced is the viewpoint of Irenaeus (pp. 55-59). He, of course, accepted types, but with a much greater appreciation of the value of O. T. history, and under the sobering restraint of Church tradition as a guide in spiritual interpretation.

[38] Bardy, *art. cit.*, p. 296.

Grant, *op. cit.*, pp. 50-51, reminds us, however, that it still had its Christological typology.

[39] Smalley, *op. cit.*, p. 3.

de Lubac, "Typologie," p. 216, points out that Philonian allegory differs from both pagan and Christian exegesis. The difference from Greek exegesis, which regards history as myth, is that Philo maintains the reality of the Hebrew past.

Grant, *op. cit.*, p. 62.

[40] Smalley, *op. cit.*, pp. 4-5.

Grant, *op. cit.*, p. 61, says there are two principal times when Philo denied the literal sense: passages containing anything unworthy of God and passages which are difficult to understand.

text is capable of a spiritual interpretation.[41] This exaggeration of spiritual exegesis was to affect the whole school of Alexandria.

* * *

The first major Christian representative of Alexandria was Clement. In him we find the inevitable encounter between Hellenistic philosophy and the Christian Gospel: his whole thought, including his exegesis, is the resultant mélange of these two elements.[42] The clue to Clement's exegesis is his concept of the *gnosis*—a philosophical notion which he baptized. For him, Christ and the Apostles taught some truths openly; but the profound truths of our faith, the mysteries, the highest spiritual experiences were conveyed secretly. Those who are initiated into this secret tradition have a special deeper knowledge of Christian doctrine—the *gnosis*.[43] Now naturally these mysteries have to be hidden from profane eyes; this is accomplished in Scripture by symbolism and allegory.[44] But the gnostic has the key to the symbolism, and by his allegoric exegesis he discovers the hidden

[41] Daniélou, "Qu'est-ce que la typologie?", pp. 203-204, gives these three characteristics of Philonian allegory:

(a) All the details of the Bible are symbolic.

(b) The realities of the O. T. are images of either the cosmos, the soul, or the intelligible world.

(c) Philo used Hellenistic symbolism to interpret the O. T.

[42] H. G. Marsh, "The Use of Μυστήριον in the Writings of Clement of Alexandria," *JTS*, 37 (1936), p. 70: ". . . we must not forget that there are two Clements—the Alexandrian philosopher and the Christian evangelist."

Claude Mondésert, "Le Symbolisme chez Clément d'Alexandrie," *RSR*, 36 (1936), p. 179, says he is more a philosopher than a Biblist.

Penna, *La Lettera*, p. 307, adds a useful caution: we cannot fully judge Clement as an exegete because we do not possess any purely exegetical writing of his (except fragments).

[43] Mondésert, *Clément d'Alexandrie*: The word *gnosis* is used both *subjectively* of the knowledge—"la science et la perception de choses présentes, futures et passées, science assurée et infallible, puisqu' elle a été transmise et révélée par le Fils de Dieu." (p. 50, from *Stromata* VI, 7, 61, 1)—and *objectively* of the secrets known, the Christian doctrine in all its wealth (pp. 108-109).

[44] Mondésert, "Le Symbolisme," pp. 167-168.

Marsh, *art. cit.*, pp. 65-67.

lore.[45] Thus, while in Clement's exegesis there are two senses, literal and spiritual,[46] it is clearly the spiritual that predominates. And in his spiritual exegesis we run the entire gamut from authentic typology through arbitrary accommodation to the Philonic concept of the Bible as a lesson in psychology or cosmology.[47] Sometimes it is a legitimate prolongation of the literal sense; oftentimes, especially in its Philonic aspects, it is not.

As a successor to Clement there came the giant of the Alexandrian school—Origen. Here we encounter a man who, unlike Clement, is primarily a theologian and an exegete.[48] In fact, he probably had more influence on Scripture than any scholar since St. Paul; nevertheless, attacks on his orthodoxy brought his exegesis into suspicion, and (at least in the last few centuries) much of his exposition was dismissed as hopeless accommodation.[49] It has been one of the great contributions of modern research to reëstablish Origen's reputation. This may be seen clearly on two points. *First of all,* it is definite now that Origen did not simply disregard the literal sense. As mentioned above, many of the

[45] Mondésert, *Clément d'Alexandrie,* p. 109: "Les vérités proprement gnostiques seront souvent proposées comme le fruit de l'exégèse scripturaire, et en particulier de l'exégèse allégorique." Clement seems to vacillate on whether or not the whole of Scripture is to be interpreted allegorically—cf. "Le Symbolisme," pp. 174-176.

[46] Mondésert, *Clément d'Alexandrie,* p. 154: "L'exégèse de Clément suppose, bien entendu, la division fondamentale des deux sens: premier et second."

[47] Th. Camelot, O. P., "Clément d'Alexandrie et l'Écriture," *RB,* 53 (1946), p. 244. Clement uses the term allegory or symbol to cover all these aspects.

[48] Jean-François Bonnefoy, O. F. M., "Origène, Théoricien de la Méthode Théologique," *Mélanges offerts au R. P. Ferdinand Cavallera* (Toulouse: Institut Catholique, 1948), p. 145: "Il faudra des siècles de labeur théologique pour arriver à la haute conception que cet homme extraordinaire s'était formée de la théologie."

[49] It is interesting to notice that Jean Steinmann characterizes him as the inventor of spiritual exegesis. ("Entretien de Pascal et du Père Richard Simon sur les sens de l'Écriture," *Vie Int,* (March, 1949), p. 248.) In view of the preceding evidence, it would seem difficult to justify such a statement.

Grant, *op. cit.,* pp. 70-71: "Harnack scornfully dismissed Origen's work with the epithet 'biblical alchemy.'"

times that he seems to deny it can be explained by his failure to recognize the metaphorical sense as literal.[50] In general, he is quite careful to establish an historical sense, almost as careful as the most exacting literal exegete among the Fathers, Theodore of Mopsuestia.[51]

Secondly, much of Origen's spiritual interpretation of Scripture is quite legitimate.[52] Some, however, it must be admitted is fanciful accommodation. It is in determining the excesses that two of his most able students, de Lubac and Daniélou, have come into disagreement.[53] Origen in the *De Principiis* gives a lucid account of his noematical tenets: [54] There are three senses of Scripture:

(a) The literal, historical sense.

(b) The psychical or tropological sense by which Scripture is applied to the individual soul. (This sense, used rather seldom by Origen himself, and soon abandoned by some of his school,[55] remains rather imprecise in its connotations.)

[50] Cf. above, Chapter I, n. 23.

Grant, *op. cit.*, p. 67, remarks that Origen held that the passages that are historically true far outnumber those which have purely spiritual meanings.

[51] Guillet, *art. cit.*, p. 264: " Sur la fidélité au sens littéral, sur le soin nécessaire pour l'élucider, Origène et Théodore sont d'accord."

[52] Grant, *op. cit.*, p. 69: Origen is humble about the value of his spiritual interpretations and never really claims certainty for them.

Smalley, *op. cit.*, pp. 12-13: ". . . Origen also founded the scientific study of the literal. He was such a giant that he could concentrate on allegory and yet leave vast monuments of literal exegesis."

[53] Henri de Lubac, S. J., *Histoire et Espirit* (Paris: Aubier, 1950).

Jean Daniélou, S. J., *Origène* (Paris: La Table Ronde, 1948).

[54] *De Principiis* (*Peri Archōn*), IV, 2 (*PG* 11, 363). "Tripliciter ergo describere oportet in anima sua unumquemque divinarum intelligentiam litterarum, id est, [1] ut simpliciores quique aedificentur ab ipso, ut ita dixerim, corpore Scripturarum [σαρκός] sic enim appellamus communem istum et historialem intellectum; [2] si qui vero aliquantum iam proficere coeperunt et possunt amplius aliquid intueri, ab ipsa Scripturae anima [ψυχῆς] aedificentur; [3] qui vero perfecti sunt . . . hi tales ab ipsa spiritali lege, quae umbram habet futurorum bonorum, tamquam a spiritu aedificentur. Sicut ergo homo constare dicitur ex corpore et anima et spiritu, ita etiam sancta Scriptura . . ."

[55] Penna, *La Lettera*, p. 307: Didymus the Blind did not use it.

(c) The spiritual sense by which the O. T. is seen to foreshadow the New. It is quite clear that these three senses are based on the Platonic trichotomy (body, soul and spirit) and probably derived from Philo.[56]

Yet in practice, as de Lubac has seen from his studies of the Homilies,[57] Origen actually uses another system of interpretation. He finds first the literal, then the spiritual, and finally a tropological sense which applies to the *Christian* soul.[58] This last sense is a true spiritual sense, not a philosophical, psychological accommodation as occurred in the first division. And so for de Lubac, in practice, most of Origen's more-than-literal exegesis is legitimate spiritualization. The only objectionable element is the false tropological application to the human soul in general (as opposed to the Christian soul) which Origen inherited from Philo.[59]

Daniélou's view is considerably simpler. Origen's spiritual

[56] Penna, *Principi*, p. 52.

John L. McKenzie, S. J., review of Daniélou's *Origène, Th St*, 10 (1949), p. 447, warns us however that we are not sure of the source of his Platonism.

[57] Origen's exegetical work can be divided into:

(a) Scholia: Notes on obscure verses and passages.

(b) Tomes: Well developed, scientific commentaries.

(c) Homilies: Familiar discourses.

The last are by far the best preserved. de Lubac has studied thoroughly the Homilies on the Pentateuch. He is responsible for the lengthy Introduction to these in the *Sources Chrétiennes*.

[58] de Lubac, "Typologie," p. 220, n. 152: "On trouve en effet chez Origène tantôt un sens moral ou tropologique précédant le sens allégorique ou mystique, tantôt un sens spirituel (appelé parfois aussi moral) qui le suit. Le premier est philonien, le second est chrétien."

Cf. also de Lubac, "Sur un vieux Distique, la Doctrine du Quadruple Sens," *Mélanges offerts au R. P. Ferdinand Cavallera*, pp. 348-351, where de Lubac traces the subsequent fate of these two different divisions into the Middle Ages.

[59] de Lubac, "Typologie," p. 199: "Ce qu' Origène doit à Philon, c'est . . . un certain mode d'explication 'moral' ou 'tropologique.'"

In "Sur un vieux Distique," p. 351, de Lubac is more specific. Philo influenced the false tropology, the theory on man's threefold composition, and the pedagogical stress on moral teaching in preparation for spiritual doctrine.

exegesis can be divided into typology and allegory. His typology is legitimate; his allegory (or his personal application of Scripture)[60] is derived chiefly from Philo and is illegitimate.[61] Daniélou's theory is attractive since it adheres to modern terminology where allegory equals accommodation, and in one sense his view is more acceptable because it shows more reserve toward Origen's spiritual exegesis than de Lubac's outlook.[62] Yet it would seem that de Lubac gets closer to the heart of the difficulty. *First,* it is not accurate to differentiate Origen's exegesis on the basis of typology and allegory since for him, as for most of the Fathers, the two terms were interchangeable. In fact allegory was far more commonly used than typology to denote a genuine spiritual interpretation of Scripture.[63] *Secondly,* Origen's inheritance from Philo is perhaps more accurately characterized as the moral or tropological sense than as allegory (which historically is Christian and comes from St. Paul). The nuances of de Lubac may be annoying, but they do present a more finely delineated picture.

[60] Daniélou, "Traversée de la Mer Rouge et Baptême aux premiers siécles," *RSR,* 33 (1946), p. 416: "Nous arriverions ainsi à cette définition de l'exégèse allégorique: elle consiste en un développement de l'exégèse typologique dans le sens d'une thése particulière. En ce qu'elle a de particulier, elle est personnelle à son auteur; par la typologie qui lui est sousjacente, elle témoigne de la tradition de l'Église."

[61] Daniélou, *Origène,* pp. 179-190.

[62] McKenzie, *art. cit.,* p. 447: "Daniélou is more cold toward Origen's allegorism than is de Lubac; it seems better, with Daniélou, to make a distinction between typology and allegorism than, with de Lubac, to identify them."

[63] de Lubac, "Typologie," pp. 180-184. Pre-Christian Greek did not use the term "allegory" to refer to a hidden sense—the term commonly employed for this was ὑπόνοια. Paul, in referring to the spiritual meanings of the O. T. as *allegories* (e. g., Gal. 5:21-24), seems to have created a new Christian terminology. (Even Philo used the term but seldom, sticking to *hyponoia.*) Paul also used the word "type"; but, in general, this designated only the first of two opposed terms, type and antitype, of which allegory was the living connection. In the whole Latin tradition allegory remained the most common terminology. "Il sert à désigner soit . . . l'ensemble des manières d'entendre le texte biblique qui débordent l'histoire ou la lettre, soit, plus précisément, le sens proprement typique, par opposition d'une part à l'histoire et d'autre part à ces autres fractions du sens spirituel que sont alors la 'tropologie' et l' 'anagogie.'" (p. 187)

And so, on the whole, Origen shows far more respect for the literal sense than Clement. Yet his exegesis is primarily spiritual, almost to the extent that he seeks a spiritual meaning behind every text of Scripture. In this spiritual sense there are legitimate elements such as typology, but also a certain amount of accommodation as when Origen tries to adapt the Scriptures to the needs of the human soul. The authority of Origen was to dominate the subsequent history of the whole school of Alexandria. There were to be other famous Alexandrian exegetes and theologians, such as Origen's pupil Dionysius (d. 265), St. Athanasius (d. 373), Didymus the Blind (d. 398), and finally St. Cyril (d. 444); but on all the influence of Origen's concepts is very strong.

* * *

Meanwhile in Antioch a new and rival movement was taking place. Unfortunately a historical study of the Antiochenes is obstructed by the paucity of their extant writings. As far as can be determined, however, the origins go back to the end of the third century when Lucian of Samosata laid the foundations of the school.[64] Its great theorician was Diodorus, Bishop of Tarsus (d. 390's), who in actual quality of exegesis was overshadowed by his pupil, Theodore, Bishop of Mopsuestia (d. 428). St. John Chrysostom (d. 407), Theodore's fellow student, although more a practical theologian than an exegete, was also Antiochene in outlook. The last great Antiochene figure in the East was Theodoret, Bishop of Cyrus (d. 460). In the West, Julian, the Pelagian Bishop of Aeclanum (d. 454), was the leading adherent; but Junilius (c. 540) also merits mention. From the names of its followers, we may see that the period of Antioch's zenith was 380-430 when Diodorus, Theodore, Julian and Theodoret were all functioning.

For centuries it has been the custom to oppose the schools of Alexandria and Antioch. The assumption was that Alexandria was guilty of unbridled extravagance in the use of allegory while Antioch was the laudable proponent of the strict literal sense. Modern scholarship has definitely modified our outlook on both

[64] Grant, *op. cit.*, p. 73, mentions that there was a strong school of Jewish exegesis at Antioch, which may have influenced Christian literalism.

sides. First, as we have seen, Alexandria respected the literal sense and maintained, at least in part, a legitimate spiritual sense. There is no doubt that part of its defamation can be attributed to Antiochene propaganda.[65] Secondly, while theoretically, at least, Antioch always defended the literal sense,[66] it also speaks of more-than-literal senses, including both typology and θεωρία. To this latter sense, *theoria,* we shall have to devote some time for it will be most useful in the study of the *sensus plenior.* Most of the information about it is taken from Theodore of Mopsuestia and Julian of Aeclanum, recent discoveries of whose works have aroused interest in Antiochene exegesis.[67]

As a beginning one must distinguish between a general usage of the term *theoria* and a more specific one. In its general usage, while most popular in Antioch, it was also employed in Alexandria, and for all practical purposes was a close equivalent of alle-

[65] This is particularly true of the two historians at Constantinople, Socrates and Sozomen, who composed their church histories about 443. They are definitely anti-Alexandrian. But even the individual Antiochene exegetes had interpreted Alexandrian allegory derogatively: *e. g.*, Diodorus' famous remark that allegory is a denial of history. As Mariès translates him: " Car là où il faut chercher à côté du texte un sens étranger il n'y a plus considération [θεωρία] mais allégorie." (*Preface to Comm. on Psalms*) Mariès, *RSR,* 9. (1919), p. 89.

[66] Guillet, *art. cit.*, p. 291, points out that sometimes even Antioch missed the real sense of a passage because its rules were often arbitrarily severe: " Victime de la même illusion qu' Alexandrie, celle qui identifiait typisme et ressemblance, Antioche risque seulement de l'être plus grossièrement encore."

[67] (a) Very little of Diodorus remains. Mariès' attribution of the *Int. to Psalm 118* to him has been contested.
(b) For the doctrine of *theoria,* Theodore's principal works are his *Commentary on the Psalms* and *Commentary on the Minor Prophets.* Devreesse's study of Theodore's works in the last few years has done much to reestablish the Antiochene's orthodoxy.
(c) Most of Julian's works have been attributed to him only recently: A *Commentary on Three Minor Prophets* (attributed to him by Morin in 1913); a *Commentary on Job* (by Vaccari in 1915); and a *Commentary on the Psalms* (by Vaccari in 1916). The latter may be a translation from Theodore or an original work. For a complete account see Adhémar d'Alès, " Julien d'Eclane, Exégète," *RSR,* 6 (1916), pp. 311-324.

gory.[68] It means a perception of the spiritual sense of Scripture. Part of this general meaning of *theoria* can be traced to the word's history and its broad significance of contemplation.[69]

But in Antiochene usage the term took on a very definite connotation also. This specific *theoria,* as can be gleaned from Julian's classical definition,[70] is the perception of the future which a prophet enjoys through the medium of the present circumstances which he is describing. The prophet is narrating some event; suddenly he realizes that this event is but a shadow, as it were, of another future event which he also sees. And so in a sort of simultaneous intuition (or *theoria*) of shadow and substance, the prophet attains to and presents not only the literal sense of what is happening but also a fuller meaning of the ultimate accomplishment. Vaccari gives four points which sum up *theoria*:[71]

(a) It supposes the historical reality of the things narrated by the author.

(b) Besides the first reality, *theoria* embraces another, ontologically posterior.

[68] H. N. Bate, "Some Technical Terms of Greek Exegesis," *JTS,* 24 (1923), p. 61. "In the Alexandrine tradition θεωρία is practically synonymous with ἀλληγορία as that word is with διάνοια."

Also P. Ternant, "La θεωρία d'Antioche dans le cadre des sens de l'Écriture," *Bb.,* 34 (1953), p. 139: "Le mot θεωρία a chez les Pères en général une signification très vaste."

[69] Francisco A. Seisdedos, "La 'teoria' antioquena," *Est Bib,* 11 (1952), pp. 39-43. It is connected with the verb *theōreō,* "to see; to examine, chiefly a festival." In Plato *theoria* was adapted to mean an intellectual contemplation especially of universal truths. The term is a *hapax legomenon* in the N. T. (Lk. 23:48). As it was used in the ecclesiastical writers, *theoria* often meant an intuitive knowledge, sensitive or intellectual, and particularly the ability to see a spiritual sense in the Scriptures.

[70] Julian of Aeclanum, *In Oseam Commentarius* (*PL,* XXI, 971 B): "Theoria est autem (ut eruditis placuit) in brevibus plerumque aut formis aut caussis earum rerum quae potiores sunt considerata perceptio."

[71] A. Vaccari, S. J., "La θεωρία nella scuola esegetica di Antiochia," *Bb.,* 1 (1920), p. 15. We might note that actually *theoria* or intuition may also be enjoyed by the Apostle or exegete when reading the Scriptures and recognizing the original *theoria* of the inspired writer—Cf. Seisdedos, *art. cit.,* p. 50.

(c) The first stands to the second as the mediocre to the perfect.
(d) Both objects are immediate termini of *theoria* but in different ways.

The ability to see these two objects *per modum unius* is due to a divine revelation,[72] usually in the form of a supernatural exaltation. The soul of the prophet is withdrawn from the material world in ecstasy, and by a divine charism contemplates the future.[73] This does not mean he loses sight of the contemporary historical panorama, but rather that by a divine light he penetrates to a further horizon than formerly seen.[74] The great feat of the inspired author upon returning from this ecstasy is to find a suitable formula to include both the contemporary meaning of events and their future fulfillment. A clever resort is hyperbole (of which Theodore and Diodorus frequently speak).[75] And so in his phrasing the hagiographer is often hyperbolical with reference to the first

[72] Ternant, *art. cit.*, p. 365, suggests that the primary objects on the contemporary level may be known naturally or by revelation; these in turn prefigure supernatural realities known only by revelation or at least borrowed from others which are known by revelation. Thus revelation is indispensable for the *theoria*.

[73] Seisdedos, *art. cit.*, p. 57: "Separada el alma del mundo material, se manifiesta en ella la acción de Dios que, en una suerte de extravío, de divagación espiritual, le hace contemplar el futuro. Estos extravíos proféticos con los cuales el profeta salta en el éxtasis al Mesías y a los bienes que en El tienen perfecto complimiento, Julian los llama *excessus, excursus*."

Theodore does not seem to have accepted fully the theory of a vision; cf. Guillet, *art. cit.*, p. 285. Theodore stresses more the hyperbolical language employed by the prophets.

[74] Seisdedos, *art. cit.*, p. 58: "El vate, por tanto, no separa en su mente lo histórico y lo mesiánico, sino que su mirada, fija en el porvenir, se remonta más allá del horizonte primitivo y abraza un campo más vasto, al penetrar profundamente, mediante la lumbre profética, el objeto de su intuicion, que sin desaparacer de su mente ni por un momento, iluminado por mayor claridad, lanza fulgores más intentos y deja descubrir tras sí una visión más grandiosa."

Cyril of Alexandria is a rare exception when he allows that the prophet's vision occurs suddenly "interrupting his perception of objects pertaining to history." Cf. Kerrigan, p. 238.

[75] Ternant, *art. cit.*, p. 357.

object, while at the same time he does not adequately describe the second object.[76]

In practice, the Antiochene exegetes greatly differ as to the application of *theoria*. Naturally the largest (and almost exclusive) field of employ was that of O. T. prophecies. Up to this time the prophecies of the O. T. had been generally taken as literal, *i. e.*, the prophet's words directly applied to the future without any contemporary reference. Theodore, recognizing that many of these "literal" prophecies seemed to refer to contemporary events, reinterpreted them as examples of *theoria*. Theodoret, on the other hand, was by no means as reluctant to admit literal prophecies as his master.

Theodore is also remarkable for the limits which he attaches to the horizon of the prophets' *theoria*.[77] In his commentary on the Psalms, he never allows David to have foreseen Christ: the future events he foresaw are all in pre-Christian Jewish history, and with rare exceptions, never after the Maccabean period.[78] In his commentary on the Minor Prophets, he is more liberal. The function of the prophet was to inform the Jewish people which part of the Davidic prophecies was being fulfilled. Yet in their role of preparing the people for such a fulfillment, the prophets' vision or *theoria* would on rare occasions carry them through the future down the great lines of God's design to the Messias.[79] The other

[76] *Ibid.*, p. 365: ". . . tout naturellement il traduit sous une seule et même formule, hyperbolique pour l'objet de premier plan et trop faible pour l'objet lointain, ces deux objets que déjà au stade du jugement spéculatif étaient intimement liés dans son esprit."

[77] Robert Devreesse, "La méthode exégètique de Théodore de Mopsueste," *RB*, 53 (1946), p. 224, finds that Theodore admits only 4 Messianic psalms. Guillet, *art. cit.*, pp. 278-279, suggests this as a reason for his condemnation by II Constantinople (a condemnation largely unjustified, Msgr. Devreesse shows in his monumental *Essai sur Théodore de Mopsueste*; Rome: Vatican, 1948).

[78] Devreesse, "La Méthode," p. 226. These might later be adapted to Christ, but only *adapted* for they had already been fulfilled (p. 222).

[79] *Ibid.*, p. 232: "Mais leur regard porte plus avant [than David's]; il suit dans le lointain les lignes du plan de Dieu . . . jusqu' à ce que se forme, au bout de la perspective, le dessin de celui qui est le terme de la prophétie: le Christ."

Antiochene exegetes do not seem to have been so restrictive in Messianic applications.

If one were then to sum up the exegetical position of Antioch, it might be compared to that of Alexandria thus:

(a) In general the greatest writers of both schools, like Origen and Theodore, respect the obvious sense and commence their exegesis of a text by looking for this sense. They are careful of the precise meaning of words and the logical trend of the text. Yet, as the product of Hellenistic culture, they all show a certain lack of understanding of many features of Hebrew writing, particularly of poetic style.[80]

(b) They are also together in admitting that the texts of Scripture have a secondary, more profound, sense. The Alexandrians always look for a spiritual sense in Scripture. The Antiochenes, especially Theodore, look for it only when there is a special reason (hyperbolical language, citation in the N. T., etc.) to do so. They admit that the whole O. T. was transfigured by Christ, but they do not search for Christ in every line of the O. T.

(c) The search of these two groups for a secondary sense is not in the same direction. Origen and the Alexandrians are primarily interested in a sort of symbolical meaning, *i. e.,* how the events and persons of the O. T. and their details prefigure Christ who relived all of Sacred History. Not the thoughts of the human author but those of the Holy Spirit are of first concern. For Alexandria, the inspired writer is not primarily one who has seen the future, but one who in ecstasy has seen the glory of God, and expresses that unutterable vision in symbols.

Antioch, on the other hand, is more interested in prophecy. The Antiochenes do not see Christ symbolized in all the passages of Scripture, but chiefly through prophecies. And so they are very much interested in the perceptions of the human author. If for Alexandria an author's vision is a vertical assumption into the majesty of God, for Antioch it is a horizontal unfolding of time. Moses, who saw God on the heights of Sinai, is the author

[80] Guillet, *art. cit.,* pp. 260-261, 265-266.

par excellence for Alexandria; for Antioch it is David the prophet who in his Psalms unrolled the subsequent history of his people.[81]

Yet symbolism and prophecy do not exclude one another; they are different aspects of a universally agreed upon spiritual sense. To sum it up with Fr. Guillet: "Between the two schools there is not, therefore, an absolute opposition; rather there is a very large area of agreement on a traditional exegesis. However, in this agreement there is a special insistence on different points of view."[82]

(d) Each point of view had its defects. (Both Origen and Theodore suffered from posthumous condemnations of some of their doctrines.) Neither school solved the basic problem of establishing a criterion for determining a legitimate spiritual sense; both often fell back on mere resemblance as a basis for a secondary sense.[83]

(e) The two schools had a very different amount of influence on subsequent Western exegesis, with Alexandria far out-distancing Antioch. The only Antiochene who had much effect on the West was the one who could teach his readers least about Antiochene exegesis—St. John Chrysostom. The ban of II Constantinople blackened Theodore's reputation.[84] Julian's commentaries were

[81] *Ibid.*, pp. 286-290.

Louis N. Hartmann, C. Ss. R., "St. Jerome as an Exegete," *A Monument to St. Jerome*, by F. X. Murphy, C. Ss. R. (New York: Sheed and Ward, 1952), p. 50, also notices this difference between Alexandria and Antioch on the awareness of the human author. For Antioch, the higher meaning is based on the literal meaning and must be understood in some way by human authors. For Alexandria, God often surpassed the understanding of the human author.

[82] Guillet, *art. cit.*, p. 274: "Entre les deux écoles il n'y a donc pas opposition absolue, il y a même accord très large sur toute une exégèse traditionelle, mais il y a insistence speciale sur des points de vue différents."

[83] *Ibid.*, p. 299. Guillet points out that in some ways Origen is a better guide than the Antiochenes; for even when the arbitrary details of his symbolism were wrong, basically he realized that true typism is more than a resemblance—it is a transfiguration—and rarely did he falsify the real sense of the Scripture. (p. 292)

[84] M. L. W. Laistner, "Antiochene Exegesis in Western Europe during the Middle Ages," *HTR*, 40 (1947), pp. 20-21. Some of Theodore's work survived in a translation by Junilius; his commentary on the Pauline

extant only in a few copies. Junilius' *Instituta Regularia,* while preserved in a good number of manuscripts, was rather seldom quoted.[85] There can be no question that Antioch had no great influence on the West; its exegesis was forgotten by the time it would have been useful. [86]

Alexandrian exegesis saturated the West. Not only were translations and excerpts from the very works of Origen popular; but also his adherents among the Latin Fathers, like Ambrose and Augustine, served as indirect channels for his ideas. In short, "To write a history of Origenist influence on the west would be tantamount to writing a history of western exegesis." [87]

* * *

And so, having compared these two great schools of Alexandria and Antioch which set the tone for all subsequent exegesis in the East, we may now turn to the West. Here we find no such prominent schools, but individual exegetes, each borrowing ideas from the East, particularly from Alexandria, and forming his own principles of exegesis. A few remarks on St. Jerome and St. Augustine as biblical interpreters should suffice to give a picture of the West in the patristic era.

In St. Jerome, the leading occidental exegete, we get an interesting example of eclecticism. Currents from Alexandria, Antioch, and the Rabbinic schools flowed into the broad stream of his scriptural exposition, and in the various periods of his life one or the other current predominates. If it is necessary to simplify, it might be said that his theoretical principles were Antiochene, but in practice he was an Alexandrian. Certainly, "in no

Epistles was popular in the Middle Ages only because it was mistakenly ascribed to St. Ambrose.

[85] *Ibid.*, pp. 28-29. Also, p. 31: "In the theological writers of the ninth century and after there are very few discernible traces of Junilius."

[86] Smalley, *op. cit.*, p. 20.

Ternant, *art. cit.*, pp. 459-474, while admitting this in general, shows instances in many writers where they were employing ideas similar to *theoria.*

[87] Smalley, *op. cit.*, p. 14.

period of the life of St. Jerome is there found a true conversion from allegorical exegesis to literal."[88]

Like Origen, Jerome admits in theory the tripartite division of the senses of Scripture into historical, tropological, and spiritual;[89] but in practice he rarely recurs to it, relying on a simpler two-fold exegesis, literal and spiritual. Jerome shows a real devotion to the literal sense, not hesitating to condemn any wild allegorizing which would be tantamount to denying it. While sometimes he seems to admit that the literal sense cannot stand as it is, it is difficult to be one hundred percent sure that he is ever really denying it.[90] One of his great contributions to this field, as already remarked, was his realization that metaphors belong to the literal sense. In dealing with prophecies, he often employs the concept of the Antiochene *theoria,* without ever using the term itself.[91]

[88] Penna, *Principi,* p. 147: "I suoi principi ricordano quelli che guidavano la *teoria* antiochena; ma in pratica, seguendo l'esempio di Origene, egli si manifestò molto meno esigente nell' accogliere interpretazioni anche assai libere." Also, p. 45: "In nessun periodo della vita di Gerolamo si trova una vera 'conversione' dall' esegesi allegorica a quella letterale."

Hartmann, *art. cit.*, p. 46, warns us not to exaggerate Jerome's turning away from Origen after the Origenist controversy of 393 A. D. He had never been an uncritical follower of Origen. "On the other hand, Jerome continued to employ Origen's allegorical method of interpretation to the very end of his life, albeit with ever decreasing frequency." Also, p. 52: "For on the whole, his exegetical method is much closer to that of the Alexandrians."

Smalley, *op. cit.*, p. 22: "St. Jerome left a tradition on one hand of fanciful spiritual, on the other of scholarly literal interpretation."

[89] S. Jerome, *Epistle CXX,* 12 (*PL* 22, 1005): "Triplex in corde nostro descriptio, et regula Scripturarum est:
Prima, ut intelligamus eas juxta historiam.
Secunda, juxta tropologiam.
Tertia, juxta intelligentiam spiritualem."

He gives a slightly different division in *Comm. in Amos* II, 4 (*PL* 25, 1027 D).

[90] Penna, *Principi,* pp. 65-69. Jerome's position is summarized on p. 76: "Egli ammetteva che ogni brano della Bibbia ha il suo senso letterale, eccettuati forse i passi dell' Antico Testamento che contengono leggi cerimoniali, per i quali egli dipende troppo da Origene."

Smalley, *op. cit.*, p. 21, points out that his last commentary, on Jeremias, is mainly literal.

[91] Penna, *Principi,* pp. 164-167.

In the realm of the spiritual (which, on the whole, he prefers to the literal), Jerome uses all the terms which the Middle Ages were later to canonize (in the famous quadruple division): tropology, anagogy, and allegory. However, with the rare exception of where they have a technical meaning, these words are for Jerome synonomous.[92] Theoretically he makes of typology almost a species within the genus of the spiritual sense, and there may be found in Jerome's works some strict criteria for legitimate typology.[93] But, in practice his types often run to sheer accommodation. Thus in all, Jerome had most of the characteristics of his contemporaries in exegesis; but at least in his underlying tendencies, he is close to our own age. Yet it was not he with all his foresight who was to be the dominant influence in the West; that role was Augustine's.[94]

The picture of St. Augustine's exegesis is much less complicated than that of St. Jerome: he was one of the principal vehicles for the dissemination of Alexandrian doctrines through the West. Always the Latin realist, even in interpretation, he usually began with the literal sense—in other words, with what actually happened according to the text.[95] He is scrupulous in accepting the literal truth of Jewish history; in fact, he fits the whole narrative of Scripture into his philosophy of history.[96] If there was something he didn't understand in the literal sense, it became simply a *mysterium*.

But above all, in true Alexandrian and Neo-Platonic fashion, the Scripture always had a spiritual sense. Augustine's attitude (at least in his sermons) may be summed up thus: "The literal sense is therefore only a foundation to be built upon; true, it is

[92] *Ibid.*, p. 124: ". . . tolti i pochissimi casi di una triplice esegesi, la terminologia di Gerolamo, anche se spesso è identica a quella degli esegeti posteriori, non riflette nessuna suddivisione particolare del senso spirituale."

[93] *Ibid.*, pp. 128-139, 146.

[94] *Ibid.*, p. 218.

Smalley, *op. cit.*, p. 23: "St. Jerome gave the medieval scholar his text and his learned apparatus; St. Augustine told him what his aim should be."

[95] Pontet, *op. cit.*, pp. 167-168. For Augustine, the literal sense is "un fait arrivé et vrai." Sometimes he could not find a real grammatical sense.

[96] Smalley, *op. cit.*, p. 23.

necessary to have it, but as soon as possible one should go beyond it."[97] In fact too much literal sense leads to heresy (didn't Satan use the Scripture to tempt Christ?). And yet when it comes to apologetics, Augustine wisely refrains from the spiritual sense and falls back on the literal. As for prophecies, he prefers the straight literal sense to the Antiochene *theoria*.[98]

Before we leave the Fathers, we might take one more glance back to the East to see how Alexandria fared at the end of the golden patristic era. We find our answer in the person of St. Cyril of Alexandria. Contrary to what we might expect, Cyril is not purely Alexandrian in exegesis: a strong breeze blows from Antioch. Cyril (like Theodore) shows a surprising interest in the background, purpose, and literal meaning of the Scriptures, in details that did not interest even Jerome.[99] And in his reflections on the psychology of the prophet he again steps outside the Alexandrian tradition.

His favorite term for the spiritual sense is *theoria* (not allegory, a term occurring but rarely). It must be admitted, however, that Cyril's concept of *theoria* is more the general sense of that word, as mentioned above. In his over-all outlook on the spiritual sense, he is the descendant of Origen. Indeed, even some of Clement's ideas on the *gnosis* find a strange recurrence here.[100] And so near the terminus of great Eastern exegesis we find an interesting funnelling of many currents of thought.

We have only sampled the Fathers, but we hope that the samplings are sufficient to give an idea of the prevailing exegesis. Practical theologians, the Fathers sought in the O. T. a means

[97] Pontet, *op. cit.*, p. 173: "Le sens littéral n'est donc qu'un sens de base; s'il est nécessaire de le supposer, il faut le dépasser presqu' aussitôt, car très souvent d'abord ce sens littéral est lui-même un sens figuré." In the latter part, the reference is to metaphors.

[98] *Ibid.*, pp. 340-342. Ternant, *art. cit.*, pp. 457-458.

[99] Kerrigan, *op. cit.*, pp. 87 ff.

[100] Kerrigan, in his chapter on the two ways of teaching, esp. pp. 140-164, shows the harmony of Clement and Origen that prevails. Cyril holds a *κήρυγμα* based on the literal sense and a more profound *παίδευσις* based on the spiritual sense.

of preparing the hearts of their listeners for the Christ of the N. T. Conceiving of the Scriptures as the Word of God, they naturally respected the literal sense; but it was the spiritual sense that best served their needs. And in their search for it, they established one grand principle of exegesis: to understand the Bible, you do not have to come out of the Bible itself—one part of the Bible explains the other. This is the principle which Augustine sums up best:

> "The New Testament lies hidden in the Old;
> The Old Testament is enlightened through the New." [101]

And so, in patristic exegesis, resemblance between the two Testaments, often superficial, became the basis of a spiritual sense. The hard facts of history, the differences counted less than artificial likenesses.[102] The unfortunate result was that a considerable portion of patristic exegesis drifted into accommodation—not an accommodation which denies the literal sense, but one which has very little basis in it.

IV. EXEGESIS OF THE MIDDLE AGES

After the fifth century there was a very definite loss of originality in patristic exegesis; the treasures of the past were preserved in the form of *catenae*, but very little of the creative appeared.[103] The upsurge of monasticism turned the Bible into a basis for ascetical discipline, as the *lectio divina* became a part of the rule. This monastic trend was to dominate from the fifth to the ninth centuries because the conditions necessary for study were found only in the monasteries.[104] Civilization was tottering before the

[101] St. Augustine, *Quaestiones in Heptateuchum*, II, p. 73 (*PL* XXXIV, 625), ". . . quamquam et in Vetere Novum lateat, et in Novo Vetus pateat."

[102] Pontet, *op. cit.*, p. 162: "Une des conséquences de cette méthode qui explique l'Écriture par l'Écriture sera la quasi suppression de l'histoire. Dans la Bible les différences compteront moins que les similitudes."

[103] Bardy, *art. cit.*, p. 304. Grant, *op. cit.*, p. 98.

[104] Smalley, *op. cit.*, p. 29. In the history of medieval exegesis we are fortunate in having two fine general works: this one of Beryl Smalley and

eyes of man; the spiritual wealth of the Scriptures raised him from the depths of despair.

The great founder of the monastic trend in biblical exegesis was John Cassian (d. c. 435) in his *Collationes.* Through him the wealth of Origen's mysticism poured into the lifestream of Western asceticism.[105] Cassian distinguished clearly the four senses of Scripture which were to be so important in the Middle Ages: history, allegory, tropology, anagogy.[106] The ideal is that, as the monk became purer of heart, his exegesis would become more skillful in the latter spiritual senses (shades of the Alexandrian gnosis!).

The use of secular sciences to determine the literal sense was not abandoned (as shown in Cassiodorus, d. 570); but the results are insignificant since the times imposed too great a limitation. "In the sixth century, *triste siècle,* all that a scholar could do was struggle to preserve his own Latin culture, and the elementary things in patristic thought."[107] The spiritual exposition came far easier to the men of God, and it is no accident that this period was to produce St. Gregory (d. 604), the master of spiritual exegesis. His reduction of the literal interpretation to a minimum and his ingenuity in discovering spiritual senses fitted the wants of a people dazed by the decline of Rome.[108]

In the early seventh century there was a glimmer of intellectual revival in the Spanish encyclopedist, St. Isidore of Seville (d. 636),[109] and in the Irish monks (adherents to the Antiochene

that of Fr. Spicq (*Esquisse d'une Histoire de l'Exégèse Latine au Moyen Age,* Paris: Vrin, 1944).

[105] Smalley, *op. cit.,* p. 28: "His hermits are a mouthpiece for Alexandrian mysticism, with its stress on the Bible."

de Lubac, "Sur un Vieux Distique," pp. 350-351, points out that he is the channel of some of Origen's Philonien tropology too.

[106] Cassian, *Collationes,* XIV, 8 (*PL* 49, 964 A). Jerusalem is his famous example. Historically, it is a Jewish city; allegorically, it is the Church of Christ;; tropologically, it is the soul of man; anagogically, it is the heavenly city.

[107] Smalley, *op. cit.,* pp. 31-32.

[108] *Ibid.,* pp. 32-35.

[109] The erudition of Isidore represented an upward trend from barbarism. In his actual exegesis, there is given considerable attention to symbolic explanations of names and numbers.

tradition). But in Venerable Bede (d. 735) we have once more a champion of spiritual interpretation, even to the point of accommodation. And it was Bede's compilations that were to have the stronger impact on medieval scholarship.[110]

The eighth and the ninth centuries witnessed the Carolingian revival. Disappointingly, the lack of originality in this period is even more oppressive. The Carolingians are compilers of patristic writings: they make up commentaries on the books of the Bible, taking passages from here and there, and with rare exceptions (like Scotus Erigena) exhibit little creativeness or critical sense in so doing.[111] Significantly, technical theological discussion began to make itself a part of biblical interpretation about this time. The quadruple division of senses was maintained although some introduced as many as seven.[112] Naturally the emphasis was on the spiritual exposition; however there is evidence of an interesting revival in linguistic studies. But all possible progress along these lines was interrupted by the tenth century (the century that is the greatest, and perhaps the only, justification for the title of "Dark Ages"). It has left us not even one important commentary and very few compilations. The Cluniac reform had shifted the emphasis from study to liturgy. Nevertheless, the love for dialectic which was hatched in this period prepared the way for the great revival of the eleventh century.[113]

* * *

The predominant factor in this revival was the Cathedral school[114] and the stimulation provided by its brilliant masters. Figuring in such famous schools as Paris, Laon, and Utrecht,

[110] Smalley, *op. cit.*, pp. 35-36.

M. D. Chenu, O. P., "Les deux âges de l'allégorisme scripturaire au Moyen Âge," *RTAM*, 18 (1951), p. 25. Bede's allegory is often not based on the real signification of the narrative but on a pulverization of the text into individual words, and on the symbolic properties of things and animals, which properties may not be even mentioned in the text.

[111] Smalley, *op. cit.*, pp. 38-39.

[112] Spicq, *op. cit.*, pp. 22-24. Grant, *op. cit.*, pp. 101-102.

[113] Smalley, *op. cit.*, pp. 44-46.

[114] It is curious but the foundation of schools has characteristically been the sign of scriptural progress, *e. g.*, witness Alexandria.

men like Berengar of Tours, Anselm of Laon, and Gilbert of Porrée were primarily theologians, true; but their theological fermentation introduced a new era in Scripture too. The compilations continued, but now far more critically; in fact, it is to this age that we owe the master compilation of the Middle Ages, its great textbook, the *Glossa Ordinaria*.[115] Yet there was also much independent exegesis of the Scriptures, as well as dialectical exposition. Sometimes this dialectic aimed to determine the original sense of a passage; often it served as a basis for constructing a theological hypothesis. From here it was just a short step to the *quaestiones* suggested by the text and corresponding responses—the favorite medieval tool of pedagogy.[116] And so the Cathedral schools of the eleventh century set an original mood in Bible studies. It was one-sided in its inclination to identify exegesis with theology, but at least it had the seeds of progress.

The twelfth century was perhaps the most significant in the whole history of medieval exegesis. Its felicitous inauguration came with the foundation of the Abbey of St. Victor at Paris in 1110, an abbey which was to combine the *lectio divina* of the monasteries with the brilliant scholarship of the universities. The best known master of the school is Hugh of St. Victor, whom Spicq calls "the great theorist of medieval exegesis."[117] With Hugh we find a real emphasis on the literal sense. He attacks the tradition of Gregory and Bede with its disregard for the letter, and maintains boldly that allegory not based on this primary meaning is useless. He was to lapse from his own standard; but

[115] Although this tremendous work, consisting of the biblical text plus marginal and interlinear glosses from the Fathers and Masters, involved the labor of many scholars over the years, the larger share of its authorship seems to belong to Anselm of Laon and his brother Ralph. The *Glossa* became the textbook par excellence, and lectures on Scripture from now on took the form of glossing it. Cf. Smalley, *op. cit.*, pp. 52-66.

[116] *Ibid.*, pp. 66-76. The *quaestiones* were eventually separated from the Scripture text into independent works, as in Lombard's *Sentences.* Finally, late in the 12th century, the *Sentences* themselves became a subject of lecture, and systematic doctrinal teaching was separated from Scripture.

[117] Spicq, *op. cit.*, p. 94.

in emphasizing the literal, he had done the world of exegesis a great service.[118]

The subsequent history of the Victorine school was to take two directions: the mystical, anti-scholastic trend (ultimately victorious) represented by Richard; and the trend in favor of literal interpretation personified in one of the most influential exegetes of the Middle Ages, Andrew of St. Victor, the man who took up the work of scriptural scholarship where Jerome had left off. Interested in Hebrew, stimulated by the best in Jewish exegesis (particularly by Rashi's literal school),[119] Andrew set his sights on the historical sense, eschewing both spiritual exegesis and theological questions. Not the Vulgate text but "Hebraic truth" was his first love, and he wanted his text to make plain sense without supernatural explanations. Almost neglected by historians, he exercised on his own times a strong magnetism away from the unbridled accommodation of former centuries. "Within the limits of his chosen subject, Andrew's influence corresponded to his master's on theology as a whole. Hugh of St. Victor seemed to his contemporaries like a 'second Augustine' Andrew was their second Jerome."[120]

The Victorine program of setting a firm literal foundation for the topheavy spiritual interpretations of monasticism made the *lectio divina* acceptable to the university schools. In the hands

[118] *Ibid.*, pp. 94-96. Smalley, *op. cit.*, pp. 83-106.
Chenu, *art. cit.*, pp. 24-25, for the difference between Hugh and Bede.

[119] An excursus into medieval Jewish exegesis would be of no real value in this chapter. It suffices to say that Rashi (1040-1105) reintroduced literal exegesis to complement the halachic and haggadic exegesis of previous centuries, and the mystical theosophic interpretations of the Cabala. His school showed a definite antagonism to the allegories of the midrashim. Cf. Smalley, pp. 149-156. Also, Penna, *La Lettera*, p. 304.

[120] Smalley, *op. cit.*, p. 185. The rediscovery of Andrew's value is one of Beryl Smalley's most important contributions (pp. 112-185). (It is interesting to note that the discovery of two of the greatest literal trends of antiquity—the Antiochenes and the Victorines—was the work of modern times. Also noteworthy is the Jewish influence on both schools. Cf. n. 64 in this chapter.) She finds that his influence was even stronger in the 13th century than in the 12th. He was worthily succeeded by his pupil, Herbert of Bosham—perhaps the most competent Hebraist produced by the Western Church between Jerome and the Renaissance.

of the latter there was to be a further metamorphosis into the academic lecture course. Three scholars responsible for this change were Peter Comestor, Peter the Chanter, and Stephen Langton.[121] These men were faithful to the Victorine tradition in their careful use of linguistics and history to determine the literal sense. Yet we must not think they neglected spiritual exposition; rather, they believed in its superiority. The traditional quadruple division came more into prominence.[122] Allegory, since the introduction of systematic theology, was less used in the schools for doctrine; it was, however, very popular in educating the laity. Tropology grew in popularity for it was helpful in satirizing social evil. Anagogy, with its emphasis on the mystical, was more widely followed in the cloister than in the classroom.[123] And so, if St. Victor modified the trend toward the spiritual sense, it never completely mastered this trend.

* * *

The thirteenth century, with its flood of Aristotelian and Arabic learning, its universities and secular masters, and the emergence of the Friars, was bound to mark a new era in exegesis. But in particular it was the Franciscans and Dominicans and their new concept of the spiritual life who were to effect a change. The

[121] *Ibid.*, c. V, "Masters of the Sacred Page." Comestor was the author of the principal medieval Bible History, *Historia Scholastica*, which just like the *Glossa Ordinaria* became a subject of biblical lectures. Andrew is one of his principal sources. Peter the Chanter is famous as a moralist. The greatest of the three was Langton (he is responsible for the division of the Bible into chapters) who served as a transition to the 13th century (cf. Spicq, *op. cit.*, p. 267).

[122] There is uncertainty about the exact origin of the famous couplet which sums up the quadruple sense (the actual division, as we saw, goes back to Cassian's time):

> "Littera gesta docet; quid credas allegoria;
> Moralis quid agas; quo tendas anagogia."

Spicq, *op. cit.*, p. 340, attributed it to Nicholas of Lyre (d. 1349)—*PL* CXIII, 28.

de Lubac, "Sur un Vieux Distique," p. 347, seems to think it older.

Penna, *op. cit.*, p. 46, lists some articles on the subject.

[123] Smalley, *op. cit.*, pp. 243-246. Spicq, *op. cit.*, pp. 100-102.

lectio divina became more intellectual; the realization of the intense ascetical value of the literal sense of the Bible made many accommodations and moralities unnecessary. Of course, there were some who tried to resist the tide (often extravagants like Joachim of Flora), but their method fell into desuetude without elaborate refutation. Aristotle was on the march. Just as Aristotelianism refused to dissect soul from body, so it refused a dichotomy between the spirit and the letter. The spiritual sense was not to be studied separately from the literal as if it were superimposed, but through and in the literal. " Scripture began to seem less like a mirror of universal truths and more like a collection of works whose authors had intended to teach particular truths; so exegesis was bound to resolve itself into the scientific study of these authors."[124] And so, with Albert the Great and Thomas Aquinas the biblical world received a theoretical justification of the literal sense in all its great value, "theology's declaration of independence from the allegorical method."[125] The literal sense is defined as the sense of the words of Scripture as distinct from the spiritual sense of "things"; it is shown clearly to contain the metaphor; it is the sense capable of scientific study and forms the only solid basis for apologetics. Contemporaneously with this theoretical justification of the literal sense, Roger Bacon showed a real fascination for textual criticism and linguistic apparatus.[126]

The movements of the thirteenth century were to carry over into the fourteenth.[127] The study of Hebrew and Rabbinics was

[124] Smalley, *op. cit.*, p. 293. Cf. pp. 264-292 for this material.

Spicq, *op. cit.*, p. 288, points out how radical Thomas was in his critique of the spiritual senses: ". . . il donnait décidément a l'exégèse littérale toute sa valeur et réduisait considérablement l'intérêt des interpretations mystiques du haut Moyen Âge."

[125] Grant, *op. cit.*, p. 106. Cf. pp. 104-105 for an evaluation of Thomas' place in the history of exegesis. ". . . he stands far closer to the school of Antioch than to the Alexandrines. This difference should not be exaggerated, however; Aquinas does not reject the allegorical interpretation, and in a way both Alexandria and Antioch can claim him as their heir."

[126] Smalley, *op. cit.*, pp. 330 ff. Yet Bacon theoretically supported the Alexandrian view of the Scriptures containing all knowledge.

[127] Spicq, *op. cit.*, p. 331: "Aucune différence réelle ne sépare ce siècle du précédent au point de vue exégètique; l'esprit et la méthode des travaux

continued and reached a culmination in the Jewish convert, Nicholas of Lyre (d. 1349). Lyre, while admitting the spiritual sense, was one of the last medieval devotees of the literal sense.[128] At the same time, in the mystical excursions of Eckhardt (sometimes based on the Scriptures), the fourteenth century was leaving the door open for a return to accommodation.[129] In the fifteenth century, allegory was once more to dominate the field until Cajetan would institute a reform.[130]

As a very short jaunt from our main path, we might notice that spiritual exegesis was not confined solely to biblical texts during the late Middle Ages. When national literature began to emerge, it was only natural that the concept of allegory would penetrate it also. This is evidenced not only in Miracle and Moral plays, but also, in descending degree, in such works as *The Romance of the Rose, The Faerie Queen, Pilgrim's Progress,* even up to Tennyson's *Idylls of the King.* The use of allegory progressively lessens in these works: in the last the story is more interesting than the allegory. But in the early period which we are dealing with, the allegory was the whole story.[131] We should notice, however, that this literary allegory is closer to metaphor than to the unconscious typism of Scripture.[132]

scripturaires se retrouvent identiques dans les commentaires de 1200 à 1400, ou plutôt les orientations dominantes de l'exégèse du XIIIe siècle s'accusent d'avantage et se scindent définitivement."

[128] *Ibid.*, pp. 335-340. Smalley, *op. cit.*, p. 355.

As noted, Lyre may have been the author of the quatrain.

[129] Spicq, *op. cit.*, p. 334: "De fait, pour Eckhart, le texte sacré n'est plus qu'une occasion de réflexions et de thèses théologiques et non le sujet d'une attention pénétrante au sens des mots."

[130] A. Vincent, "L'Exégèse Moderne et Contemporaine de l'Ancien Testament," *Initiation Biblique*, p. 306: "Cette ligne scientifique ne devait malheureusement pas être suivie et au siècle suivant Gerson (+ 1429), Tostat (+ 1455), Denys le Chartreux (+ 1471) s'attachent surtout à mettre en valeur les sens spirituels, allégoriques et moraux."

Also, Penna, *La Lettera*, p. 318.

[131] To those interested in this facet, we recommend C. S. Lewis, *The Allegory of Love* (Oxford: Univ. Press, 1936). We have cited only a few examples from one language, but the notion of a meaning hidden beneath the words had a profound effect on much of early European national literature.

[132] McCasland, *art. cit.*, p. 3.

V. EXEGESIS FROM THE REFORMATION TO THE PRESENT

We shall treat this period much more summarily than the preceding sections: first, there seems to have been less detailed investigation of this era; and secondly, it offers little that is of real importance to our main topic.

Apparently Cajetan fulfilled the role of leader in returning from the decadence of scholastic exegesis to a real appreciation of the literal sense.[133] This return to the literal was just in time: the Protestant Reformation was to demand an apologetical use of Scripture in which accommodation would have little importance.[134] When men reject the tradition of the past as the authoritative guide in exegesis, much more reliance is bound to be placed on the apparent, face-value meaning of the Scriptures. Among the Reformers, however, we find an interesting dichotomy in exegesis. In studying Protestant interpretations of the O. T. with reference to the persecution of idolaters (Catholics) and blasphemers (other Protestant dissenters), Lecler finds that the famous leaders, *e. g.*, Luther, Melancthon, Calvin, Bucer, in general interpreted literally.[135] If the O. T. gave the Jewish king the right to kill such

[133] Jaak Seynaeve, W. F., *Cardinal Newman's Doctrine on Holy Scripture*, Louvain Dissertations, Series II, T. 45, p. 308.

Smalley, *op. cit.*, p. 351.

[134] G. Ernest Wright, " Exegesis and Eisegesis in the Interpretation of Scripture," *Exp T*, 48 (1936-37), p. 354. " But with the advent of the Reformation the extreme method of allegorical exegesis largely disappeared." By eisegesis, he means the reading into Scripture of preconceived ideas, as opposed to exegesis, or the taking out of Scripture what is already there. As he wisely notes, apologetics which supplanted allegory was often an abusive form of eisegesis too.

Grant, *op. cit.*, p. 111, quotes Luther's remarks on how much he allegorized while a monk before 1517; later on his work concentrated more on historical backgrounds. But the change must not be exaggerated: his exegesis of the O. T. was always Christocentric and (p. 110), " Such a view requires the typological understanding of the Old Testament, and often permits allegorical interpretation to reenter exegesis."

[135] Joseph Lecler, " Littéralisme Biblique et Typologie au XVIe Siècle," *RSR*, 41 (1953), pp. 76-95.

de Lubac, " Typologie," p. 224, n. 158: Calvin had a horror of spiritual exegesis.

On Calvin we might append a note. He, too, vigorously maintained the

heretics, the same law could be literally invoked by the Reformation princes. On the other hand, the smaller, dissenting Protestant groups, like the Anabaptists and Antitrinitarians, who were on the receiving end of the punishment, favored a more spiritual interpretation with spiritual penalties.[136]

In the Catholic counter-Reformation it is natural that the literal sense, which better served apologetics, would receive attention. The theologians of the time present some fine examples of real scriptural exegesis. A catalyst in much of this literalism was the new scientific interest in philology engendered by the Renaissance—an interest which was to fructify ultimately in Rationalism. But once the immediacy of the Reformation was over, a recrudescence of the spiritual sense was inevitable. This time (the seventeenth century) it came under the banners of Jansenism and eventually included names such as Pascal, de Sacy, and Duguet.[137] That this spiritual revival did not succeed in monopolizing Bible studies is witnessed in the works of Maldonatus (d. 1583), Cornelius a Lapide (d. 1637), and Richard Simon (d. 1712). And so in subsequent Catholic thought until the nineteenth century, both literal and spiritual streams are mixed.

In the Protestant realm also, the spiritual sense had its day. With the Pietistic movements of the seventeenth and eighteenth centuries, it was natural that the ascetic wealth of the Scriptures should be tapped through all available channels, including typology and accommodation.[138] In the nineteenth century, the higher

value of objective, non-allegorical interpretation—perhaps even more than Luther. Yet in determining the "objective" sense of Scripture, faith is the only guide. Grant (Protestant), *op. cit.*, p. 114, remarks: "By his acceptance of the primacy of faith in exegesis Calvin opened the way for subjectivism even while he tried to exclude it." And so neither he nor Luther was so complete an innovator in exegesis as is sometimes claimed.

136 These trends still give certain Protestant exegesis a curious blend of subjective objectivity. Grant, p. 117, phrases the Protestant position thus: "The Bible is not one standard of authority among others, as it was for medieval Catholicism. It is the sole standard. And it is not an objective standard, as it was for Thomas Aquinas. It is a standard at once objective and subjective, for in it and through it God Himself speaks to the human heart. The Bible authenticates itself."

137 Coppens, *Harmonies*, p. 79.

138 *Ibid.*, p. 81. He cites many names involved.

critics and their influence are all too well known to require repetition here.[139] Their effect on much of Protestant exegesis was towards literalism, even to the excess of denying the spiritual.

Catholic exegesis of this period, distrustful for a while, was slow to accept the fruits of higher criticism. As the textbooks of the period witness, the twofold division of senses into literal and spiritual (or typical) was always theoretically maintained. In practice, however, as the spirit of the times infiltrated Catholic ranks, little emphasis was placed on seeking the typical sense. Since revelation was thought to be the only guide to typology, the exegete shied away from innovations.

One figure of the nineteenth century must receive a few lines of special attention, that of Cardinal Newman. The great theologian presents almost an anachronism in his Noematics, for his admiration of the Alexandrian Fathers and his deep love of the spiritual sense made his works savor of patristic times. In his Anglican days especially, he often overemphasized mystical interpretations and seemed quite suspicious of literalism's proclivities toward heresy.[140] "Yet with the passing of the years he attached more and more importance to the critico-literary methods of biblical interpretation."[141] As has been seen more and more in theology, Cardinal Newman was often a century ahead of his times. The leading student of his exegesis claims that it includes the concept of the *sensus plenior*.[142] If so, it is one more example of the Cardinal's foresight; perhaps his exegesis may in some ways be more of a prolepsis than an anachronism.

* * *

[139] Cf. J. Coppens, *The Old Testament and the Critics* (Patterson: St. Anthony Guild, 1942). Also, the last cc. of Grant.

[140] Seynaeve, *op. cit.*, pp. 320-322. Also, pp. 343-347. Sometimes Newman uses pure accommodations, but it is difficult to say whether he attached a real scriptural value to them.

D. Divo Barsotti, *Il Mistero Cristiano nell'anno Liturgico* (Florence: 1950), p. 33: "Con razione Newman vedeva legati i destini dell' ortodossia a quelli dell' esegesi spirituale: non ci può essere sviluppo del dogma che in un approfondimento del senso della Scritura."

[141] Seynaeve, *op. cit.*, p. 312.

[142] *Ibid.*, pp. 339-342.

In the twentieth century, after a hundred years of higher criticism, we are seeing once more a revival of the spiritual interpretation. The tendency of the nineteenth century to deny the spiritual sense justifies such a revival; but, as this history should have shown, such a revival always has within it the potentialities of exaggerated accommodations.

In Protestant circles, the movement is obvious.[143] Serious scholars (Dodd, Wright, Rowley, to mention a few) speak of an exegesis which will restore the religious values of the O. T. Some go further: Hebert and Vischer approach very closely to pure accommodation in their works.[144] Karl Barth speaks of a pneumatic sense: the unknowable realm of the spirit is perceived indirectly and vaguely through Scripture if we strip its false, human veil and approach it spiritually. In the end, although Barth has earnestly striven to restore the religious import of the Bible, his agnostic concept of Scripture goes beyond the extreme positions which the school of Alexandria was supposed to have held.[145]

[143] Raymond V. Schoder, S. J., "The Rebirth of Scriptural Theology," *AER*, 117 (1947), p. 87: "Fortunately, a revulsion from the intrinsic religious barrenness of this myopic 'historical' approach to the Sacred Scriptures seems to be setting in."

Cf. Coppens, *Harmonies*, p. 14, for extensive bibliography.

Grant, *op. cit.*, pp. 114, 117, points out that if theology and exegesis began their separation in the Middle Ages, the divorce was furthered by Calvin's refusal to read theological views into Scripture. The Lutheran trend is much more favorable toward a theological interpretation of the Bible.

[144] A. G. Herbert, *The Throne of David* (London: Faber, 1941).

W. Vischer, *Das Christuszeugnis des Alten Testaments* (1936-46).

For comments, cf. J. Coppens, "Miscellanées Bibliques," *ETL*, 23 (1947), p. 183. England has been slow in moving toward allegory. Germany began before the First World War. Sweden has a strong typology school. In comparing Herbert and Vischer, Coppens finds the latter the more audacious, "san doute l'incarnation la mieux réussie de la nouvelle exégèse allégorisante protestante." (p. 184)

Also cf. A. Bea, S. J., "L'Enciclica Humani Generis' e gli Studi Biblici," *CC*, 101, v. 4 (1950), p. 424. He sees Vischer, Hebert and Barth as the three great Protestant spiritualizers.

[145] Dubarle, *art. cit.*, p. 47, shows the possibilities of this.

Coppens, *Harmonies*, p. 134, is more unsympathetic: "Barth aboutit

Catholics too have been witnessing a movement in the direction of the more-than-literal. Some have approached this trend through studies of patristic exegesis (de Lubac, Daniélou), some through ascetic or liturgical interests (Congar, Chifflot, Charlier), some through literary interests (Claudel); but whatever the background, the movement has been gaining apace. That there are dangers present has been recognized by the Holy See. In 1941, a document of the Biblical Commission was directed against an Italian pamphlet which would substitute symbolical allegory for literal exegesis.[146] *Humani Generis* attacks those who replace the literal sense with the spiritual and seek justification in research on the school of Alexandria.[147] And to add to this fermentation has come the *sensus plenior,* the discussion of which has caused the greatest reconsideration of the whole field of Noematics in the three thousand years of scriptural exegesis.[148]

en dernière ligne a des positions qui dépassent, conclut le Père Hammer, l'alexandrinisme le plus discutable."

Grant's judgment is interesting (*op. cit.*, pp. 158-159): "No one has done more to recover the authority of the Bible for our day. . . . If at times he has exaggerated the impotence of human reason, his exaggeration has been a salutary correction to the somewhat jejune liberalism of early twentieth-century exegesis. . . . In this rediscovery of the God of the Bible, Barth leads Protestant exegesis to new tasks."

[146] *AAS,* 33 (1941), pp. 465-472. *Rome and Scriptures,* pp. 129-138.

[147] We must not consider this an attack on all Catholic authors in their studies of Origen. de Lubac, for instance, clearly favors a spiritual sense, but nowhere does he deny the literal sense. The Pope is attacking exaggerations of the spiritual sense, not the spiritual sense itself (which he praised in *Divino Afflante Spiritu*).

Cf. A. C. Cotter, S. J., *The Encyclical Humani Generis,* 2nd. ed. (Weston, Mass: 1952), pp. 91-92.

[148] In "The History and Development of the Theory of a *Sensus Plenior,*" *CBQ,* 15 (1953), pp. 141-162, the present writer attempted a non-partisan, bibliographical summary of all the major articles on the subject.

Chapter Three

CURRENT PROBLEMS AND SOLUTIONS

The first two chapters have reviewed briefly the usual classification of the senses of Scripture and the history of exegesis. Now comes an all important question: does a classification into the literal and typical senses meet all possible needs? For instance, can all the valid exegesis of the last three thousand years be classified as either literal or typical? Can the valid use of Scripture (we use the word "valid" to exclude accommodation) in the liturgy and in the documents of the Magisterium be classified as either literal or typical? Do these forms of exegesis fully succeed in harmonizing the two Testaments? It is time to examine such questions one by one in the light of what we have already seen. If the answer is a unanimous yes—that the usual classification is sufficient—we need go no further in proposing a reclassification. If it is no, we shall have to investigate some possible solutions to these problems.

I. THE PROBLEMS

First, and most logically, comes the question of the exegesis of the past: can it all be classified as literal or typical? To reply it is not necessary to cover each of the five sections of c. II. If we investigate the two most important, the N. T. and the patristic periods, we should have enough information to give a fair reply.

(A) As was already pointed out, the N. T. in its exegesis often goes beyond the literal meaning of the O. T. In a judgment on this more-than-literal interpretation, a great deal of caution is desirable. As Fr. Cerfaux firmly insists, the Apostles were the recipients of a special charism to interpret Scripture, a charism which in some ways defies human rules.[1] Consequently, the N. T.

[1] Cerfaux, "Simples Réflexions," p. 35. He bases the idea of a charism on the reception of the Holy Spirit in Jn 20: 22-23, and the parallel passage Lk 24: 45, "Then he opened their minds, that they might understand the Scriptures."

p. 36: "Le charisme les place, d'une certaine manière, au-dessus des règles humaines."

authors sometimes see the O. T. being fulfilled in ways which escape our poor classifications and even our understanding. "One has the feeling that New Testament writers were often driven to use any image, derived from whatever source, and used in however confused a fashion, to express the truth which was the overwhelming, and essentially inexpressible, fact of their lives—that the living God was at work amongst them."[2] Well does Fr. Coppens advise us that such exegesis is hardly a norm for indiscriminate imitation.[3]

However, even if we are facing an element of the divine before which at times we must admit defeat, a good part of the N. T. exegesis can none the less be classified.[4] Truly within its confines there is a certain typology.[5] Yet, here again we must be careful, for this typology has definite limits. There is no general theory that all the details of the O. T. were types of the N. T.[6] Typology was never as popular in the N. T. as it became among the Fathers.[7] Well then, if all the more-than-literal exegesis in

[2] Dentan, *art. cit.*, p. 216.

[3] Coppens, *Harmonies*, pp. 40, 92. He suggests that there might be a Rabbinic influence on it. See above, c. II, n. 28, for Bonsirven's cautious approach to Rabbinic influence on St. Paul, who would be the most likely suspect.

[4] Cerfaux, "Simples Réflexions," p. 36. Also p. 42: "Même dans son exercice direct, le charisme ne supprime pas l'usage réel—jusqu'à un certain point inconscient—des règles d'exégèse."

C. H. Dodd, *According to the Scriptures* (London: Nesbet, 1952), p. 126, passes a remark which should serve as a further caution in passing judgment on N. T. exegesis: certain large selections from the O. T. were quite familiar to the Apostles and their listeners; a citation of a single verse from one of these is often to be taken not as an interpretation of the verse itself, but as a pointer toward the meaning of the whole section.

[5] Balthasar Fischer, "Le Christ dan les Psaumes," *MD*, 27 (1951), p. 106: "D'une part le Nouveau Testament, quand il s'agit de l'Ancien, voit partout les types du Christ et du Laos . . ."

[6] Cerfaux, "Simples Réflexions," pp. 42-43.

[7] Cerfaux, "L'Exégèse," p. 144: "La typologie ou l'allégorie, telle qu'elle apparaît dans le Nouveau Testament, exception faite pour l'épître aux Hébreux, ne prend point encore dans l'exégèse la place prépondérante qu'elle occupera plus tard. A peu près inexistante comme procédé apparent dans les évangiles synoptiques et dans le livre des Actes, elle marque surtout, dans saint Paul, quelques sections particulières."

the N. T. is not typology, how can we classify it? Some of it may be accommodation, but this is a very insignificant section.[8] The N. T. hagiographers certainly give no evidence that they are using the Scriptures in a sense not intended by God (accommodation); on the contrary, they make it clear that their spiritual meaning is precisely the meaning intended by God, but not realized by the Jews.[9]

Whatever other elements may be present, some of the most proficient students of N. T. exegesis claim that much of it is a deepening of the literal sense of the O. T.—a sense coming from the text itself, rather than from types. Fr. Cerfaux calls it a development from the strict literal sense to a Christian literal sense.[10] Fr. Van der Ploeg, speaking of the author of Hebrews, says: "He recognizes the existence of types and consequently of typical exegesis; but what he is giving an exposition of is, above all, a sense of texts and not of persons."[11] Fr. Spicq, also in reference to Hebrews, mentions typology (or more exactly—the Christian parable);[12] but in explaining how O. T. texts are used in a

[8] Cerfaux, "Simples Réflexions," p. 43. Venard, "Citations," cols. 49-51. de Lubac, "Sens Spirituel," pp. 554-555.

Dodd, *op. cit.*, p. 127-128: ". . . the New Testament writers do not, in the main, treat the prophecies of the Old Testament as a kind of pious fortunetelling, and seek to impress their readers with the exactness of correspondence between forecast and event. . . . They interpret and apply the prophecies of the Old Testament upon the basis of a certain understanding of history, which is substantially that of the prophets themselves."

[9] Cerfaux, "L'Exégèse," p. 134. He admits allegory in St. Paul, especially in Hebrews (p. 145). As remarked above, others disagree.

Fischer, *art. cit.*, p. 106: ". . . tandis que l'allégorie proprement dite dans le sens de Philon lui est à peu près étrangère."

Van der Ploeg, "L'Exégèse," p. 193.

[10] Cerfaux, "Simples Réflexions," p. 44: "Le but de Dieu, qui inspira la Bible en vue des réalités chrétiennes, entraîne cette adaption et ce développement d'un sens littral [sic] strict (notre sens littéral) à un sens littéral chrétien (notre sens plénier?)."

[11] Van der Ploeg, "L'Exégèse," p. 228: "Il reconnaît l'existence de types, et, par conséquent de l'exégèse typologique, mais ce qu'il explique, c'est avant tous le sens de textes, et non pas de personnes."

[12] Spicq, *Hébreux*, I, p. 346. O. T. realities, besides having historical value, are sacramental, receiving their ultimate and decisive application in the N. T. "Ce caractère sacramentel ou préfiguratif de l'Ancien Testament est appelé

fuller application in Christian times he says it is through arrival at the density of the literal sense.[13] Fr. Fischer has something similar: he calls attention to how often the N. T. will apply to Christ what was said of Yahweh in the O. T. Elsewhere he has said that such an application does not belong to the domain of typology, but to that of fulfillment.[14] How are we to classify a deeper literal sense which is neither purely literal nor purely typical?

(B) If caution was desirable in approaching N. T. exegesis, how much more perilous is a judgment on the immense field of patristic exegesis—the "vast forest" as Origen calls it. Here we face a period of some four hundred years, replete with diverse currents of influence and theories of interpretation. The exegesis of the Fathers runs the range, all the way from the spiritual exaggerations of Pseudo-Barnabas to the over-strictness of Theodore of Mopsuestia, and has as many facets as authors. Besides this in-

de nos jours typologique, selon l'acception que saint Paul donne au mot τύπος. . . . Mais on caractériserait plus exactement l'enseignement symbolique de l'Ancien Testament, selon l'exégèse propre de *Hébr.*, en le rangeant dans le genre parabolique."

[13] *Ibid.*, p. 348: " C'est ce qu'on pourrait appeler la densité du sens littéral des textes bibliques ou selon une acception plus courante depuis R. Cornély, mais peut-être équivoque, leur sens plénier." N. 4 explains the latter part of his remark: " Il serait inexact de parler d'un élargissement du sens littéral, et absolument faux d'une multiplicité de significations. C'est un phénomène d'ecsémie si l'on veut, mais dans la ligne même de la lettre, un approfondissement de la richesse du contenu réel de la Parole de Dieu."

[14] Fischer, *art. cit.*, p. 106: " D'autre part, la compréhension " christo "-logique des expressions " théo "-logiques de l'Ancien Testament, c'est-à-dire ce que nous avons appelé la christologisation à partir d'*en haut*, est un des traits les plus distinctifs de la christologie néo-testamentaire."

On pp. 93-94 he says of such christologisation d'*en haut*: " Le phénomène d'exégèse que nous constatons ici n'appartient plus, il est vrai, au domaine de la typologie, mais à celui plus vaste du sens de l'accomplissement."

Dodd, *op. cit.*, p. 133: " Without pursuing this problem further, I would submit that, while there is a fringe of questionable, arbitrary or even fanciful exegesis, the main line of interpretation of the Old Testament exemplified in the New is not only consistent and intelligent in itself, but also founded upon a genuinely historical understanding of the process of the religious—I would prefer to say prophetic—history of Israel as a whole."

itial problem of vastness and variety, there are several other complications. First, in dealing with the literal exegesis of the Fathers, we must remember their dependence on the LXX rather than on the Hebrew text. Second there is the question of terminology (largely a personal preference with each Father); many of the terms used in those times now have a different connotation, *e.g.*, allegory. Then too we have to face the thorniest difficulty of all—to determine when the Fathers were really giving the exegesis of a passage and when they were merely using it as a catechetical example (without the intention of presenting the true meaning of the text itself). Fr. de Riedmatten reminds us that the work of the Fathers "in the field of Scripture is a theology."[15] At this period Scripture and Theology were not diverse sciences, and scriptural commentary was the vehicle of theological reasoning and catechetical exhortation.

These obstacles render a universal classification of patristic exegesis impossible. Of course, one can recognize literal exegesis in varying quantities; but the more-than-literal exegesis offers a fascinating variety. As was pointed out, accommodation often plays a role (not always easily distinguishable). And surely there is valid typology too. Fr. Daniélou has worked hard on isolating certain groupings in the typology of the Fathers.[16] Yet once again it seems that we cannot confine all valid spiritual interpretations to typology.

Indeed, the *theoria* of the Antiochenes is hardly typology. We shall enter into a detailed discussion of the classification of *theoria* in the next chapter, but for now we may state that those who have studied it in detail distinguish it from typology.[17] They consider it as a prolongation and sublimation of the literal sense.[18]

[15] Henri de Riedmatten, O. P., "Typology in the Scriptures," trans. by K. Pond, *Blackfriars*, 33 (1952), p. 133.

Charlier, *art. cit.*, p. 22: Patristic exegesis is not a method.

Guillet, *art. cit.*, pp. 270-271, on the formulas of Origen's interpretations: "Elles ne prétendent pas fixer le sens définitif du texte, mais amorcer les prolongements scripturaires qui donnent à ce texte un sens plus plein."

[16] Jean Daniélou, S. J., "The Fathers and the Scriptures," *ECQ*, 10 (1954), pp. 270-271.

[17] Seisdedos, *art. cit.*, p. 60. Vaccari, *art. cit.*, p. 22.

Ternant, *art. cit.*, pp. 151-152.

[18] Grant, *op. cit.*, p. 76, describes Antiochene *theoria* thus: ". . . a sense

Thus this considerable portion of patristic exegesis is not adequately covered by the present classification of senses. And in fact, it is most probable that among the Fathers in general, typology does not satisfy as a term for covering the whole of more-than-literal exegesis. Penna does not think it does,[19] and de Riedmatten observes that some Fathers do not use much typology at all.[20] Yet more investigation is needed.

And so, in summary, on the basis of past exegesis practiced both in the N. T. and the Fathers, a new classification seems desirable.

* * *

Second, we encounter the exegetical employment of Scripture in the liturgy. Is it enough to pass off all liturgical exegesis as mere accommodation, or does it sometimes attain to a legitimate sense of Scripture which is neither literal nor typical? We must remember that the Bible contains God's message to man. This message has been entrusted to the Church to teach all generations, and nowhere is her teaching office more frequently exercised than in the liturgy. Then does it not seem rather strange to say that the meaning given by the Church to the Bible when using it in the liturgy is *always* pure accommodation, not intended by God, the Author of Scripture? Bouyer says, "The Bible is the Word of God, not a dead word imprisoned in the past, but a living word addressed immediately to the man of today taking part in the liturgical celebration."[21] The liturgy may

of Scripture higher or deeper than the literal or historical meaning, but firmly based on the letter."

[19] Penna, *Principi,* p. 93: "Ma non è lecito sorvolare sul fatto che difficilmente si possono ridurre tutte le interpretazioni offerte dai Padri, oltre quella letterale, al vero senso tipico, come è inteso nei moderni trattati di Ermeneutica."

Also p. 146: For St. Jerome typology is a species within the genus of the spiritual sense.

[20] de Riedmatten, *art. cit.,* p. 139: He mentions Jerome, Apollinaris of Laodicea, Chrysostom, Theodore of Mopsuestia.

[21] Bouyer, *art. cit.,* p. 30: "La Bible est la Parole de Dieu, non une parole morte, emprisonée dans le passé, mais une parole vivante, qui s'addresse immédiatement à l'homme d'aujourd'hui prenant part à la célébration liturgique."

sometimes accommodate Scripture; yet occasionally at least it attains to a real meaning of Scripture which is admittedly not literal.

Now, once again, does typology cover this exegesis? An answer to this question is rendered extremely difficult, if not impossible, by the fact that a scientific attempt to classify liturgical exegesis in exact modern terminology has, to the best of our knowledge, not been made.[22] But one observation of Fr. Fischer is worthy of being called to attention. In investigating why the Psalms were accepted into the liturgy of "the Church of the Martyrs," he finds that it was because they were considered prophetic, receiving fulfillment in Christ. A few of them are literally prophetic, but the majority are used in the liturgy in a spiritual sense.[23] They are seen as being spoken either by Christ or by the Church (about or to Christ). In the former case, it is a typical exegesis. But when the liturgy uses the Psalms as being spoken by the Church to Christ, "we are dealing with a method of interpretation which is sharply distinct from typology."[24] It is rather a fulfillment of what was said in the O. T. to God the Father. Investigation of other facets of the liturgy might well lead to a similar conclusion.

* * *

Third, there is the exegesis used by theologians and particularly by the Magisterium in the definition of dogmas of faith. This is especially a problem in the application of texts to Our Blessed Lady in the definition of the Immaculate Conception and the Assumption. Coppens reacts against employing the role of Scripture in the development of doctrine as a proof for a new classification of Scripture—the problem is already complicated enough.[25]

[22] Barsotti, *op. cit.*, has some observations on the spiritual or mystical interpretation used in the Liturgy: it is based on the typical sense. Yet, p. 30: "Il senso mistico non è altro dal senso letterale, è il medesimo senso letterale e storico veduto in profondità . . ."

[23] Fischer, *art. cit.*, p. 92.

[24] *Ibid.*, p. 93: ". . . nous avons affaire à une méthode d'interprétation qui se distingue nettement de l'interprétation typologique."

[25] Coppens, *Harmonies*, p. 41: "L'évolution du dogme est un problème en soi, encore très obscur par certains aspects. Le sens plénier souffre lui

Besides it is difficult to be sure that the Church is presenting us with a real exegesis of such Marian texts. For instance, *Ineffabilis Deus,* when referring to Marian references, invariably says that *the Fathers* (or someone else) saw such a meaning in the passages; it does not say that such *is* the meaning.[26] The attitude of *Munificentissimus Deus* is very much the same.[27]

We can formulate, however, some observations on the employment of the O. T. to refer to the B. V. M. It would certainly be temerarious to say that all such exegesis is pure accommodation. Some of it probably is, but tradition is too universal on a few of the Marian texts for them to be dismissed so summarily. Are these texts, then, Marian in a literal or a typical sense? Let us take Gen 3:15 as an example. One is more and more impressed by the difficulty of interpreting the text in a rigorously literal application to Christ and Mary. The typical sense of the passage is also hard to establish, because the great struggle of the human race against evil (a suggested literal interpretation) is scarcely a strict type of Christ's victory over Satan, nor are the mothers of all good men a type of Mary.[28] Of course, these remarks are only opinions open to much dispute; but when we give a list of examples of the *sensus plenior* in c. IV, the reader will see that many writers have sought refuge in a new classification for the Marian exegesis of this[29] and other texts, *e.g.,* Is 7:14, Lk 1:42,

aussi d'un manque de clarté. Allons-nous expliquer *obscurum per obscurius*?"

[26] St. Anthony Guild ed., pp. 11-13. This is the case with references to Gen 3: 15, a whole series of patristic types, and Lk 1: 28.

[27] Paulist Press ed., pp. 14-15. It even says that theologians and preachers "have been rather free in their use of events and expressions taken from the Sacred Scripture to explain their belief in the Assumption."

[28] Miller, *art. cit.*, pp. 428, 429.

Buzy, *art. cit.*, pp. 392-393. Both deny categorically the typical sense of the text.

[29] Dominic J. Unger, O. F. M. Cap., in his exhaustive work (*The First Gospel, Gen 3: 15,* St. Bonaventure, N. Y.: Franciscan Institute; 1954) lists those who favor each interpretation of Gen 3: 15.

Pp. 282-284: For the *strict* literal sense of "Her seed" as referring to Christ, he lists about 70 authors; for an *inclusive* literal sense (the fuller sense: it refers primarily to something else, and secondarily to Christ) he

Jn 19:27, Ap 12.[30] These writers feel that the usual classification does not cover such exegesis.

Also, as a related problem, there might be mentioned the fact that today Catholic exegetes are calling into question the strict *literal* Messianic import of some O. T. prophecies (Is 7:14, Dn 7:13-14, Psalms 8 and 69, 2 Sam 7:14), and turning toward a secondary Messianic sense. It is claimed that such prophecies had a fulfillment in their own times. The habit of apologetical treatises of listing the prophecies of the O. T. on one side of the page and literal fulfillments in Christ on the other presents a distorted concept of the prophetic charism. This charism was primarily directed toward the reform of its own time, and the prophetic message was often fulfilled in contemporary circumstances. Only secondarily but more perfectly then would it be fulfilled in Christ.[31] Yet the typical sense, with the necessity of finding type and antitype, does not attract many of these exegetes who are dissatisfied with the literal interpretation of Messianic prophecies. The fulfillment seems to be of the text itself, rather than of a figure. And so, if it is found necessary to present another classification among the senses of Scripture, one may well expect to find these prophecies as examples of the new sense.[32]

Therefore, in the employment of Marian texts by theologians (or perhaps by the Magisterium) and in the case of some Messianic prophecies, objectively there seems to be an exegesis which is neither strictly literal nor typical.

* * *

lists about 50 authors. (Yet since 1925, 20 new authors support the strict literal sense; 27 new authors support the fuller sense.)

Pp. 288-289: For the sense of "the woman," a much larger percentage favors the strict literal sense.

We are not sure that Unger's inclusive literal sense is always the same as the *sensus plenior*.

[30] For one or the other of these texts we may list Buzy, Moriarty, Steinmann, Coppens, Rivera, Laridon, Sutcliffe, Tuya, and others.

[31] Most interesting is a remark which Pascal made of prophecies (cited by Seisdedos, *art. cit.*, pp. 62-63): If prophecies have only one sense, the Messias is not yet come; if they have two senses, he is certainly come.

[32] Cf. c. IV, on examples of the *sensus plenior*.

Fourth and finally comes the problem of the harmony that should exist between the two Testaments. The questions that we have hitherto discussed were *a posteriori* ones. Faced with the objective evidence of the exegesis practiced in the N. T. and the Fathers, in the liturgy and the Magisterial documents, we investigated to discover if the usual classification of senses fitted this evidence. Here the difficulty is more subjective.

The O. T. and the N. T. have a common principal Author; both are inspired; both contain revelation; both narrate the story of God's action in history for the salvation of man. Consequently, even *a priori,* we should expect to find a certain amount of harmony between the two. The whole of the Fathers' scriptural outlook was based on the assumption that such a harmony did exist. Before the beginning of the patristic period, St. Paul stated that the O. T. or "the Law has been our tutor in Christ."[33] Near the end, St. Augustine said "The N. T. lies hidden in the Old."[34] Between these two poles the theme of unity was repeated over and over again. As Kerrigan remarks, some of the Fathers stressed it even to the point of identity.[35] (The only discordant voices were heretical, *e. g.,* Marcion.) Why did the two Testaments harmonize? — because they both dealt with the central figure of time, Christ. The O. T. dealt with him in symbol, type and prophecy; the N. T., with him in word and deed. We might say that the two Testaments form a triptych with Christ as the center piece.[36] Or as Claudel beautifully puts it, "Behold the page between the two Testaments all set in vivid red."[37] Or still, with an even greater writer, "For us the Testaments are both new; they have not the same age; but they have for object the same novelty."[38] Thus the Christocentric ordination of the O. T. has always been the key to keeping the two Testaments one book.

[33] Gal 3: 24.

[34] Cf. above, c. II, n. 101.

[35] Kerrigan, *op. cit.,* p. 132.

[36] Coppens, *Harmonies,* p. 41.

[37] Quoted in de Lubac, *Catholicism,* p. 90.

[38] Origen, *In Num. Hom.* 9: 4 (*PG,* 12: 628-629): ". . . et utrumque nobis novum Testamentum est, non temporis aetate, sed intelligentiae novitate."

It is not by accident that the title of Coppens' work on the *sensus plenior* is *Les Harmonies des Deux Testaments.* The question of whether or not the usual classification of senses is enough to effect such a harmony is vital to the whole outlook of Hermeneutics. Of course we must not expect a miracle. No new exegesis, no matter how it stresses the Christological aspect of the O. T., can ever suppress the individual characteristics of each author nor the historical outlook of his work: a perfect harmony with the N. T. is impossible.[39] But the way we interpret Scripture should allow us to see, besides individual and historical peculiarities, the whole of God's plan in the O. T.—His orientation of history toward His Son.

No one can deny that literal exegesis helps toward this goal. (Of course, we refer to literal exegesis in the hands of believers. In the hands of rationalist critics it is another affair. It is a myopic and barren science, not of the living word of God, but purely of documents and emendations, of hieroglyphs and ostraca. A Protestant scholar has truly remarked that this exegesis belongs "far more appropriately in a faculty of liberal arts than in a faculty of theology."[40]) The true literal sense narrates how the Jews received progressive revelation, preparing their minds and hearts for Christ. It shows God working in history to purify His vehicle of Redemption, the Chosen People. It even gives us some literal prophecies of Christ (of which the recognized number seems to be ever decreasing). Yet it leaves untouched, as far as Christology is concerned, vast portions of the O. T. in history, wisdom and prophetic literature.[41] These sections, of course, play a role in the human development of the Jews. But are they not in some way more closely connected with Christ? Do they not play more than a human role in God's plan?

[39] Coppens, *Harmonies*, pp. 41-44. P. 44: "Sans doute, l'unité d'auteur divin confère à la Bible une unité minima de dessein et de finalité . . . Mais cette inspiration et cette trame générales laissent intacte la physionomie de chaque livre."

[40] A citation in Schoder, *art. cit.*, p. 85.

[41] Jean Daniélou, S. J., "Exégèse et Dogme," in "Sur l'Exégèse Biblique," by Claudel, Massignon and Daniélou, *DV*, 10, p. 93: "Et que nous importerait l'Ancien Testament, s'il n'était qu'une documentation sur les moeurs d'une tribu de bédouins durant les deux millénaires qui précèdent le Christ."

The affirmative answer to these queries has led the Church to recognize a typical exegesis of the Scriptures which would relate to Christ figures and objects in the O. T., things which are not literally Christological. Thus the typical sense aids in establishing the harmony of the two Testaments, for it brings them together as type and antitype, as shadow and reality. But, when all is said and done, the strict typical sense does affect only a limited number of realities in the O. T. and *not the text of the O. T.*[42] Are we then to say that all passages of the *text* of the O. T. which are not literally applied to Christ have in no way been fulfilled in Christ? Is there not in some instances a deeper, fuller meaning of the text itself so that, although it was accomplished literally at the time it was uttered, it is even more profoundly accomplished in Christ? If such a meaning exists (and more and more scholars say that it does on the basis of the objective evidence presented above), we have come a long way toward solving the problem of the harmony of the two Testaments, a harmony that is a fact and must be accounted for in our exegesis.

And so we finish our presentation of problems which a correct classification of senses must resolve. In the first problem, it was clear that to the minds of many top scholars the usual classification of senses into literal and typical (as strictly defined above) does not account for all valid N. T. and patristic exegesis. The second question, that of liturgical exegesis, was hampered by the lack of scientific study. Yet, at least, with the liturgical use of the Psalms, we often seem to have a sense of fulfillment which is neither really literal nor typical. Thirdly, the exact use of Marian texts in Magisterial documents is difficult to determine. Many authors, however, are not satisfied with calling the Marian application of certain O. T. texts (as well as prophecies) either literal or typical, and find refuge in a new classification. And finally, it does seem as if a reclassification would facilitate a recognition of the harmony between the two Testaments. The burden of all this evidence has forced Scripture men to reexamine the fundamental

[42] As will be pointed out below, when it does overflow into the words and we have a typical sense of the text itself, this can hardly be classified under the strict typical sense (which, by definition, is not a sense of the text), but needs a new classification.

tenets of Hermeneutics, and there have been several modern attempts toward a solution. It is convenient to distinguish four trends and to treat them separately.

II. THE SOLUTIONS

(1) More inspirational use of literal interpretation. Perhaps the most widely followed policy among Catholic exegetes is one which, while interesting itself chiefly in the literal historical sense, points out the religious mission of the Jewish people, their close contact with God, the spiritual value of their poetry and prayers, etc. Many seminary courses and Catholic books of exegesis accept this outlook on the O. T., and indeed are bitter opponents of any rationalistic tendencies in contemporary interpretation. To the scholarship of these exegetes we owe an immense debt of gratitude: they have enabled the Church to maintain proudly its position of leadership in biblical studies, and have kept Scripture free from the Scylla of unrestrained allegory and the Charybdis of skepticism. A complete understanding of the literal sense of the Bible will always remain the prime duty of exegetes, and any secondary sense of Scripture which departs from a literal basis will be little else than a chimera.[43] Yet the question may arise whether the noblest use of the literal sense is enough to solve the problems presented above. Many Scripture scholars feel that it is not; their solutions however must presuppose the literal sense and be based on it.

* * *

(2) Revivifying the typical sense. A second trend, which has as its object more properly the solution of the difficulties mentioned above, turns to the typical sense. A revival of interest in the typical sense has long been a desideratum. As Coppens remarks, typology has often been considered an article of luxury and of

[43] The primacy of the literal sense is well treated in Coppens, *Harmonies*, pp. 104-119.

Pius XII, *Divino Afflante Spiritu* (Trans. in *Rome and Scripture*), p. 92. " In the performance of this task let the interpreters bear in mind that their foremost and greatest endeavor should be to discern and define clearly that sense of the biblical words which is called literal."

doubtful taste.[44] This revival has taken place both in Catholic and Protestant circles. *Facile princeps* of the movement is Fr. Daniélou. He assures us with utmost confidence: "It is in fact the notion of type . . . which permits us to posit the relation between the two Testaments."[45] For Daniélou, the Apostolic exegesis had for its principal object a demonstration that O. T. types had been realized in Jesus Christ; and thus typology had a predominant role in the N. T.[46] There are only two senses, the literal and the typical; and the great contribution of the Fathers was the development of the typical or Christological sense.[47] In his resistance to a new classification in the senses of Scripture, he is vehement. In fact he accuses those who favor the *sensus plenior* of a sort of conspiracy to deny the typical sense.[48]

[44] J. Coppens, "Pour une meilleure intelligence des Saintes Écritures," *ETL*, 27 (1951), p. 504: "Trops longtemps le sens typique a été considéré comme une article de luxe, d'un luxe et d'un gout douteux."

L. Bouyer, *Le Mystère Pascal* (Paris: Cerf, 3rd ed., 1950), p. 41, n. 44: "La question de l'exégèse allégorique n'a guère été sérieusement étudiée à l'époque moderne. Cela est dû, sans doute, à une juste réaction contre les extravagances médiévales; mais aussi un rationalisme inconscient paraît, sur ce point, obnubiler encore le sens historique des meilleurs patrologues."

C. Spicq, O. P., "L'avènement de la théologie biblique," *RSPT*, 34 (1951), p. 569, is of a different outlook: "Cette insuffisance, en effet, conduit maints auteurs à minimiser la signification et la valeur du sens obvie ou littéral, et à lui superposer un sens supplémentaire proprement divin, voire un sens spirituel, notamment typique, et ce qui est encore pis, à deviner une polysémie. Les plus avisés parlent d'un sens plénier, ou mieux *plenior*." Yet cf. n. 13 above in this chapter.

[45] Daniélou, "Traversée de la Mer Rouge," p. 420: "C'est en effet la notion de type, qui marque à la fois continuité et infériorité, qui permet de penser la relation des deux Testaments."

[46] Jean Daniélou, *Sacramentum Futuri* (Paris: Beauchesne, 1950), p. 257. "Les écrits du Nouveau Testament nous montrent un stade déjà évolué de cette typologie apostolique."

Also, "The Fathers and the Scriptures," p. 270, "The New Testament did not have to invent typology. Its essential message is that the types are fulfilled in Jesus Christ."

[47] Daniélou, "Les divers sens," p. 120.

[48] Daniélou, Review of Coppens' *Harmonies*, *DV*, 16, p. 150: "Ce qui en effet obscurit actuellement la question, c'est que les exégètes littéraux, se

In judgment and appreciation of these ideas, we face some difficulties. What does Daniélou mean by type? Does he mean type in the strict sense, confined to realities, exclusive of the text, outside the ken of the hagiographer, etc.?[49] If so, it is not easy to reconcile his statements about typology in the N.T. with those of Frs. Cerfaux, Fischer, and Van der Ploeg, mentioned in this chapter. And again, on the exegesis of the Fathers, Daniélou runs contrary to Penna, Mondésert, de Lubac, Vaccari, Devreesse, and Guillet, all of whom in very specialized studies distinguish between typology and other valid patristic secondary senses. Part of the dispute, of course, is centered around the Antiochene *theoria,* which is not strictly typical. Daniélou's judgment on Antioch is concise: "And so, through their refusal to accept historical typology, they ended up in a Platonic kind of allegorization which was entirely foreign to genuine tradition."[50] We are in no position to solve the question; but on the weight of authority, it seems that Daniélou is guilty of oversimplifying. On the other hand, if by typical sense Daniélou means something beyond the ordinary narrow connotation of type, his terminology may confuse some.[51]

In his studies on the typical sense, Fr. Daniélou makes it quite plain that he is opposed to innovations in typology, and prefers the patristic types.[52] Of course, within the scope of patristic typology he admits that there is much false allegory; but there are also many true and valid types which should not be neglected in present day exegesis. (Fr. Coppens finds some of these types, how-

refusant à admettre autre chose que le sens littéral, s'enforcent de ramener le sens figuratif à celui-ci."

Coppens denies any such refusal to admit the typical sense ("Bibliographie," p. 89); so does Fernández ("Nota Referente," p. 75). And we must confess that our reading, which would include all the major proponents of the *sensus plenior,* has failed to uncover any such denial.

[49] He certainly confines it to realities, "The Fathers and the Scriptures," p. 268: "It is the realities themselves that are types."

[50] *Ibid.,* p. 272.

[51] Burghardt, *art. cit.,* p. 111. "A patient, protracted effort by the present writer to put unity and clarity into Daniélou's terminology has resulted in an admission of defeat." He has found five different subdivisions of the typical sense.

[52] Daniélou, Review of Coppens' *Harmonies,* p. 152.

ever, to be of little value to the man of today, *e.g.*, Rahab and her red rag.)[53] Claudel seems to share Daniélou's ideas on the exclusive value of patristic types.[54] Yet this movement to revivify patristic typology is not without opposition; Charlier claims that such an outlook constitutes an active danger of becoming simply a negative reaction against the scientific instead of a combination of patristic method with scientific technique.[55] In any case, one may well ask whether, even with new studies being made of the typical sense and of its usage in the Fathers, typology in its usual meaning solves the questions we have broached. Or is there needed some legitimate secondary sense of Scripture which can be based on modern discoveries and can be applied to the text itself without some reality or "thing" as a necessary intermediary?

* * *

(3) A plea for the Spiritual Sense. Bouyer, Charlier, Chifflot, Congar, de Lubac, Dubarle, Hamman, Kehoe, and Russel all speak of a "spiritual" sense of Scripture. However, it is very difficult to formulate an exact definition of this sense as it is presented in the various authors. Bouyer, for instance, says that two principles dominate "spiritual" exegesis: that the Bible is the living word of God addressed to modern man (taking part in a liturgical celebration); that the O.T. is enlightened by the New, while the N.T. only reaches its depth when confronted with the Old.[56] "Spiritual" exegesis then would seem to be one which would bring out the living value of the Bible and effect a harmony

[53] Coppens, *Harmonies*, p. 93. Cf. also n. 88, p. 93.

Penna, *op. cit.*, p. 139, gives some examples of fanciful types in St. Jerome.

Kerrigan, *op. cit.*, p. 460, doubts if Cyril's exegetical principles are likely to be of much value to modern exegesis.

[54] Paul Claudel (with Massignon and Daniélou), *art. cit.*, p. 81.

[55] Charlier, *art. cit.*, p. 16, "L'Église ne se penche pas sur son passé que pour en construire l'avenir." Cf. also p. 22.

Coppens, "Nouvelles Réflexions," p. 8, presents an incisive criticism of exaggerations in the pan-typology movement. Of particular interest is his observation that the ability of typology to give the uneducated an insight into the Scriptures has been exaggerated.

[56] Bouyer, *art. cit.*, p. 30.

between the two Testaments. He seems to equate it to allegory (in the pristine sense) which is composed of typology and anagogy.[57] Charlier says that all the senses of the Bible can be narrowed down to two: literal and "spiritual."[58] He tells us, "Spiritual exegesis for the Fathers consisted in uncovering the deep and objective meaning of a text in the light of the entire economy of salvation."[59] This meaning uncovered by "spiritual" exegesis is not distinct from the literal sense, but a recognition of its fullness through the light of revelation.[60] For Chifflot, the "spiritual" sense flows from the connection that God has established between different realities existing at various stages of biblical revelation. The Bible may be considered as a fibrous structure consisting of threads of connection between its different parts, and thus permeated with a vast "spiritual" sense.[61] It is probably de Lubac who has gone deepest into the "spiritual" sense. Certain points of his treatment are clear: it is a meaning of "things" and seems to have escaped the awareness of the human author;[62] it goes beyond the narrow confines of typology.[63] However, as Coppens

[57] *Ibid.*, pp. 30-31: "Il faut préciser davantage: le lien entre les deux [Testaments] se définit par l'allégorie, au sens précis que l'antiquité donnait à ce terme." He then mentions the threefold sense of the O. T.: literal, typical, anagogical. Later on p. 48, he has a very interesting remark on this typical sense: "Ainsi, le sens typique faisant converger sur le Christ et l'Église toutes les *paroles* apparemment dispersées qui constituent l'Écriture, se prolonge-t-il de lui-même dans le sens anagogique . . ." Italics ours.

[58] Charlier, *art. cit.*, p. 23.

[59] *Ibid.*, p. 24. "L'exégèse spirituelle, pour les Pères, consiste à dégager la portée profonde et objective d'un texte, à la lumière de l'économie entière du salut."

[60] *Ibid.*, p. 27, the literal sense is the only sense. P. 32: "Ce que l'on appelle le sens spirituel n'est donc pas à proprement parler un sens distinct du sens littéral: il est contenu objectivement à l'intérieur de la lettre, comme un aspect—le plus profond et le plus décisif—qui ne se révèle qu'à la lumière, divinement acceptée par la foi, de la Révélation achevée."

[61] Chifflot, *art. cit.*, pp. 253-254.

[62] de Lubac, *Histoire et Esprit*, p. 390: "Et puisque, sens des choses, il n'est pas mis en elles par l'auteur humain d'un livre, il vient tout entier de l'Esprit."

[63] *Ibid.*, p. 387.

remarks, there remains much that is imprecise about de Lubac's "spiritual" sense; for at times he seems to equate it with a sense obtained through reading the sacred books piously under an interior illumination of the soul.[64]

Nor is this confusing use of "spiritual" confined to individual authors; official Church documents use it in various meanings. In the 1941 Biblical Commission decree, spiritual is a synonym of typical.[65] Both the 1950 Instruction and *Divino Afflante Spiritu* seem to include in "spiritual" all non-literal senses intended by God.[66] But in *Humani Generis*, those who desert the literal sense for "a new exegesis, which they are pleased to call symbolic or spiritual," are criticized.[67]

With all these divergent views, a general definition of the "spiritual" sense is impossible at the present time. But this idea appears to be prevalent: the "spiritual" sense includes typology and a certain plus value beyond it—in other words, any valid meaning of Scripture that is not literal. Fr. Kehoe gives a good hint when he says that the typical sense is an instance of the "spiritual" sense but does not exhaust it.[68] This sense then approaches a desirable solution to the problems mentioned above. Yet a study of the literature on the "spiritual" sense almost inevitably leaves a certain feeling of vagueness and a desire for a little more precision.

Of interest is Fr. Braun's judgment on the "spiritual" sense.

[64] *Ibid.*, pp. 391 ff.

Cf. Coppens, "Nouvelles Réflexions," p. 17.

Also, "Pour une meilleure intelligence," p. 506, he accuses Schildenberger of sharing de Lubac's imprecisions: "Tantôt ce sens paraît se confondre avec le sens typique, tantôt il paraît plutôt consister dans le sens chrétien et vital que chaque fidèle peut dégager des Écritures saintes à titre privé, grâce aux dons, peut-être à un charisme spécial de l'Esprit."

[65] *Rome and Scriptures*, p. 131: "The spiritual or typical sense . . ."

[66] *AAS*, 42 (1950), p. 501. *Rome and Scriptures*, p. 93.

[67] NCWC trans., p. 11.

For observations on some of these usages, cf. de Ambroggi, 1950 article, pp. 444-445.

[68] Richard Kehoe, O. P., "The Spiritual Sense of Scripture," *Blackfriars*, 27 (1946), p. 247.

Incidentally, St. Jerome was of the same opinion. Cf. Penna, p. 146.

He says that it can be made equal to the typical sense plus the *sensus plenior*; it is a generic title under which there are two species with various subdivisions.[69] Among the other authors, Fr. Coppens approached this same idea once (however, he added a third species, the allegorical sense [70]), but has changed his table of senses at least twice since then.[71] Gribomont too may be near this point of view when he suggests that, "The *sensus plenior* and the typical sense would really be only correlative aspects of the organic development of the literal sense in the framework of the progress of revelation." [72]

Thus the exegetical trend behind the "spiritual" sense may well run in harmony with the idea of a *sensus plenior*. Of course, there are differences and the respective proponents are not entirely in agreement; but the important thing is that there are similarities which may be capitalized on. Any possibility of obtaining unity of terminology (without sacrificing precision) in this much confused field is to be grasped at. The greatest obstacle is set up by those who deny that the *sensus plenior* has any relation to the spiritual sense, because they consider the *sensus plenior* as literal (in a broader usage of the word than we have given). This is a problem that deserves much discussion—which will be given to it in the next chapter—but in the meantime the words of Fr. Congar deserve attention: "I don't understand at all the fanaticism which drives certain exegetes to haunt everyone who uses what they call a spiritual or symbolic sense, while in practice they them-

[69] Braun, *art. cit.*, pp. 297-298. His definition of the *sensus plenior*, however, excludes any consciousness of it on the part of the human author. Cf. appendix.

[70] Joseph Coppens, "Le problème du sens plénier," *Problèmes et Méthode*, p. 18. Yet cf. also "Nouvelles Réflexions," p. 17. He points out disapprovingly that de Lubac uses "spiritual sense" in two meanings: (a) equal to typology; (b) a religious reading. Therefore he finds the term too vague.

[71] Coppens, "Bibliographie," p. 89.

Coppens, "Nouvelles Réflexions," pp. 16, 19.

[72] Gribomont, "Sens plénier," p. 31. "Sens plénier et sens typique ne seraient en effet que les aspects corrélatifs du développement organique du sens littéral, dans le cadre du progrès de la Révélation."

selves bring back under different names the real substance of the sense they have attacked in other authors."[73]

* * *

(4) The introduction of the *sensus plenior.* The final attempt to solve the problems we have mentioned in this chapter is the introduction of a new classification into the scriptural senses. The next chapter is dedicated to this subject.

[73] Congar, Review of Vischer's book, p. 337. "Je comprends d'autant moins l'archarnement que mettent certains exégètes à poursuivre tout usage de ce qu'ils appellent sens spirituel ou symbolique, que practiquement, ils réintroduisent sous des noms différents la substance réelle de ce qu'ils ont pourchassé chez les autres."

Chapter Four

THE *SENSUS PLENIOR*

I. THE DEFINITION

And so finally we are led to a study of the *sensus plenior* as a possible solution to the problems proposed in the classification of scriptural senses. This study will constitute the rest of our work. Since the term *sensus plenior* is of recent origin, it might be of interest to comment very briefly on its history.

One must distinguish carefully between the *sensus plenior* as a specific title of a sense of Scripture, and the general usage of the term meaning any more profound interpretation of the Bible. There are many instances of the latter where an author writing in Latin about a text will say that "more fully" it has a certain meaning. For instance, Benedict XV speaks of a "*sensum plenum*" which we are to draw from the Scriptures.[1] Cornely refers to "*accuratiorem et pleniorem . . . sensum,*" but this is in connection with the consequent sense.[2] The honor, however, of having first used the term "*sensus plenior*" to designate clearly one of the senses of Scripture belongs, to the best of our knowledge, to Fr. Fernández, writing in the 1920's.[3] Since then the term has been accepted by many authors.

Now as to the actual value of the term *plenior,* some like it and others do not. Coppens says it is a most natural title and almost

[1] Benedict XV, *Spiritus Paraclitus, Enchiridion Biblicum,* no. 485 ". . . ad plenum ex Sacris Libris sensum eruendum." This seems to mean some sort of a synthesis derived from the literal and spiritual sense taken together.

Cf. Courtade, "Les écritures," p. 483. Braun, *art. cit.*, p. 295.

Also Coppens, *Harmonies,* p. 35, n. 3.

[2] Cornely, *op. cit.*, p. 528. Yet he thinks it is not really a consequent but a literal sense.

[3] Andrea Fernández, S. J., "Hermeneutica," *Institutiones Biblicae* (2nd ed., Rome: Biblical Institute, 1927), p. 306. We have been unable to ascertain whether or not it is mentioned in the first edition of 1925. Both Coppens and Courtade say that Fernández was the first to use the term "*sensus plenior,*" and Courtade attributes it to the first edition.

scriptural.[4] Van der Ploeg suggests its affinity to the Greek word πληρόω, so often used in the N. T. as "to fulfill, to render full," the meaning of the O. T.[5] The main objection to the term *plenior* or "fuller" is a logical one:[6] "full" has no comparative —a thing that is full cannot really be fuller. And so some propose another title such as "plenary sense"[7] or "evangelical sense."[8] But as Sutcliffe remarks, a thing can be fuller in the sense of approaching closer to an absolute fullness not already achieved.[9] The O. T. was a partial revelation—it had meaning in itself, but it attained to fullness only with Christ. It is the case of something being full in one respect and not in another; and thus from an overall position, it is capable of being fuller. Therefore, in the ordinary universe of discourse, there is no real objection to the term "fuller" or *plenior.* In any case, the term *sensus plenior* seems here to stay.

* * *

If this classification in the senses of Scripture received a definite name some thirty years ago, we must not assume that the idea behind such a classification is a new one. Even such a decided opponent as Fr. Courtade admits its antiquity.[10] In the nineteenth

[4] Coppens, "Le problème," p. 19, n. 11. He points out that the term has been especially popular in Italy.

[5] Van der Ploeg, "L'Exégèse," p. 193. He suggests examples such as Mt 1:22: "Now all this came to pass that there might be *fulfilled* what was spoken by the Lord through the prophet." Italics ours.

[6] Fr. Spicq (cf. above: c. III, n. 13) says the term may be equivocal, but his objection seems to be that it might lead one to think of a multiple literal sense.

[7] Sutcliffe, *art. cit.*, p. 335. In Italian de Ambroggi uses *senso pieno.*

[8] Colunga, *art. cit.*, p. 451: "La teologia nueva pregona le existencia de este sentido *pleno*, que mejor llamaríamos *evangélico*."

[9] Sutcliffe, *art. cit.*, p. 335.

[10] Courtade, "Les Écritures," p. 481: "L'idée est ancienne. Se rencontre-t-elle chez les Pères? On discute. Elle se rencontre chez beaucoup de scolastiques, chez saint Thomas, chez Suarez."

Colunga, *art. cit.*, p. 451: "No es éste un hallazgo de los modernos. . . . Pero nos atrevemos a afirmar que la única novedad que en el existe se reduce a la afirmación de la revelación progresiva, cosas enseñadas y por los Padres y por Santo Tomás, y la unidad de la revelación en sus múltiples etapas."

century in particular do we find a proximate preparation for the new classification: several of the finest theologians and Scripture scholars of the period suggest a sense of the Bible very close to that which we now call the *sensus plenior.*

Cardinal Newman believed in a more profound interpretation which would uncover truths adumbrated in the O. T.[11] In the words of Jaak Seynaeve in his masterful study on Newman and the Scriptures: "Let us say at once that, in our view, Newman seems to admit the existence of a *sensus plenior* as a definite kind of mystical meaning not to be identified with the typological sense."[12] Cornely, too, favored such a sense.[13] He distinguished two divisions of the consequent sense: the second is that which we usually call consequent, i. e., the meaning derived through a syllogism built on a scriptural text. But the first consists in a richer meaning which a passage assumes long after it has been written, through a certain evolution in the meaning of its words. Thus wisdom has a certain meaning when spoken of as human wisdom, but an even fuller meaning when applied to God. Although Cornely calls this "*accuratiorem et pleniorem sensum*" a consequent sense, he admits that it does not go beyond the limits of the literal sense.

[11] John Henry Newman, *The Arians of the Fourth Century* (London: Burns and Oates, 5th ed.), p. 56: "The word *allegorizing* must here be understood in a wide signification; as including in its meaning, not only the representation of truths, under a foreign, though analogous exterior, after the manner of Our Lord's parables, but the practice of generalizing facts into principles, of adumbrating greater truths under the image of lesser, of implying the consequences or the basis of doctrines in their correlatives, and altogether those instances of thinking, reasoning, and teaching, which depend on the use of propositions which are abstruse, and of connexions which are obscure, and which, in the case of uninspired authors, we consider profound, or poetical, or enthusiastic, or illogical . . ."

[12] Seynaeve, *op. cit.*, p. 339. Cf. also pp. 390-391.

[13] Cornely, *op. cit.*, pp. 527-530. Especially p. 528: "Iam vero, quum hi sensus non primarie quidem voci illi subsint, sed secundarie et consequenter ad eius cum hoc subjecto conjunctionem exoriantur, aliqui accuratiorem et pleniorem hunc sensum vocant consequentem, monentque hac ratione explicari multa, quae ab aliis multiplicem sensum habere dicuntur . . . quoniam ea quae vocis in suo contextu consideratae vim exhauriunt quidem, sed non excedunt, etiam limites sensus literalis non transgrediuntur."

Fr. Lagrange proposed the hypothesis of a sense in some way "*supra-littéral.*"[14] He seems to mean by it that additional meaning which is grasped from a scriptural text which has been placed in the context of the whole Bible, or which has been confronted with other and clearer revelation on the same subject. Fr. Pesch sees the possibility of an "*altiorem sensum*" which the human author did not foresee, but which God intended to express in the words of Scripture[15] (therefore, not a typical sense, which is a sense of "things" rather than of words). After citing many authorities for this sense, he says, "These authorities teach that underlying the words of Scripture there is frequently a deeper sense than that which can be obtained by the common rules of interpretation, and that the hagiographers themselves did not always understand in its full amplitude the sense of the inspired words."[16] Prat was still another who insisted that we cannot confine the divine message to those points of which the human author was fully conscious, for the Church is justified in finding in obscure prophecies a hidden sense which may not have been understood by the prophets themselves. He confines this hidden sense to prophecies.[17]

[14] M. J. Lagrange, O. P., "L'interprétation de la Sainte Écriture par l'Église," *RB*, 9 (1900), pp. 141-142: "Ces paroles [Providentissimus Deus] semblent faire allusion à un sens en quelque sorte supra-littéral qui ne peut être déterminé que par une autorité compétente . . . À prendre un texte en soi, on n'en tirerait pas cette conclusion: elle apparaît cependant comme une résultante par la confrontation avec une autre verité, affirmée par le même Esprit de Dieu."

The passage in *Prov. Deus* to which he refers is this: (*Rome and Scriptures*, p. 14) "For the language of the Bible is employed to express, under the inspiration of the Holy Spirit, many things which are beyond the power and scope of the reason of man—that is to say, divine mysteries and all that is related to them. There is sometimes in such passages a fullness and a hidden depth of meaning which the letter hardly expresses and which the laws of interpretation hardly warrant."

[15] Pesch, *op. cit.*, pp. 509-511.

[16] *Ibid.*, pp. 510-511: "Hae igitur auctoritates docent subesse saepe verbis scripturae altiorem sensum, quam qui communibus interpretandis praeceptis inveniri possit, et ipsos hagiographos non semper totam amplitudinem sensus verborum inspiratorum comprehendisse."

[17] F. Prat, S. J., "Les historiens inspirés et leurs sources," *Études* 86 (1901), pp. 494-496.

With such precursors as Newman, Cornely, Lagrange, Pesch and Prat, we need not wonder that the theory of a *sensus plenior* attracted many followers once promulgated by Fr. Fernández.

* * *

It is now indeed time to turn to a definition of the *sensus plenior.* Practically each of its proponents and attackers has his own definition: in an appendix we list a good number of these. But for clarity's sake, it seems best at the start to select a common denominator definition with which nearly all can agree, and to leave till later all disputed points. The following definition is serviceable:

> *The* sensus plenior *is that additional, deeper meaning, intended by God but not clearly intended by the human author, which is seen to exist in the words of a biblical text (or group of texts, or even a whole book) when they are studied in the light of further revelation or development in the understanding of revelation.*

Perhaps a dissection of the definition is called for. The fuller sense is an *additional, deeper meaning*: this is evident from the word *plenior,* as well as its frequently used synonyms: *amplior, eminentior, uberior.* It is a meaning *intended by God,* which fact enables us to call it a sense of Scripture. Since God is the principal author of the Bible, whatever He intended to have expressed by its words is truly a scriptural sense, whether or not the human author fully intended it. That *the hagiographer did not clearly intend* the fuller sense of the text he wrote would be conceded by all scholars. The exact extent of his knowledge and intent, however, is greatly disputed and will be discussed later.

The fuller sense exists *in the words of a text.* This clearly distinguishes it from the generally accepted notion of the typical sense which is primarily a sense of "things" written about in the text: the *sensus plenior* needs no such intermediary. Likewise this sense is already present or latent in the text; it is not adjoined by mere accommodation. The fuller sense thus presupposes the literal sense of the passage and is a development of that literal sense. And to be sure that some deeper meaning is really a legitimate *sensus plenior,* we must show its very real connection to the literal sense, of which it is an evolution, an *approfondissement.*

The definition continues with the words: "*or group of texts.*" This indicates that not only a single text but also an idea running through many passages is capable of having a *sensus plenior.* Thus the many texts referring to Emmanuel in Isaias, chapters 7, 8, and 9, are cited by some as taking on a fuller meaning in the light of what we know about Christ. Indeed, a fuller sense is possible even when the texts in the group are in quite different contexts, perhaps separated by many years and by a difference of authorship.[18] Finally, a whole book, such as the Canticle of Canticles, can assume a fuller sense.

The words "*further revelation or development in the understanding of revelation*" are so phrased as to admit both the Old and New Testaments to the scope of the *sensus plenior.* In the texts of the O. T., the constantly developing Jewish revelation could throw light on events of earlier history. Bouyer distinguishes two levels in Jewish history: first, the historical events themselves; and second, their later interpretation by the prophets and by the authors of the Sapiential Books.[19] But of course the great key to the *sensus plenior* of the O. T. was the revelation that is Christ; he is the key that unlocked the treasures of the Jewish Scriptures. Nevertheless one must not suppose that the full meaning of the N. T. was immediately evident to the early Christians. Even though there is no new public revelation, development in Christian doctrine has enabled us to penetrate more to the core of N. T. texts and understand their *sensus plenior.*

II. THE PROOFS

Once a working definition of the *sensus plenior* has been established, the next logical step is the presentation of the evidence responsible for the definition. Actually in chapter III the reader has already seen in some detail the basic problems which led men to propose the new classification known as the *sensus plenior.* Since

[18] Buzy, *art. cit.,* p. 400.

[19] Bouyer, *art. cit.,* pp. 35-36.

Cf. above, c. II, section I on Jewish exegesis.

these problems serve as our proofs, it is well here to point up more directly, but very, very briefly, the relevancy of these problems to the fuller sense.

(A) The exegesis practiced by the N. T. writers and the Fathers is the first reason for positing the *sensus plenior.* As was mentioned, modern studies show that much of this exegesis was more than literal (in the strict sense) and yet not exclusively typical. The words of the O. T., as distinguished from the "things," were interpreted in a more profound way than the human author seems to have had in mind. Such an exegesis is precisely what the classification of the *sensus plenior* covers.

(B) The problem of the interpretation practiced in the liturgy too may achieve at least a partial solution in the acceptance of a fuller sense. The Church, teaching through its liturgy, attaches to the Psalms, for instance, a meaning surpassing the literal but sharply distinct from typology. This meaning seems to be a harmonious development of the text of the O. T., a fulfillment of its words—is not this the *sensus plenior?*

(C) With regard to the exegesis of certain Marian texts by theologians (at least mentioned in magisterial documents), we are faced with the same problem. Many authors deny that such exegesis is literal, and yet refuse to recognize it as typical because no clear types are involved. The more profound meaning flows from the text itself. And as for Messianic prophecies, it will be seen that the principal application of the fuller sense is in the classification of prophecies. It is a refuge for those who know that a text is truly Messianic, but again fail to find such Messianism adequately accounted for in previous classifications. As pointed out, the admission of a *sensus plenior* allows a partial fulfillment of the prophecy in contemporary Jewish history, and thus restores the prophet to his proper perspective as a reformer of his own times.

(D) And finally the fuller sense aids in harmonizing the two Testaments. Positing a *sensus plenior* implies that the text of the O. T. attains to its full meaning not in isolation but only when conjoined to the N. T. and to the Christian Tradition, strictly so-called. Likewise the N. T. becomes a direct organic outgrowth of the O. T., the fulfillment of the destiny of Israel. The very possibility of a *sensus plenior* is hinged to the common authorship of the whole Bible by the one God who so ordained His plan of salvation that His Son fulfilled what was said in the Scriptures before him.

These then are our proofs. They are for the most part *a posteriori.*[20] (On the other hand it will be noted that the arguments against the *sensus plenior* are chiefly *a priori, e. g.,* nature of instrumentality, demands of inspiration. To the best of our knowledge there exists as of this date no real attempt to refute the *sensus plenior* by a confrontation of the *a posteriori* evidence presented above.[21]) Many different competent scholars, whose very words we have quoted, and who worked independently, often with this problem not even in mind, conclude that not all the exegesis practiced by the N. T., the Fathers, the liturgy, and the theologians (the Magisterium?) can be classified as strictly literal or typical. There is still to be accounted for a meaning of the O. T. text itself deeper than that intended by its hagiographer and made clear in later times (which sense seems a prerequisite for a *thoroughgoing* harmony of the two Testaments). The *sensus plenior* classifies exactly such a meaning. *Ergo,* we may conclude to the validity of this classification.

* * *

Now, in a way, such a proof is not apodictic. It is based on interpretation of evidence, something which never allows the certitude of mathematics or metaphysics. Any single one of the arguments when taken alone might not be convincing. But is this not just the sort of proof that underlies the apologetics of many of our most important doctrines? To outsiders we present a series of texts which, separately considered, might be taken otherwise, but whose cumulative effect demands one interpretation. It is a

[20] Fr. Weisengoff (Review of *Problèmes et Méthode, CBQ,* 14 (1952), p. 85), who is not at all a proponent of the fuller sense, admits that its backers do often advance *a posteriori* evidence for it.

[21] By presenting first *a posteriori* evidence, and then attempting to answer *a priori* objections, we are working on the principle of *ab esse ad posse valet illatio.*

case of what Newman calls a convergence of probabilities.[22] Yet "... from probabilities we may construct legitimate proof, sufficient for certitude."[23] It is, as Pope Pius XII points out, a case of the application of the metaphysical principle of sufficient reason.[24] That the arguments for the *sensus plenior* do constitute a proof is witnessed by an impressive list of those who have acknowledged their acceptance in writing: (Most probably its forerunners: Newman, Cornely, Lagrange, Pesch and Prat), Aubert (?), Ayer, Benoit, Braun, Buzy, Cerfaux (?), Colunga, Coppens, Cotter, de Ambroggi, de Riedmatten, de Vaux, Fernández, Fuller, Gribomont, Leal, Miller (?), O'Flynn, Perrella, Renié, Rivera, Schildenberger, Seynaeve, Simon and Prado, Steinmann, Sutcliffe, Ternant, Turrado, Tuya, Van der Ploeg.[25] This list

[22] John Henry Newman, *A Grammar of Assent* (London: Longmans, Green, 1901), p. 293: "... for a syllogism is at least a demonstration, when the premisses are granted, but a cumulation of probabilities, over and above their implicit character, will vary both in their number and their separate estimated value, according to the particular intellect which is employed upon it. It follows that what to one intellect is a proof is not so to another, and that the certainty of a proposition does properly consist in the certitude of the mind which contemplates it. And this of course may be said without prejudice to the objective truth or falsehood of propositions ..."

[23] *Ibid.*, p. 411.

[24] Allocution of Oct. 1, 1942, *AAS* 34 (1942), p. 338. *Clergy Review*, March 1943: "Sometimes moral certainty can be reached only by means of a number of indications and proofs which, taken singly, are not capable of grounding a true certainty, and only by their accumulation succeed in excluding any reasonable doubt in a man of sound judgment. This is not a case of passing from probability to certainty by the simple process of adding probabilities together: that would be an illegitimate transition from one species to another essentially distinct. ... The process is one in which it is recognized that the simultaneous presence of each one of these indications and proofs can only find a sufficient ground in the existence of a common source or basis in which they have their origin; that is to say, in objective truth and reality. The certainty in this case, therefore, arises from the wise application of an absolutely certain and universally valid principle: the principle of sufficient reason ..."

[25] This list is reasonably complete; we most sincerely hope that we have not misrepresented anyone's opinion. The question marks in parentheses indicate authors who mention the *sensus plenior* favorably, but about whose personal opinion there might be some doubt.

contains theologians and Scripture scholars of the most varied interests; there are members of the diocesan clergy and of numerous religious orders; a great many nationalities are represented as well as the great Catholic intellectual centers all over Europe and in Jerusalem. The movement behind the *sensus plenior* is not confined to any group or school; it is a cosmopolitan trend in modern Catholic thought.

III. THE DIVISION

A working notion of the *sensus plenior* has been established from available evidence; there now arises the necessity for a more detailed presentation. To obtain further clarity, it seems useful to discuss a division of the fuller sense. Probably the best method of procedure is to use as an outline Fr. Coppens' tripartite division.[26] This author has been criticized for a too mechanical division of the indivisible.[27] Perhaps such an objection has validity; certainly it is arbitrary to assume that this is the only possible division.[28] Nevertheless, through his dissecting, Coppens has presented a clearer idea of the *sensus plenior* than that hitherto achieved. Actually, the ideas in his division are often common to other authors, but had never been systematically organized before. In any case, it provides a good point of departure.

(1) *The General Sensus Plenior.* (Coppens has coined the word *périchorétique*: he has now recognized that perhaps his neologisms are too forbidding.[29]) This is best described as the homogeneous enrichment in meaning that a text assumes when placed in its setting in the whole Bible. As Coppens puts it, there is a mutual compenetration of the various elements in the Scriptures,[30] so that a passage means more when one has read the whole Bible. Since the various books of the Old and New Testaments are the

[26] Coppens, *Harmonies*, pp. 58-61.

[27] de Vaux, Review of Coppens' *Harmonies*, p. 280.
Fernández, "Hermeneutica," 6th ed., p. 384.

[28] Buzy, *art., cit.*, p. 406, suggested a division into comprehensive and extensive according to whether the fuller sense is derived through greater comprehension or greater extension.

[29] Coppens, "Nouvelles Réflexions," p. 19.

[30] Coppens, *Harmonies*, p. 59.

works of one Author, it is natural that the totality should enable us to understand better the parts. Fr. Chifflot tells us: "Assuredly therefore there reigns from one end of the sacred text to the other a vast spiritual sense which, by placing each event or each thought in its total context, not that of the particular book, . . . confers on it in the eyes of our faith a sense pregnant with future values." [31] Once the mind and plan of the author have been seen, the part fits more easily into the whole.

Perhaps this division of the *sensus plenior* is the answer to Fr. Courtade's plea for a historical sense of Scripture. He says that there is an orientation toward Christ in the whole history of the O. T. which gives new meaning to isolated happenings.[32] If it is true in secular history that our outlook on an event is colored by our philosophy of history, how much more true is this of the history of the Jews, a nation living by its Messianic faith. Both of the ancient schools of exegesis, Alexandria and Antioch, were in accord on a very special historical sense in the O. T.[33] It is probably the very narrowness of the usual classification of scriptural senses into typical and literal that has caused us to forget this historical sense. As Fr. Courtade points out, the historical sense is not literal because it is not clearly intended by the hagiographer; nor is it typical because the significance of history does not reside exclusively in types.[34] It does fit very well, how-

[31] Chifflot, *art. cit.*, p. 253: "Il règne donc assurément, d'un bout à l'autre du texte sacré, un vaste sens spirituel qui, replaçant chaque événement ou chaque pensée dans son contexte total, non pas celui du livre particulier, . . . lui confère aux yeux de notre foi un sens prégnant de l'avenir . . ."

[32] Courtade, "Le sens de l'histoire," p. 136: "L'Ancien Testament annonce Jésus-Christ non seulement par ses paroles, mais par l'inclinaison de toute cette histoire qu'il nous raconte."

However, we should note with Coppens (*Harmonies*, p. 58) that all this new meaning must come from orientation toward Christ and union with the N. T. A fuller meaning which might come from a mere knowledge of contemporary ancient history or archaeology is scarcely a *sensus plenior*.

[33] Guillet, *art. cit.*, p. 272: "Toutes deux s'accordent à voir dans l'histoire du peuple hébreu une préparation à l'Incarnation."

[34] Courtade, "Le sens de l'histoire," pp. 138, 140. Also p. 141: "La classification habituelle des sens scripturaires présente une lacune. Elle ne fait pas au sens de l'histoire biblique la place qui lui revient de droit." However, we must note that a year later Fr. Courtade reacted adversely to Coppens' *Harmonies*, and denied the existence of the *sensus plenior*.

ever (although Fr. Courtade would never say so), into the *sensus plenior* as its first division.[35]

* * *

(2) *The Typical Sensus Plenior* (a name which is not wholly satisfactory since it is open to misunderstanding). Coppens speaks of this as "*historico-typique*" and more recently as "*typisme verbale.*"[36] In chapter I, we pointed out that all biblical types

[35] Albert Gelin, S. S., "Le problème de l'Ancien Testament," *Recherches et Débats,* 13 (1951), p. 11, goes further and defines the whole spiritual sense in terms of this historical sense: "J'appelle sens spirituel l'orientation 'réelle' de l'Ancien Testament vers le Christ, se réalisant dans l'histoire par ces voies privilégiées, dont la direction mystérieuse à ceux qui les pratiquaient est manifestée d'un coup par le fait du Christ."

[36] Coppens, "Bibliographie," p. 89, n. 147. Also "Nouvelles Réflexions," p. 19. In this section we must caution the reader that we are not certain that we have fully understood Fr. Coppens' ideas. We formed our conclusions on the Typical *Sensus Plenior* at least in part from his observations, but the end result may not be at all what he intended. (Perhaps many of the objections levelled at his suggestions are no longer applicable to the above remarks.) There may have been some fluctuations or development in his thought.

(a) At times he seems to mean, in part at least, what we mean above.

(b) At other times he seems to mean that the *text itself* in one part of Scripture is a type of the text of another part of Scripture: the two texts assume the role of type and antitype. *Harmonies,* p. 60: "Voir le sens plénier consistera donc à percevoir un texte de l'Ancien Testament dans son aspect de réalité inchoative du Nouveau, dans sa valeur de type, de figure, de symbole historico-réel . . ." Also, "Le Problème," p. 13: "Si l'on ajoute que les *paroles scripturaires* peuvent à leur tour être considérées comme des réalités posées par Dieu dans l'histoire, le typisme et le sens plénier qui en rejaillit sur elles aboutissent à leur conférer *un sens 'réel'* qui déborde le sens littéral."

To us it would seem very unlikely that one text could stand in relation to another as type to antitype. Coppens himself refers with favor to Charlier's twofold criterion for true typology: internal proportionality and efficient causality (cf. c. I, p. 11 above). There can be resemblance between two texts, but hardly causality. Efficient causality exists between "things" because they enjoy an extrabiblical existence; but it is rather difficult to conceive of a text on one level of revelation *causing* a text on another level of revelation. If this be Coppens' real meaning of "verbal typism," further explanations and some examples are most desirable.

Fernández, "Sentido Plenior," p. 324, disagrees with Coppens: "No cono-

are expressed in words, and that there are types which have only a literary existence. Consequently, while remaining a sense of "things," the typical sense has a certain relation to the words of a text. Beyond this and truly distinct from it is what we call here "the typical sense of words." This is the old idea of Fr. Patrizi [37] that typism sometimes overflows into the text itself.[38] For example, David is a type of Christ: if we study certain events in the life of the Savior, we see how they were foreshadowed by similar events in David's life. That is the typical sense—it concerns David and "things" in David's life which are expressed in certain biblical passages. Yet the fact that David is a type of Christ influences not only the texts which *directly* concern David as a type of Christ, but also many other texts which have really nothing essential to do with making David a type. For instance, we might mention some of the things that David has said in the Psalms, *e. g.*, Psalm 2. That these words of David can be placed on the lips of Christ and have a fuller meaning is in no small

cemos ningún relato bíblico, que como tal, como realidad puramente literaria, encierre un sentido típico propiamente dicho; es decir, que sea figura, tipo de otra cosa, es decir del antitipo."

(c) In still another place, Coppens might be interpreted to identify verbal typism with types which had only a literary existence. In "Nouvelles Réflexions," p. 19, he divides the typical sense into:

1. sens typique historico-verbal	suivant que les réalités, sur lesquelles le typisme s'appuie, ont eu une existence *historique* ou purement *littéraire*.
2. sens typique verbal	

As remarked in Chapter I, the case of types with only a literary existence appears to us to be a case of strict typology, since the type is not the words themselves but the "thing" conjured up by the words. It does not belong to the realm of the *sensus plenior*. Cf. Fr. Fernández' remark, c. I, n. 61.

[37] Patrizi, *op. cit.*, pp. 205 ff.

Coppens, *Harmonies*, pp. 84 ff., has greatly developed Patrizi's thought. The above remarks reflect opinions of both authors.

[38] Patrizi, *op. cit.*, p. 213: "Quod autem sensus spiritalis subesse verbis potuerit, ex eo est, quod de typis ea sint prolata seu quod illa, de quibus prolata sunt, typi fuerint."

Edmund F. Sutcliffe, S. J., "The Plenary Sense as a Principle of Interpretation," *Bb* 34 (1953), p. 338: "The typical sense necessarily overflows from the type itself to the words used about it."

way due to David's being a type of Christ. It is a sense that the type has reflected back on the text:[39] here there is no question of the meaning being directly attached to the "thing"; the richer sense accrues directly to the words (because of the "thing"[40]), and is a development of the literal sense of those words. (In fact, by a sort of *a posteriori* reasoning, it is the deeper signification found in the words which often leads the reader to suspect that there was a type in the first place.[41]) Since this sense is more directly connected to the words than to the "things," it would violate a long accepted terminology to classify it as a typical sense. It fits the definition of the *sensus plenior*, and would seem to be most satisfactorily classified as such.

* * *

[39] Fernández, "Sentido Plenior," pp. 312-313, objects to this idea of Patrizi's that things can throw back a spiritual sense on the words, that a text which describes a type can have reflected on it a spiritual meaning by medium of the antitype. Fernández says that God does not see first the type and then the antitype, but both simultaneously; and He expresses them both simultaneously too, so that any fuller spiritual sense is there directly and not through the antitype. "La palabra inspirada tiene por objeto inmediato próximo y directo así al tipo como al antitipo; uno y otro estan expresados inmediatamente sin intermedio alguno, por la letra del texto sagrado."

The question is a subtle one. God's vision of the two is simultaneous, but is not the expression (in human terms) determined by human laws? Should we demand of human language and thought such simultaneity as Fernández claims, or isn't it more logical to suppose that the antitype is not as proximate and direct an object as the type?

[40] Patrizi would not say this directly. Yet on pp. 213-214, his remarks allow for a close connection between "the spiritual sense of words" and the literal sense.

Coppens, *Harmonies*, p. 85: "On peut même se demander si les textes sacrés ne peuvent pas devenir à l'occasion *directement* l'objet d'une exégèse typologique. Patrizi le nie, mais la raison qu'il invoque est faible."

Does Fr. Miller's idea have any relation to this? Cf. *art. cit.*, p. 428: "Oftmals redet man auch von typischem Sinn, wo der Wortsinn eine ganze Fülle von Gegenständen, handelnden Personen und Ereignissen in sich schliesst, die zwar in sich die Beziehung von Typus und Antitypus haben, aber hier als *Ganzes* unmittelbar erfasst werden."

[41] Patrizi, *op. cit.*, p. 205.

(3) *The Prophetical Sensus Plenior.* The third division of the *sensus plenior,* and perhaps the one most readily admitted, is what Coppens calls "*prophético-typique.*" This is the *sensus plenior* which a prophecy is seen to possess once it has been fulfilled. (Almost all the proponents of the fuller sense agree on this third division; indeed it was in relation to the problem of prophecies that Fernández first conceived the *sensus plenior.*[42]) It is a historical fact that many of the great O. T. prophecies were understood fully only when Christ came. Their vague and even seemingly contradictory character left the complete fulfillment of prophecies a riddle to contemporaries and even to their own authors; but now with the Christian revelation we can see far more clearly what they mean. This species of the *sensus plenior* is especially valuable in our own days when investigation is portraying the prophets less as all-knowing seers and more as men of divinely-inspired and yet unclear presentiments. As shall be seen later on, most of the examples of the fuller sense cited by the various authors belong to this division.

* * *

(4) These are the three divisions suggested by Coppens. Do they exhaust all possibilities? We see no *a priori* reason why they should. At least one case comes to mind which is not exactly covered by any of the three divisions. There are many passages in the O. T., particularly in the Sapiential literature, which are really devotional prayers. A Psalm, such as 22, "The Lord is my shepherd, I shall not want," is often just such an act of devotion. If we repeat these prayers in exactly the same meaning the author intended, *e. g.,* when we use the *Miserere* as a prayer for forgiveness, we are using them in their literal sense. Patrizi wisely warns us not to confuse accommodation with an application of the literal sense to our daily lives.[43]

[42] Fernández, *op. cit.* (2nd ed.), pp. 306-307.

[43] Patrizi, *op. cit.,* p. 278.

Höpfl-Gut, *op. cit.,* p. 466, provides a similar thought by remarking that it is a literal sense to use a proverb like "Obedience is better than a victim" (I Sam 15:22) to inculcate obedience: "Notandum est, non adesse accommodationem, sed verum sensum litteralem si *praecepta vel*

Yet, because of the Christian dispensation, many O. T. prayers and proverbs now take on a fuller meaning.[44] Baptism highlights verse 4 of the *Miserere*: " Wash me thoroughly from my fault and from my sin cleanse me." Christ, the Good Shepherd, gives more meaning to Psalm 23. This type of richer insight is precisely what is at the core of liturgical exegesis. It is not accommodation; rather it fits the definition of the *sensus plenior*. As a fuller sense, the only existing category that might cover it is the General *Sensus Plenior* (although it is preferable to confine this division to historical developments). Really, does it not form another division?—a division for which we would not dare conjure up a name.

And this is only one possibility.[45] As more authors study the *sensus plenior*, surely other classes of instances will appear. And so we believe that Coppens has made a great advance in proposing his division; yet this very advance should show us that the *sensus plenior* is a huge classification, capable of many subdivisions. It started as a category for prophecies. To confine it to prophecies, as some authors seem to wish, is to unduly narrow its scope, and to make necessary a still further classification for these other cases. In an already confused field, more new codifications are most undesirable, especially when a broad interpretation of this one can suffice.

proverbia proferuntur, quae per se omnes homines respiciunt, licet in S. Scriptura ad unum tantum vel ad plures directa fuerint."

[44] We owe the seeds of this idea to Dom M. J. Farrelly, O. S. B., who placed in our hands his unpublished essay on the *sensus plenior*.

[45] de Ambroggi mentions a sense which he calls *senso letterale eminente* (cf. 1950, article, p. 450: " intendiamo un'oggetto che poteva essere *perfettamente* inteso *anche* dall'autore humano, como al vertice di una serie "). An example he proposes is Deut 18:15; Moses, in speaking of the prophet, foresaw (clearly?) a whole series of prophets with Christ as the consummation. Since de Ambroggi allows perfect foreknowledge of this " eminent " sense, it is for him literal. We would suggest that in many cases (including the one cited), the foreknowledge may have been vague. This would reduce de Ambroggi's sense to a *sensus plenior* and perhaps a new subdivision.

IV. RELATIONS TO THE OTHER SCRIPTURAL SENSES

After the definition and division of the *sensus plenior,* the next step is a treatment of the many difficulties created by this new classification. Up to now these difficulties have been avoided for they would have only caused confusion. But once the main ideas have been presented, it is absolutely necessary to face squarely the problems that have divided the proponents of the fuller sense. These problems may be grouped about the relation of the *sensus plenior* to the literal sense, to the typical sense, and to the consequent sense.

(1) Let us begin with the relation of the *sensus plenior* to the literal sense. This is a question that has aroused some dispute. Coppens in three of his classifications has listed the fuller sense as a literal sense;[46] in a fourth he places it under the spiritual sense.[47] Fernández, de Ambroggi, Simon and Prado, Höpfl and Gut, and Ayer are all quite clear in maintaining that it is a literal sense.[48] On the other hand, Benoit insists it is spiritual.[49] Miller says that strictly speaking it is literal, but it will always be classified under the spiritual.[50] The key to the dispute lies in the answer

[46] Coppens, *Harmonies,* p. 99; "Bibliographie," p. 89; "Nouvelles Réflexions," p. 19.

[47] Coppens, "Le Problème," p. 18. This is not a case of inconsistency, but reflects Fr. Coppens' keen awareness of the intricacies of the problem.

[48] Fernández, *Institutiones Biblicae,* 6th ed., p. 383. It should be noted that Fernández excludes from a definition of the literal sense any question of the hagiographer's knowledge.

de Ambroggi, 1932 article, speaks of this as "letterale pieno." Also in the 1952 article, p. 233, he divides the literal into ordinary and "pieno."

Simon and Prado, 3rd ed., 1938, p. 210. The *sensus plenior* is distinct only subjectively, *sine fundamento in re,* from the literal sense. This has been eliminated from the latest edition.

Höpfl and Gut, *op. cit.,* p. 462. It is a *consectarium* of the literal sense.

Ayer, *op. cit.,* p. 108: "Sensus plenior est ille sensus litteralis (latius sumptus) . . ."

[49] Benoit, *op. cit.,* pp. 358-359. It is not literal because it is unknown by the human author.

[50] Miller, *art. cit.,* p. 433: "Für gewöhnlich handelt es sich aber hier doch nur um dem sogenannten *Vollsinn,* der streng genommen zum Literal-

to two questions: how does one define the literal sense? And does one allow the hagiographer any knowledge of the fuller sense?

The question of the definition of the literal sense is the old one of terminology.[51] In Chapter I we mentioned that there is a fundamental division on this point. For those who define the literal sense solely in terms of what God intended in the words of a text, and entirely eschew the human author's consciousness and intention, the *sensus plenior* can certainly be classified as literal. For those who define the literal sense as that which the human (as well as the divine) author intended, the classification is not so simple. If the literal sense is to be confined to what he *clearly* intended, then the *sensus plenior* is not literal; if the literal sense is to cover what he intended even vaguely, then at least some of the fuller sense would be literal. As stated before, we see absolutely nothing to be gained by imprecision; we found it better to consider the literal sense as that which the human author clearly intended when he wrote the text; consequently it seems better now to say that the *sensus plenior* is not strictly speaking a literal sense.

The question of the extent of the hagiographer's knowledge of the fuller sense is much more interesting than the previous one, and throws a great deal of light on the nature of this sense.[52] Many of its proponents define it as a sense which God intended but of which the human author had no knowledge at all. Benoit, Braun, Cotter, Ayer, Leal and Fuller would appear to be among those who hold this opinion.[53] Others, however, claim that the

sinn gehört, praktisch aber zu allen Zeiten auch unter den geistigen Sinn eingereiht wurde."

[51] Gribomont, "La Lien," p. 73, points this out clearly.

[52] *Ibid.*, p. 71: "Le noeud du problème se trouve dans la psychologie de l'auteur sacré."

[53] Benoit, *op. cit.*, pp. 358-359.

Braun, *art. cit.*, p. 297: "de dépasser la compréhension de l'hagiographe."

Cotter, *art. cit.*, p. 459.

Ayer, *op. cit.*, p. 108: "nonnisi a Deo comprehenditur necnon ab eis qui divinitus dictis aut factis illustrati sunt." (The latter seems to refer to readers.)

Leal, *art. cit.*, p. 476: "trasciende el alcance de autor humano."

Fuller, *art. cit.*, 39k, "a sense of which the writer was not conscious."

sensus plenior lay within the purview of the human author (at least indistinctly). Coppens, Fernández, and Gribomont are leading this trend which seems to be gaining force.[54] In our definition above, by using a negative approach ("not *clearly* intended by the human author"), we avoided the issue for the moment; and certain authors, such as Tuya and Sutcliffe, seem to have adopted the same policy.[55] Actually such a definition is more than a mere escape, for the *sensus plenior* as a classification includes instances where the hagiographer had a vague foreknowledge and instances where he had no knowledge at all.

The question of the hagiographer's purview is something that can never be solved with certitude.[56] Our only evidence is circumstantial, *e. g.*, the manner in which the text is phrased.[57] If there is some indication in the text that the writer may have suspected the fuller meaning, fine. But, if not, we are certainly not justified in an *a priori* assumption either that he could not have suspected it[58]

[54] Coppens, *Harmonies*, pp. 46-52.

Fernández, *Institutiones Biblicae*, 6th ed., p. 383.

Gribomont, "Le Lien," pp. 75-78. Simon and Prado, 3rd ed., p. 210.

[55] Manuel de Tuya, O. P., "Si es posible y en qué medida un *sensus plenior* a la luz del concepto teológico de inspiración," *C Tom*, 79 (1952), p. 372: ". . . desconocido por el hagiógrafo. Por lo menos explicitamente en su plenitud . . ."

Sutcliffe, *art. cit.*, p. 334, "but not necessarily known to the human author."

de Ambroggi, in his 1932 article, p. 299, said: ". . . non era conosciuto dall' agiografo." In the 1952 article, p. 233, he says that it was known perfectly by God and imperfectly by man.

[56] Colunga, *art. cit.*, p. 451.

[57] We might choose as an example Is 7:14, which Steinmann (*Isaïe*, pp. 88-93) says is an example of a *sensus plenior*. The Hebrew prophet is speaking of a young girl who shall conceive and bear a child. He could have chosen many words to refer to the girl; but his vague consciousness of the importance of the event in the Messianic role of Israel led him under the inspiration of God to choose the word *'almah*. This word, which can mean "virgin," allows the text to be applied to Mary in a *sensus plenior*.

[58] Buzy, *art. cit.*, pp. 389-390, was one of the first to question the assumption that the hagiographer was never aware of the fuller meaning. He says unconsciousness is not essential to the definition. "Ce qui importe, c'est de percevoir si réellement et indépendamment de la conscience qu'en

or that he had to have suspected it.[59] Without evidence, we simply do not know. To a certain degree, the particular type of *sensus plenior* can help us to estimate the author's consciousness. Coppens points out that the consciousness of the fuller sense may have been more frequent in the Prophetical *Sensus Plenior* than in the General *Sensus Plenior* or the Typical *Sensus Plenior*.[60] But in all branches of the fuller sense, there will occur some instances where the author was vaguely aware[61] of the deeper import of his text.

Once we have taken this position, we are forced to account to the reader on how the author could have possessed such a foreknowledge. Three suggestions have been proposed; let us see the advantages of each: (a) Origen suggested that the prophets were the recipients of a mystical experience which immersed them in the deepest of divine mysteries. Consequently, though incapable of expressing this fullness of knowledge to their contemporaries, they so composed their books as to leave room for its un-

pouvait avoir l'auteur, son texte a parfois un sens plural . . ., s'il a un sens plénier."

[59] Perhaps the reason for demanding consciousness on the part of the human author is the fear that without it the sense could not be an inspired one. We hope to show below that inspiration in no way requires consciousness of the full sense by the hagiographer.

[60] Coppens, *Harmonies*, pp. 123-124: "Nous l'admettons [consciousness], on se rappellera, pour cette espèce de sens plénier que nous avons intitulée *sens prophético-typique*. Pour les deux autres espèces, nous estimons qu-en règle générale les auteurs inspirés n'y ont pas participé. Une exception manifeste à la règle, ajoutions-nous, est la conscience du Christ . . ."

On the basis of remarks made in c. I about the hagiographer's awareness of the typical sense, we would go further than Fr. Coppens in allowing consciousness for instances of the typical *sensus plenior*.

[61] Perhaps we should explain what we mean by "vague awareness." It means that the hagiographer, without foreseeing the future in detail, had a premonition or even certitude that what he was saying would have a more important role in God's plan than its contemporaneous function. He could not say exactly how, but in an undetermined way he knew that it would one day reach its fulfillment. Naturally there are an infinite number of possible degrees in this awareness; at times it must have approached quite closely to the clear awareness which the literal sense demands.

derstanding by future generations. By a symbolical use of the things they wrote about, they preserved their mystic vision until Christ would unveil it. Thus, for the Alexandrian exegete, the human author was less prophet than mystic; he is primarily one who has seen the glory of God. This solution of Origen might cover some instances of the *sensus plenior*; however, it is not really satisfactory as a general solution since there is seldom proof of such a mystical vision. The text betrays but little evidence of radiant immersions.[62] (b) The Antiochian doctrine of *θεωρία* deserves more attention.[63] As we have explained, *theoria,* in its specific sense, is the perception of the future which a prophet enjoys through the medium of the present circumstances he is describing. Upon return from this vision in which God has revealed to him the future, the prophet attempts to convey what he has seen by using hyperbole in narrating the present. But just what sense of Scripture is involved in *theoria?* The fact that the Antiochenes, even Theodore of Mopsuestia, admitted the existence of *direct literal* prophecies[64] shows that there is some distinction between the strict literal sense and *theoria.*[65] The difference consists in this: literal Messianic prophecies could have only one application—Christ; *theoria,* however, occurred in prophecies which had both a meaning in Jewish history and a fuller meaning in Christ.[66]

Yet the meaning perceived through *theoria* is not a typical sense either. In typology, the prophet (generally) does not foresee the future; all the futurity is in the type or the "thing." In *theoria* the prophet foresees the future and tries to express it in *words.*[67] He sees the fuller meaning through objects, but it is

[62] Coppens, *Harmonies,* pp. 48-50.

[63] *Ibid.,* p. 51. Coppens prefers this to all other explanations.

[64] Guillet, *art. cit.,* pp. 279-80.

[65] Some of the authors speak of *theoria* as literal, but seemingly they are using "literal" in a broad sense of pertaining to the text itself. This they make clear by saying that, while *theoria* is literal, it is not historical (by this is probably meant our narrow definition of literal). Cf. Seisdedos, *art. cit.,* p. 60, and Vaccari, *art. cit.,* p. 28.

[66] Seisdedos, *art. cit.,* p. 59. Julian of Aeclanum offers this criterion.

[67] *Ibid,* p. 60. Vaccari, *art. cit.,* p. 22.

Ternant, *art. cit.,* pp. 151-152. All three agree on this point. Ternant points out that there were real types too at Antioch.

Also Guillet, *art. cit.,* p. 279.

primarily attached to the text.[68] Consequently all the major scholars agree that *theoria* is something in the literal rather than the typical line.

The basis of this observation lies in the consciousness which the Antiochenes attribute to the hagiographer.[69] Theodore allows the least awareness of any; for him the prophets in their *theoria* had only a very obscure foreknowledge—just enough to allow them to use hyperbole so that subsequent generations could discover in their text traces of the Messias.[70] He never accepted the ecstatic visions proposed by his fellows. The majority opinion at Antioch allowed a more generous consciousness of the future.[71] Even this foresight, however, was not a clear awareness, but imprecise in

[68] There may be an element of the Typical *Sensus Plenior* in *theoria*. The following passages are worth noting:

Ternant, *art. cit.*, p. 143: "La Theôria, dans ce contexte technique qui sera le nôtre désormais, servirait ainsi à déceler une véritable typologie au creux du sens littéral, ou, si l'on veut, un sens que nous pourrions appeler typico-littéral."

Mariès, *Études préliminaires à l'édition de Déodore de Tarse sur les Psaumes* (Paris: 1933), p. 136: "Dans le cas où joue la *θεωρία*, le premier objet est, si l'on veut, un type, mais un type où est déjà appréhendé dans sa *plenitudo* l'objet supérieur, l'antitype si l'on veut, et ce par la vue pénétrante qui est justement cette *θεωρία*. Le premier objet est pour elle un *medium* de connaissance par lequel est signifié et dans lequel est connu le second objet d'ordre supérieur."

[69] Ternant, *art. cit.*, p. 143, makes awareness the distinguishing factor between Antioch and Alexandria in their outlook on the spiritual sense.

[70] Guillet, *art. cit.*, p. 284: "De cette portée ultérieure, du sens typique de leur message, si les prophètes n'ont eu 'qu'une connaissance très obscure,' ils en ont vu assez pour éclater en mots hyperboliques et nous permettre d'y découvrir une annonce authentique de Messie."

Vaccari, *art.cit.*, p. 23.

[71] *Ibid.*, p. 22: "Il profeta realmente prevede l'uno e l'altro personaggio, l'uno e l'altro fatto."

Ternant, *art. cit.*, pp. 145-149, 354-359, proves this point in detail. P. 145: "Mais, en de très nombreux cas de *Theôria* découverts par les Antiochiens . . . la conscience que le prophète (ou le psalmiste considéré en tant que prophète) est supposé posséder de la valeur figurative du premier objet visé par ses paroles, est nettement affirmée ou clairement insinuée par nos auteurs."

details and as to the time of realization.[72] And so the writer could only haltingly present the richer import of his words.[73]

Theoria then involves a fuller meaning of the text itself, evident to later generations through a development in revelation, and foreseen somewhat vaguely and imprecisely by the prophet. Truly it seems to be an instance of the *sensus plenior.* Now Ternant is quite definite in denying the connection between *theoria* and the *sensus plenior.*[74] He admits the existence of the latter, but defines it as being absolutely unknown by the hagiographer.[75] Since *theoria* demands consciousness, the two are not the same: this is the only cleavage he makes between them. Such a distinction seems rather unnecessary on several accounts: (1) as stated above, the trend is definitely away from defining the *sensus plenior* in terms of lack of awareness. Most authors today allow some awareness, particularly in the prophetical instances of the fuller sense. (2) If we make such a division, we now have two new classifications in an already crowded field. The *sensus plenior,* correctly defined, would easily suffice. (3) How can we possibly decide in many cases whether there was awareness or not, whether it should be classified as *theoria* or as *sensus plenior?* Our broader definition of the fuller sense obviates such decisions. And so it seems much wiser to agree with Coppens and Gribomont that the deeper meaning derived through *theoria* is a division of the fuller sense; it is the Prophetical *Sensus Plenior* of which the author was aware.

The Antiochene concept of *theoria,* therefore, is another possible

[72] Vaccari, *art. cit.*, p. 35.

Seisdedos, pp. 65-66.

[73] Ternant, *art, cit.*, p. 158: "Nous avons là un sens littéral unique qu'on peut appeler 'métaphorique' par rapport au premier objet, à cause de la 'disproportion par excès' dans l'application des paroles aux réalités imparfaites, mais que l'on ne peut vraiment appeler propre par rapport à aucun des deux objets, vu qu'à cette disproportion par excès s'ajoute 'une disproportion par défaut' dans l'application aux réalités messianiques que le regard du prophète atteint à travers les premières."

[74] *Ibid.*, pp. 153-155.

[75] *Ibid.*, p. 153: There is a *sensus plenior* "distinct du sens littéral mais le continuant et l'approfondissant dans une ligne homogène et qui, réalisé lui aussi a l'insu de l'auteur sacré, se deduit de 'la portée fonctionelle du texte dans l'économie de la Révélation entière.'"

explanation of how the hagiographer might have foreseen the future. In many ways it would seem far more practical than Origen's solution. True, *theoria* requires revelation and a sort of ecstatic vision, but not the mystical assumption into the heights of the divinity which Alexandria would have. It is a more simple insight into the future through the present. Prophecy is supernatural no matter how we explain it; but the simpler explanation is still more attractive and better suits the evidence.

(c) A third explanation of the human author's awareness is that of Fr. Gribomont. He is not proposing something entirely distinct from *theoria*; [76] he is simply working more in the line of Thomistic psychology,[77] and some of his observations are novel and useful. He sets the tone of his treatment by stating firmly, "Clear consciousness is not the only form of consciousness." [78] If a man is conscious of a certain idea, is he not in a way conscious of many developments latent in that idea? [79] There is nothing anti-psychological in saying that a statement has a plural meaning as long as one meaning is contained in the other. Have we not often had the experience of remarking, "That's just what I meant!" when someone expands a little on our statements? Do we not hold a philosopher partially responsible for the logical developments of his ideas worked out by his pupils? Rather frequently then it may be said that a man is imperfectly conscious of and intends the

[76] Gribomont, "Le Lien," pp. 84 ff. In fact he maintains that *theoria* is a historical example of his ideas.

[77] Gribomont's article is "selon la théologie de S. Thomas." The whole purpose of it is to show that the idea of the *sensus plenior* and its psychology corresponds perfectly with Thomistic thought.

[78] *Ibid.*, p. 72: ". . . la conscience claire n'épuise pas la conscience."

[79] *Ibid.*: "Outre la zône qu'éclaire vigoureusement le regard lucide de *l'attention, l'intention* se porte sur tout un monde plus vaste qui se révèle a l'esprit."

Dodd, *op. cit.*, p. 131: "It would not be true of any literature which deserves to be called great, that its meaning is restricted to that which was explicitly in the mind of the author when he wrote. . . . The ultimate significance of prophecy is not only what it meant for the author, but what it came to mean for those who stood within the tradition which he founded or promoted, and who lived under the impact of the truth he declared. . . . The meaning of the writings cannot remain static while the life to which they belong changes with the centuries."

fuller meaning of what he says. This is especially true, Gribomont insists, of the biblical authors who were quite aware that they were playing but a small role in the vast drama of the religious history of the Chosen People. Since they realized that God was guiding every action in history toward the fulfillment of His plan, the Messias, is it unreasonable to hold that at the back of their minds they were sometimes conscious that what they said and did would have a fuller meaning when the whole of the plan had been unrolled? Nay, on occasion might they not even have suspected from the development they had already seen just what sort of *sensus plenior* their words would receive? [80] Indeed, Fr. Gribomont phrases this whole idea nicely when he observes that the *explicit* knowledge of the religious value of the present was for the hagiographers an *implicit* knowledge of future things.[81] Thus in many cases there is no reason to deny to the human author at least an undetermined knowledge of the *sensus plenior.*

In summary then there are at least three possible explanations of the vague consciousness which the human author had at times of the *sensus plenior.* These suggestions are not to be opposed to each other; each has validity in particular cases. Origen's solution of mystical ecstasies would probably have the most limited application; but there does exist mystical symbolism in the O. T., *e. g.*, Ezechiel, Daniel, where it might be of use. The *theoria* holds sway principally in the realm of the Prophetical *Sensus Plenior.* Gribomont's psychology may account for some instances of foreknowledge in the General *Sensus Plenior* and the Typical *Sensus Plenior.* In any case, there is no inconsistency in maintaining that the hagiographer could have been vaguely conscious of the fuller sense.

Perhaps an objection has formed in the reader's mind: the explanations offered are certainly possible, but only *possible*; where is the proof that they correspond to fact? [82] True, we cannot prove

[80] This is not necessarily true in every case. Observe the cautions of Fernández mentioned above, c. I. p. 14.

[81] Gribomont, "Le Lien," p. 77. He attempts to show that much of this is in accord with Thomist philosophy.

[82] For instance, Roland E. Murphy, O. Carm., *A Study of Psalm 72 (71)*, (Washington, C. U. A.: 1948), p. 103, says of *theoria* with reference

it apodictically. It is once again a question of persuasion from evidence. The context of many of the Messianic prophecies demands that the statement have had contemporary meaning; Chris tian exegesis demands a future Messianic meaning. Are we to say that the prophet had no consciousness of this second meaning which is a development of the first? Often the very way the text is phrased indicates that he did have some awareness. Is it not curious how often in prophecies we have such a hard time to figure out just what the prophet meant for his own times; and yet when we see the future fulfillment, the prophecy makes perfect sense? The words are almost distorted as far as contemporary connotation, but they always leave room for the future. (Wisely the Antiochenes observed that is because in one poor phrasing the prophet was trying to straddle both realities, so that he is hyperbolic for the first meaning, and deficient for the second.) The convenient phrasing of such prophecies indicates awareness, for it would be beyond credibility that it was always accidental. The explanations given above for such supernatural awareness are not far-fetched and are as well attested as possible. The Fathers support two of them; the other is based on ordinary experience and Thomistic psychology. They are more than merely another possible explanation; they are the most probable explanation.

We have now finished our remarks on the relation of the *sensus plenior* and the literal sense. They are closely related because both deal with the text of Scripture. The fuller sense of a text does not constitute a second literal sense, but is an *approfondissement* of the one and only literal sense. Yet, since by definition the hagiographer was not fully and clearly aware of the *sensus plenior* of his text, it is not a strict literal sense. But it is worth noting that the lack of clear awareness may run all the way from absolute ignorance to near clarity. Consequently, while we maintain the theoretical distinction between the two senses, there undoubtedly

to Psalm 72: "Such an explanation is practically impossible to prove. There is nothing intrinsically impossible in it; but perhaps that tells against it—it is merely another possible explanation. . . . Such a method of exegesis is an *a priori* psychological deduction."

Ternant, *art. cit.*, pp. 360 ff, presents a rebuttal.

will be many borderline instances where it is impossible to decide whether clear awareness was present or not. The human mind in its thought and intention has many shades of intensity; at dividing lines these shades do not remain distinct, but blend into one another.[83]

* * *

(2) The second problem concerns the relation of the *sensus plenior* to the typical sense. Once again we encounter a preliminary question of terminology. Is the typical sense to be confined to a sense of things or realities (as expressed in the words)? If so, then the *sensus plenior,* being a sense of the words themselves, is theoretically quite distinct from it. On the other hand, were one to give to typology a broader connotation, *i. e.,* not only the meaning of realities but the fuller meaning reflected back on the *text* by types, then the Typical *Sensus Plenior* might be considered a typical sense.[84] Once again it would seem better to accept the traditional and more precise definition and confine the typical sense to realities.

Coppens insists quite strongly that the Typical *Sensus Plenior* is not a true typical sense. Real typology involves a "transposition of meaning." When typology is in question, one goes beyond all bonds of the literal sense. The object described becomes a sign, a figure of future realities, realities which have nothing to do with the literal sense of the passage itself,[85] (*e. g.,* Melchisidech's lack

[83] Benoit, *op. cit.,* p. 361, has some interesting observations on this: "Les effets de l'inspiration se diffusent sur les divers sens du texte d'une manière progressivement décroissante qui ne se peut résoudre en étapes tranchées."

[84] Daniélou, Review of Coppens' *Harmonies,* p. 150, insists that it is. Daniélou, we must remember, rejects the *sensus plenior* entirely.

Coppens, in reply ("Bibliographie," pp. 89-90), says that if Daniélou will accept a broader definition of the typical sense, they might more or less agree.

Bouyer's remark on the typical sense is interesting (*art. cit.,* p. 48): "Ainsi, le sens typique, faisant converger sur le Christ et l'Église toutes les *paroles* dispersées qui constituent l'Écriture se prolonge-t-il de lui-même dans le sens anagogique . . ." (Italics ours.)

[85] Coppens, "Nouvelles Réflexions," p. 6: "La caractéristique la plus importante du sens typique consiste selon nous dans le fait qu'il se réalise uniquement moyennant une transposition de sens. Là où le typisme

of genealogy as a figure of Christ). But in the Typical *Sensus Plenior,* this is not true.[86] To take the example already given, David is a type of Christ. Therefore, words said by or to David (which have nothing to do with making David a type of Christ) take on a fuller meaning when applied to Christ. For instance, "Thou art my son, this day have I begotten thee." ; "My God, My God, why hast thou forsaken me?" (naturally one need not accept the choice of examples)—in all these cases it is a fuller meaning of the *literal* sense than is involved. The face value of the words is the foundation of the growth, which is not true in strict typology.[87] Consequently on a theoretical basis, the *sensus plenior* is really distinct from the typical sense.

A second point arises: what should be the interrelations of the two senses? Do they have anything in common? The remarks of several authors should be discussed. Fr. de Vaux says the two should be kept entirely separate: the fuller sense is a homogeneous development of the literal sense; the typical sense is heterogeneous to the literal sense. He criticizes Coppens for confusing the two senses by introducing "verbal typism" as a *sensus plenior.*[88]

intervient, le sens littéral est dépassé; il devient le signe, le chiffre, la figure des réalités que la lettre n'incluait pas."

[86] Coppens, *Harmonies,* p. 61: "Entre les deux sens, comme nous le verrons encore mieux plus loin, la distance est grande. Pour prévenir toute confusion, il suffit de remarquer que le typisme dont il est question ici, est naturel et qu'il n'implique, d'aucune façon, la transposition de sens, propre a l'exégèse typologique."

[87] As remarked, we found in Coppens' remarks on the typical *sensus plenior* some confusion. That seems to pervade here too: his remark on p. 137, *Harmonies,* scarcely blends with previous observations: "Seule la troisième forme de sens plénier que nous avons distinguée plus haut: *le sens plénier historico-typique,* est le moins homogène au sens littéral et obvie, puisqu'il ne se réalise que par la voie d'évolution, voire, . . . par voie de greffe. En fait, comme nous l'avons déjà insinué (p. 54, note 46), souvent l'enrichissement est tel qu'il vaudra mieux parler d'un sens ajouté, augmenté, greffé, recréé. Dans ces conditions, il sera dû soit aux auteurs qui ont récrit le texte, soit aux rédacteurs ou compilateurs inspirés qui, en l'enchâssant dans un contexte nouveau, plus large et plus dogmatique, lui ont donné son sens profond, plénier."

[88] de Vaux, *art. cit.,* p. 280. "La confusion est d'autant plus aisée que

In commentary, it might be pointed out that Coppens was not the first to posit an interrelation between the two senses. In 1932 de Ambroggi clearly stated that the fuller sense was a literal, not a typical sense.[89] Yet he foresaw a case where, "In the confrontation of a prophecy with its fulfillment, we might perceive an intermediary reality, a real figure, a type." [90] This remained a typical sense for him, however, because the *sensus plenior* referred only to the words themselves. Buzy, who seems to represent an intermediary stage in the development of the fuller sense, holds that the typical sense is only an application or species of the *sensus plenior*. The only difference is that the fuller sense compares the realities on a verbal plane, while the typical sense juxtaposes them on the plane of "things" represented by the words.[91] In this observation we have the germ of a Typical *Sensus Plenior.*

Coppens has replied to de Vaux's critique. He points out that de Vaux is inconsistent in basing the fuller sense on "the economy of salvation." If the *sensus plenior* is attached to a text because of the way that God has ordered His plan of salvation, must we not admit that types play a role in this plan, and therefore can give a fuller meaning to the text? [92] Besides, did not the prophet

l'auteur, tout en rattachant essentiellement le sens plénier au 'texte' et le sens typique aux 'faits' de l'Écriture, admet que certains sens pléniers découlent des faits et que certains sens typiques découlent des paroles du texte."

We feel that de Vaux is objecting to the idea that one text may stand to another in relation of type to antitype (cf. n. 36, above), something which does seem unacceptable. Perhaps he would not be adverse to what we mean by the Typical *Sensus Plenior*?

[89] de Ambroggi, *art. cit.*, p. 298.

[90] *Ibid.*, p. 309. "Può accadere talora che, nel confronto del vaticinio coll' adempimento, noi scorgiamo una realtà intermedia, una figura reale, un tipo insomma . . ."

[91] Buzy, *art. cit.*, p. 403. ". . . le sens typique peut se ramener au sens plural ou plénier, dont il est une application, ou une espèce . . . La seule différence à noter, c'est que les personnes ou les objets signifiés, au lieu d'être juxtaposés sur un même plan, sont ici étagés sur divers plans superposés, d'abord sur le plan des mots, ensuite sur le plan des choses représentées par les mots."

[92] Coppens, "Bibliographie," p. 88: "Il paraît perdre de vue le critère que lui-même assigne en second lieu pour retrouver le sens plénier. Qu'est-ce, en effet, '*l'économie du salut*' sinon les faits et les personnages

often foresee the future through the medium of present objects and realities (*theoria*)? [93] Thus, while Coppens maintains the distinction between the *sensus plenior* and the typical sense, he allows for certain interrelations.[94]

If Fr. de Vaux would completely separate the two senses, Fr. Gribomont goes to the opposite extreme of making them completely correlative.[95] He says that the ultimate basis both of the typical sense and of the *sensus plenior* is the unity of biblical revelation. This unity is objective and subjective: objective because the institutions of the Jewish religion were types of our institutions; subjective because our religious mentality is a development of the Jewish religious mentality. Now we should unite subject and object, and not divide them. The *sensus plenior* (subjective) and the typical sense (objective) are but two different aspects of the same reality, and there is a relation of mutual causality between them. After all, typology is not an attribute of things in themselves, abstracted from the subjective religious attitude of the Jews,[96] and vice versa. To sum it up: "Depending on whether he holds a realistic or an idealistic philosophy, the historian will say that it is the objective side of revelation, implied in types, which calls for the 'plenitude' in the reactions of the believer; or on the contrary, it is the progressive revelation of God the Savior in the minds of the prophets that sublimizes little by little

de la Bible suscités et ordonnés par Dieu en vue du salut? En d'autres termes, le R. P. de Vaux fait lui-même appel à la typologie pour justifier en certains cas le présence du sens plénier."

[93] *Ibid.*

[94] Yet here once again Coppens seems to fluctuate to some degree. In critique of Schildenberger, he writes ("Pour une meilleure intelligence," p. 506): "Le typisme peut y contribuer [toward a *sensus plenior*], certes . . . mais il n'est pas requis. Il vaut mieux qu'il ne s'y mêle pas, car le vrai sens plénier se situe dans la ligne du sens littéral philologique qu'il prolonge et qu'il approfondit."

[95] Gribomont, "Sens Plénier," pp. 22-24.

Schildenberger's work has not been available to us; but seemingly from Coppens' remarks, it maintains a somewhat similar thesis—"que le sens plénier ne se dégage qu'à travers le typisme." (Coppens, "Pour une meilleure intelligence," p. 506.)

[96] Cf. *supra*, p. 14.

their religious environment."[97] This correlativity of the *sensus plenior* and the typical sense which Gribomont proposes applies to all three branches of the former. Since the typical sense must be foreseen by the hagiographer, it is also prophetical: thus the Prophetical *Sensus Plenior* and the Typical *Sensus Plenior* coincide. The General *Sensus Plenior* is presupposed in the subjective attitude of the author who obscurely knows that his types play a part in the whole biblical schema.[98] And so Gribomont goes further in identifying the fuller sense with the typical sense than any of his predecessors.

His ideas may be very helpful in passages where the author was obscurely conscious of the *sensus plenior* and where there are types present. Yet it is hard to see that in every example of the fuller sense these two conditions are verified. As remarked when treating the typical sense, while it must be admitted that the author could have been conscious of the typical sense (and indeed many times probably was), we are unjustified in demanding this consciousness. And without this consciousness, Gribomont's parallel between the typical senses and the Prophetical and General *Sensus Plenior* no longer stands. In general, Gribomont's position, although entailing some most valuable observations, is rather an oversimplification.[99]

And so in summary, the *sensus plenior* and the typical sense are two different things: one deals primarily with words; the other, with "things." Yet since they both outstrip the *clear* consciousness of the author, they have a very basic attribute in common. Consequently, it would not seem wise either to deny all interrelation or to posit complete correlation between the two—the truth

[97] Gribomont, "Sens Plénier," p. 24. "Selon la pente réaliste ou idéaliste de sa philosophie, l'historien dira que c'est l'objectivité de la Révélation, impliquée dans les types, qui commande la 'plenitude' des réactions du croyant, ou qu'au contraire c'est la Révélation progressive du Dieu Sauveur dans la conscience des prophètes qui sublimise peu à peu le cadre religieux. Le progrès est corrélatif."

[98] *Ibid.*, p. 27. Also, p. 31: "Sens plénier et sens typique ne seraient en effet que les aspects corrélatifs du développement organique du sens littéral, dans le cadre du progrès de la Révélation."

[99] Coppens, "Bibliographie," p. 88, disagrees with Gribomont. "Nous croyons la thèse exagerée."

lies in between. In practice, especially in the case of the Typical *Sensus Plenior,* it may be quite difficult to decide whether some interpretations belong to the typical sense or to the fuller sense. This is only natural: the *sensus plenior* stands between the literal and typical senses and shares some qualities with each. Borderline cases will exist on both extremes.

* * *

(3) The third problem concerns the relations of the *sensus plenior* to the consequent sense. Historically it was under the general title of a consequent sense that Cornely first spoke of "*accuratiorem et pleniorem sensum,*" although he wondered could this fuller sense be truly called consequent, ". . . since those interpretations which indeed draw forth the full meaning of the word considered in its context, but do not exceed it, do not pass beyond the limits of the literal sense."[100] This hesitation of Fr. Cornely was somewhat dissipated by Simon and Prado who clearly distinguished the *sensus plenior* from the implicit consequent sense.[101] The fuller sense is directly intended by God; the consequent sense, indirectly. Like the strict literal and typical senses, the *sensus plenior* can be a basis for the consequent sense since it supplies concepts implicitly containing other concepts that are obtainable by a reasoning process. The authors put the difference into scholastic terminology. The fuller sense gives a meaning which is subjectively distinct *sine fundamento in re* from that of the hagiographer; both God and the hagiographer intend the same formal concept, only God sees it in its fullness. The consequent sense, as intended by God, is subjectively distinct *cum fundamento in re*

[100] Cf. n. 13, in this chapter.

[101] Simon and Prado, *op. cit.*, 3rd ed., p. 209. All of this has disappeared from the 6th ed. (Cf. pp. 250-251), but whether this constitutes a denial of the former position is not stated. The work now has adopted the division of the consequent sense mentioned in c. I, n. 89. The authors remark: "Ad sensum implicitum iure trahi potest sensus plenior." (They acknowledge in a note that the Höpfl and Gut manual calls the fuller sense a *consectarium* of the literal sense, but say that this is only a question of terminology!) This *sensus plenior* is also called supralitteralis (Lagrange), "quatenus veritates refert verbis quidem hagiographi divinitus expressas, sed quas idem hagiographus neque explicite tradere intendit nec, seclusa speciali revelatione, assequi valet."

from the literal sense; the concept it contains is formally distinct from that of the human author.[102] To some this may seem a decisive clarification; yet one may wonder if it can be successfully applied to all instances of the *sensus plenior.* Wherever the human author was even vaguely aware of a deeper meaning in his words, the fuller sense is within the same formal concept; but where he was completely unconscious of such a deeper meaning, a new formal concept would be involved.

Fr. Coppens' position on the relation of the fuller sense to the consequent sense shows an interesting variation. Naturally the greatest problem is centered on that division of the consequent sense where explicative reasoning is employed, *i. e.,* an explanation, often very simple, of what is implicit in the terms. Merkelbach seems to call this a *sensus plenior*; Coppens rejects the identification on the grounds that any deduction, even by explicative reasoning, should be kept distinct from the *sensus plenior.*[103] Also he would appear to deny that cases of strict illative reasoning belong to the fuller sense. Yet he suggests (following Grandmaison and Gardeil) that one might distinguish a certain class of derived meanings whose relation to an original revealed proposition one cannot prove by strict reasoning. Some claim this insufficiency is made up by the Church. Coppens proposes that such derived meanings might be instances of the *sensus plenior,* and thus strictly scriptural.[104] They would form a bridge between the fuller sense and the consequent sense.

Elsewhere Coppens hints that, if one does not accept his explanations of the *sensus plenior,* one might say that it is a case of explicative reasoning within the consequent sense.[105] And finally

[102] *Ibid.,* p. 210.

[103] Coppens, *Harmonies,* p. 74.

[104] *Ibid.,* p. 78. ". . . en supposant que le révélé confus dont ils [Grandmaison and Gardeil] nous entretiennent, et qui se situe en quelque sorte entre l'objet d'une analyse purement conceptuelle et celui de la conclusion théologique, coïncide en réalité avec le sens plénier tel que nous avons essayé de le définir. Nous serions alors en présence de ce sens littéral plénier et conséquent . . ."

Tuya, "Si es posible," p. 405, says that if one follows Marin Sola, such illative consequent senses (theological conclusions) can be examples of the *sensus plenior.*

[105] Coppens, "Le problème," pp. 15-16. "Si l'on n'accepte pas les

in his latest article, Coppens admits that it is very difficult to distinguish the fuller sense from the consequent sense derived through explicative reasoning; but if philosophical analysis is introduced, he holds a clear distinction. He even suggests the reservation of the term "consequent sense" to conclusions derived by non-scriptural reasoning.[106]

Coppens' rather wavering reflections are a tribute to the intricacies of the problem. As we remarked in Chapter I, the consequent sense is, in our opinion, a rather haphazard classification introduced to explain problems in the development of doctrine. If a better solution to these problems is accepted, the consequent sense may cease to be employed as a classification. In any case, the *explicative* consequent sense (which we prefer not to call "consequent" at all) seems to be nothing more than the literal sense, phrased in a different manner. If at times a deeper connotation is conveyed by the difference in phrasing, the new meaning may well be a *sensus plenior*. Thus the so-called explicative "consequent" sense can be broken down and classified as a literal sense or a *sensus plenior*.

In the case of the *illative* consequent sense (the only true "consequent" sense), it would seem best to make a distinction: (1) if both major and minor are in Scripture, then a *sensus plenior* may

explications exposées ci-dessus, on dira donc que le sens plénier est un sens greffé sur le sens littéral et s'en dégageant par un raisonnement explicatif réduit à sa plus simple expression: il coïnciderait dans ces conditions avec ce que *Les Harmonies des deux Testaments* ont appelé '*le sens conséquent explicatif*.' Les frontières, on le voit, apparaissent parfois confuses."

[106] Coppens, "Nouvelles Réflexions," p. 14: "Concédons que plus d'une fois il est difficile de distinguer nettement les sens plénier et conséquent. C'est notamment le cas chaque fois que le sens conséquent se dégage du texte par une simple explication des termes du donné révélé, du moins quand cette explication se fait uniquement à l'aide de thèmes bibliques et sans aucun recours à l'analyse philosophique. Aussitôt que celle-ci intervient, la distinction s'impose. Qu'on réserve donc l'appellation de sens conséquent aux conclusions qui se déduisent des textes inspirés moyennant des raisonnements non-scripturaires; en revanche, celles où seuls des thèmes et des rapprochements bibliques interviennent, relèveront du sens plénier."

be involved. The General *Sensus Plenior* means that a passage of Scripture may have a fuller meaning when viewed in the light of other sections of Scripture. This is just as well the case if one passage (the minor) throws light on another passage (the major), so that a deeper meaning (conclusion) is perceived. We must remember that in such cases the syllogism is often an artificial construct to fit the process into the scholastic pattern. (2) if the major is of Scripture and the minor is of pure reason, the conclusion is not a *sensus plenior* (or, for that matter, a real scriptural sense at all). The real fuller sense already exists in the Scriptures; it is not extrinsically adjoined by human reasoning. But, it must be repeated, many of the cases suggested as examples of this illative reasoning are not consequent senses at all. The conclusion is not derived by a minor of reason but by the Church's insight into the depths of divine revelation. When this is true, the *sensus plenior* may well be involved, as Coppens suggests.

* * *

We come at last (perhaps to the reader's relief) to a conclusion of our remarks on the relation of the *sensus plenior* to the other senses of Scripture. To summarize, we are really concerned only with its relation to the literal and the typical senses. (The consequent sense disappears from the picture. Where no real illative reasoning is involved, it is to be resolved into the literal or the fuller sense. Where philosophical illative reasoning is involved, it is not a sense of Scripture at all.)

The sensus plenior *is a distinct sense from either the literal or the typical, holding a position between the two, but closer to the literal. Like the literal sense it is a meaning of the text; unlike it, it is not within the clear purview of the hagiographer. It shares this latter characteristic with the typical sense; but unlike the typical sense, it is not a sense of "things" but of words. In practice, there will be many borderline instances in both directions where it is impossible to decide just what sense is involved.*

If we are to indulge in the latest fashion of making a schema of the senses of Scripture, we propose *either* of the following (the first division has the advantage of effecting a *rapprochement* with those writers who use the term "spiritual" sense; the second, of being closer to the traditional Thomistic division):

I. A Division on the basis of *the Hagiographer's Knowledge.*
   1. Clear understanding—The Literal Sense
   2. Lack of clear understanding—The Spiritual Sense:
      a. Flowing from the text—The Sensus Plenior
      b. Flowing from "things" described in the text—The Typical Sense.

II. A Division on the basis of *the Material Object.*
   1. Sense of words: ("Literal" in a very broad sense)
      a. With *clear* knowledge by the hagiographer—The Literal Sense
      b. Without *clear* knowledge by the hagiographer—The Sensus Plenior
   2. Sense of things—The Typical Sense

V. OBJECTIONS TO THE *SENSUS PLENIOR*

And now, after this consideration of the definition and division of the *sensus plenior,* and its relation to the other scriptural senses, we owe it our reader to consider the objections that are leveled against it by its opponents.

(1) We are told that the new meaning which constitutes the *sensus plenior* does not come from within the text but is added on by new revelation.[107] The O. T. presents a gradual development of revelation. When the Christian now reads more into its texts than the author clearly intended, he is doing so in virtue of an increased knowledge of revelation, not because such a fuller mean-

[107] Weisengoff, *art. cit.,* p. 84.

de Lubac, *Catholicism,* p. 90. "Yet the act of redemption is not like a key which by unlocking the Old Testament reveals a meaning already present in it. This act in some sort creates the meaning."

Steinmann, "Entretien," p. 247, has Richard Simon say: "Avec l'Église, je tiens pour juste l'interprétation de l'Ancien Testament par le Nouveau, à condition de maintenir que cette exégèse est une création du Nouveau Testament, une révélation nouvelle."

La Vie Intellectuelle, "Autour de l'exégèse biblique," December, 1949, p. 508. (No author is given, but the article defends Steinmann.) The article states that the spiritual sense does not come from the text itself, but from outside.

ing is latent in the text. "Surely God reveals only what and as much as He wants to reveal; hence, if in the Old Testament certain data of revelation are obscure or give only some notes of a doctrine, may it not well be that at that time God wants to reveal the doctrine obscurely or partially? It will be only later that God by another revelation will add a note or notes to something already given or will clarify what was obscure. . ."[108]

The answer to this difficulty seems to lie in two points. The first is that the O. T. besides being a partial revelation was a pedagogic revelation. When God revealed something, He was at the same time preparing His hearers for the Messianic fullness of that revelation. The Hebrew writers not infrequently betray the fact that they themselves do not understand the full import of what they are saying, but that eventually all will be clear. This is certainly true too of the N. T. where Christ told the Apostles that the Paraclete would enable them to understand the full meaning of his words. Therefore it would not be at all foreign to God's pedagogic plan to increase our knowledge of revelation by drawing more advanced doctrines out of what has been already learned, instead of mere external additions. Indeed Fuller is right when he asks, "Why should it surprise us if God put into words a meaning which only revelation would bring out?"[109] Would it not be more surprising if, foreseeing as He did the fulfillment, He deliberately eschewed it from the text?

And this is not pure speculation: as even Fr. Weisengoff admits, N. T. exegesis often seems to speak more as if the doctrines were already spiritually contained in the O. T.[110] It approaches the O. T. with the idea that what was already written there is being fulfilled. In fact, Fr. Cerfaux tells us that the Apostles had a special charism for reading and seeing the fuller meaning in the Scriptures.[111] This same exegetical outlook was common among

[108] Weisengoff, *art. cit.*, p. 85.

[109] Fuller, *art. cit.*, 39k.

[110] Weisengoff, *art. cit.*, p. 85.

Bouyer, *art. cit.*, p. 34, says that the N. T. does not use the O. T. as a *deus ex machina*: its interpretations come from the heart of the O. T. itself: "Rien n'est plus certain aujourd'hui que le fait que ce procédé est intérieur à l'élaboration même de l'Ancien Testament."

[111] Cerfaux, "Simples réflexions," pp. 35-36.

the Fathers: "To repeat a saying of Loisy about St. Paul, they do not prove their theories by the Scriptures, they see them in the Scriptures."[112] And so we have valid reasons for believing that the *sensus plenior* is not simply a question of an external addition of meaning to the text (especially since those who say that it is are singularly ungenerous in supplying objective evidence for their view). Further revelation makes clear a sense that was already there; it does not create a new one.

A second point that is useful in answering this difficulty is the peculiar adaptability of the Hebrew language to carry such hidden meanings. In all languages, the *adaequatio verbi et intellectus* is rarely achieved, for the abstract concept often overflows its material instrument. Consequently when we read, we must go beyond the written word and attain to the fullness of the author's mind. This is what Fr. Coppens speaks of as the homogeneous plus-value of language.[113] Furthermore, it is inevitable that a written text objectively conveys more to one reader than to another; and it may occur that it engenders some ideas not clear to the author himself, but certainly implied in what he says. But besides these general features of language, Hebrew offers special difficulty. It is a simple language with a small vocabulary, lacking the fine technical precision of Greek and Latin. In literary form, written Hebrew is full of metaphors, elastic and vague; sometimes indeed it is capable of more than one meaning at a time.[114] Now God knew this when He chose Hebrew as the vehicle of His word. He knew that future generations would see in the vagueness of the text deeper meanings than the hagiographer understood. Is it

[112] de Riedmatten, *art. cit.*, p. 133.

[113] Coppens, *Harmonies*, p. 53.

[114] Louis Massignon, "Soyons des Sémites Spirituels," part of "Sur l'exégèse biblique" written with Claudel and Daniélou, *Dieu Vivant*, 14 (1949), p. 84. "Surtout dans les langues sémitiques, le sens des phrases . . . n'est pas un sens unique, mais complexe, polyédrique . . ."

Coppens, "Le problème," p. 16, "La pensée hébraïque n'a pas la netteté de la pensée grecque. Tournée souvent vers l'avenir, chargée de métaphores elle s'habille de formes littéraires floues, imprécises, imagées, qui s'ouvrent à des compléments, qui les appellent, qui les contiennent déjà . . ."

not reasonable to suppose that God accepted this, and so arranged His plan as to take advantage of these homogeneous possibilities of language? And even in the case of the human author, is it not possible that, suspecting that his message might have a fuller meaning later on, he deliberately chose elastic terms to allow for that eventuality[115] (*e. g.,* Isaias' use of *'almah*)? Thus, even on a very objective level, the idea of a *sensus plenior* already in the text is not too strange.

* * *

(2) A second objection raised against the fuller sense is that, by classifying it as an homogeneous development of the literal sense, one distends and overstuffs the literal sense, and opens the way for abuses. This charge is not unimportant since the determination of the literal sense is the first duty of exegetes. Daniélou charges that this forcing of the *sensus plenior* into the literal sense is caused by the obstinate refusal of some exegetes to give any credit to the typical sense, or indeed any sense but the literal.[116] de Lubac adds that the modern tendency to place fuller spiritual meanings under the literal sense is dangerous since it might establish the explicit consciousness of the hagiographer as a requisite for all scriptural meanings.[117]

In reply, it must be admitted that the inclusion of the *sensus plenior* under the strict literal sense can be confusing; and it is for this very reason that such a classification is best rejected. On the other hand, to classify the *sensus plenior* as a sense separate from the literal, although related to it, avoids the objection. As for Daniélou, of all the proponents of the fuller sense consulted, we have not found one who denies the typical sense. Daniélou's objections are colored by his own refusal to recognize the fact that not every spiritual sense can be classified as a typical sense.

[115] Massignon, *art. cit.,* p. 83. ". . . une intention maîtresse; celle qu'avait, assurément, l'auteur, lorsqu'il en modalisa l'idée par une phrase, dans l'unique but, je pense, de nous faire participer à son dessein."

[116] Daniélou, Review of Coppens' *Harmonies,* p. 150. ". . . c'est que les exégètes littéraux, se refusant à admettre autre chose que le sens littéral, s'enforcent de ramener le sens figuratif à celui-ci."

[117] de Lubac, "Sens spirituel," p. 550.

Fr. Bierberg's objections along this line are much more interesting.[118] He points out that it is maintained that the *sensus plenior* is merely an *approfondissement* of the literal sense and not something substantially different from it. Therefore, it must be either identical with the comprehension and the correlative extension of the author's concept, or included in it. If it is *identical,* then it is the same as the literal sense and should not form a separate classification. If it is *included,* how can it have greater extension without becoming the object of a new concept? "Thus the *sensus plenior* is different rather than fuller." He cites the example of an idea in Psalm 8 (man is the lord of creation) being applied to Christ in Heb 2:6-8. "Therefore, David could not in this text have intended Christ as the object of his term without automatically adding an exclusive note to the comprehension of his idea 'man.' Nor can it be said that the text refers to Christ inclusively, except in so far as it refers to all men inclusively and equally as man: thus it would apply to Christ in no fuller sense but rather in the same sense that it applies to each of us."

In answering Fr. Bierberg we must distinguish between those instances of the *sensus plenior* of which the author had a vague awareness and other instances where no awareness at all was present. In the former case, there is no new formal concept in the fuller meaning. The greater extension, which the author intended but did not know *clearly* (and therefore is not a strict literal sense—this is a distinction which Fr. Bierberg does not bring forth explicitly when speaking of the literal sense[119]), has simply been made clear. Fernández makes the apt comparison of seeing a room in the very dim light of evening and then returning in the bright light of day. Nothing has been changed; nothing new has been added; but now we see all the furniture and paintings clearly where before we could just make out the dim outline. Applying this to the *sensus plenior,* he says: "It is certain that this meaning, now better illuminated and more intimately pene-

[118] Bierberg, *art. cit.*, pp. 187-188.

[119] If Bierberg applies the literal sense, as he seems to do, to everything that the human author knew and intended, whether clearly or unclearly, then he is perfectly right: this type of *sensus plenior* is no more than a literal sense.

trated, was already comprehended implicitly in the sense which the sacred writer clearly knew and intended."[120]

On the other hand, for any fuller meaning of which the author was totally unaware, Fr. Bierberg is, of course, quite correct on a purely logical basis. (Need we point out, however, that supernatural verities, of which inspiration is one, have a way of not fitting into nice logical categories.) As remarked when we commented on Simon and Prado's proposals about the *sensus plenior,* there is often a new formal concept involved. When we say that the fuller sense is a development of the literal sense, we are not referring to the terminology of Aristotelian logic. We mean the *sensus plenior* draws out the potentialities of the literal sense, potentialities placed there through God's pedagogical plan of salvation. In the example cited (let us suppose for the moment that the author of the Psalm was totally unaware of any fuller application of his words), according to strict logic, Christ as the special king of the redeemed universe is not contained in the formal concept of man as the lord of creation. But when God made man the lord of creation, He also intended that one day His Incarnate Son would be in a special way Christ the King. One doctrine was to complete the other: man was to rule the universe and the God-man was to rule men. And He so guided the phrasing of the first doctrine (Psalm 8) that St. Paul could exegete the Psalm to refer to the second doctrine, and thus bring out the connection between the two. For Bierberg this is a pure accommodation;[121] to us this would mean that it was not intended by God. But Paul gives no such indication: he seems to take it for granted that God intended it.[122] The argument that it is a new formal

[120] Fernández, "Sentido Plenior," p. 305: "Lo cierto es que este sentido mejor illuminado y más intimamente penetrado se hallaba ya implicitamente en el sentido bien conocido y querido del escritor sagrado. A esto llamamos nosotros *sensus plenior.*"

[121] Or if it be thought that such a sense is really biblical, Bierberg would allow that it might be typical—hardly, the deeper sense springs from the words themselves, not from the fact that man is a type of Christ.

[122] One may argue about the case in hand (we accept it because Bierberg has used it); but about the general attitude of the author of Hebrews there should be no doubt. Cf. Van der Ploeg and Spicq, notes 30, 31, c. II, above.

concept as far as the hagiographer is concerned does not destroy the fact that the literal meaning of the Psalm (man's ruling over creatures) is seen to have a more sublime sense when applied to Christ's reign, and that St. Paul points out a relationship between the two doctrines in God's plan of salvation—which is what we mean by development, fulfillment, *approfondissement.*

Well then, one may cry out triumphantly, if you admit that the *sensus plenior* and the literal sense may consist of different formal concepts, you have returned to the bizarre theory of a multiple literal sense. Not at all; such a theory allows for an application of one passage to entirely *unrelated* realities. Here—and this is our control—we insist: (1) that the doctrines concerned be related, and there be some authoritative testimony of this relation; (2) that the fuller meaning be close to the literal meaning, so that the words are not used in an entirely different sense, but in one closely connected to the original. As far as we know, not one adherent of the fuller sense accepts the theory of a multiple literal sense.[123]

* * *

(3) A third objection concerns the hagiographer's awareness of the fuller meaning. Most of the authors admit that in at least some examples of the *sensus plenior* the human author was unconscious of the increase in meaning that his text would later receive. Now can one really speak of a text having a meaning which its author in no way conceived or intended? If the human author of Scripture was not even vaguely aware of the *sensus plenior,* how can we call it a sense of Scripture?

The answer to this objection (an objection which is indeed basic to most of the adverse criticism which is encountered) lies in a renewed emphasis on the instrumentality of the human author. God is, after all, the principal Author of Scripture; His awareness and His intentions are the criteria for scriptural senses, not those of the hagiographer.[124] Of course, the hagiographer was

[123] Buzy, *art. cit.,* refers to a plural sense, but (p. 388) he points out clearly that he is speaking of a homogeneous, not a heterogeneous, one.

[124] Leal, *art. cit.,* p. 478: "Si un texto no ha sido entendido plenamente

a free instrument and real author, and therefore was generally aware of the complete meaning of what he wrote. However, he was still a deficient instrument and could be moved to say something which he understood only partially, but which God intended fully. Perhaps Fr. Coppens' distinction between the human author as hagiographer and as prophet might be of use.[125] As hagiographer, the author understood and intended the literal sense. But sometimes the hagiographer was also a prophet; and in this case it is not required that he have understood all. St. Thomas says: "Since the mind of the prophet is a deficient instrument, even the true prophets do not know everything which the Holy Spirit intends in their visions, their sayings or their deeds."[126] This

por el hagiógrafo, con tal que el Espíritu Santo lo haya así visto y querido 'est eius sensus.'"

For definitions of what constitutes a scriptural sense, cf. c. I, n. 65.

Also, St. Thomas, *Q. Disp. de Potentia*, q. 4, a. 1, # 8: "Unde si etiam aliqua vera ab expositoribus sacrae Scripturae litterae aptentur, quae auctor non intelligit, non est dubium quin Spiritus sanctus intellexerit, qui est principalis auctor divinae Scripturae. Unde omnis veritas, quae salva litterae circumstantia, potest divinae Scripturae aptari, est eius sensus."

[125] Coppens, *Harmonies*, p. 47.

Tuya, "Si es posible," pp. 384-386, makes a threefold distinction: prophet; hagiographer relating God's words; hagiographer writing his own thoughts.

[126] *Summa Theologica*, II-II, p. 173, a. 4: "Sciendum tamen quod, quia mens prophetae est instrumentum deficiens, ut dictum est, etiam veri prophetae non omnia cognoscunt quae in eorum visis, aut verbis, aut etiam factis Spiritus Sanctus intendit."

Courtade, *art. cit.*, p. 497, appends to his article a note on this text. He admits that our interpretation is incontestably the most probable. He proposes, however, another one: the prophets would know all that their words signify but not everything about the object dealt with. Such an interpretation does seem a little far-fetched especially when we consider other Thomistic texts below. (Cf. n. 132).

Among those who favor the *sensus plenior* a minor dispute has arisen over whether the text applies to prophets in the proper or improper sense. (The proper sense refers to those prophets who receive a supernatural lumen for interpreting the species infused by God.) Benoit, *art. cit.*, pp. 291-292, says improper; Tuya, "Si es posible," pp. 389-391, says proper. It would not seem to disturb our argument at all since we are simply trying to prove that there can be some sense of Scripture of which the prophet was unaware, which is true in either case.

observation is not peculiar to St. Thomas, but is agreed upon by some of the greatest theologians of all time.[127] For them, the prophet reported what God had said; he could not confine the scope of the message to what he understood. This is also true of the Evangelists quoting the words of Christ.

This answer does not satisfy the opponents of the *sensus plenior*. They argue that from the very nature of instrumental causality one can prove the impossibility of the fuller sense. God is employing as an instrument an intelligent creature whose proper action involves understanding and volition. Now an instrument exerts its instrumental action only when it exerts its proper action. Consequently, when the hagiographer is being used as an instrument by God, he must understand and intend what he writes. If we say the *sensus plenior* goes beyond the hagiographer's knowledge and intention, then he is not the instrumental cause of it.[128] We must not attempt a vivisection; no text can possess a sense which would entirely escape the human author's intention and have its origin in God alone.[129]

[127] Sutcliffe, *art. cit.*, p. 336, lists Sts. Jerome and Augustine, Suarez, and cites *Divino Afflante Spiritu.*

Tuya, "El Sentido Típico," pp. 632-641, mentions in addition Chrysostom, Marin Sola, Hugon, Benoit. The following seem worthwhile quoting:

St. Jerome (*Comm. in Ep. ad Ephesios, PL,* 26:479 D): "Aliud est enim in spiritu ventura cognoscere, aliud ea cernere opera completa."

Suarez, *De Fide*, disp. 8, sect. 4, N. 2: "Cum prophetae lingua et mens sint Spiritus Sancti instrumenta, quae non adaequant virtutem principalis agentis, non est necesse omnia intelligi a prophetis quae Spiritus Sanctus intendit."

Hugon, from *La Causalité Instrumentale en Théologie* (Paris: 1907), pp. 26-28 (as cited by Tuya): ". . . et il n'est pas besoin que leur activité soit proportionel avec l'effet à produire." This refers to God using creatures.

Benoit, *op. cit.*, p. 357: "L'Esprit divin qui se sert d'un esprit humain pour communiquer avec les hommes ne se condamne pas de ce fait à ne jamais dépasser ses étroites limites."

Quite a contrast with these is presented by Courtade's statement, *art. cit.*, p. 492: "Ainsi les prophètes, pas plus que les autres écrivains sacrés, n'exprimaient par leurs paroles des vérités qui leur fussent inconnues."

[128] Muñoz, *art. cit.*, pp. 163-164.

[129] Courtade, *art. cit.*, pp. 486-487: "Ne la soumettons donc pas à une

In reply to this, we must study more closely the nature of instrumentality. From the outset let us admit that the philosophy of the instrument is difficult and disputed: there are still many aspects of which we cannot be sure. (Yet the greatest authorities on instrumentality, like St. Thomas and Suarez, have no difficulty in admitting that God could intend in the Scriptures more than the human instrument intended, which rather militates against instrumentality rendering such a sense impossible.) These pertinent observations, however, seem fairly well established: [130]

(a) An instrument is not a mere occasion, but has its proper form by which it acts. Man's proper action is cognitive and volitive.

(b) The instrument must be actuated by a principal cause which sets it in motion and raises its power transitorily.

(c) The resulting action is wholly the effect of each cause, but each acts in its own manner. The exact way they cooperate is not clear.

(d) The action of a *created* principal cause is limited by the proper action of the instrumental cause.

(e) The action of an *uncreated* principal cause is not so limited; [131] God can raise an instrument's action over natural obstacles. Yet even with such elevation, it still remains an instrument. Thus, for instance, there is a whole school of theologians who hold that the sacraments are the physical instrumental causes of grace. They see no difficulty in saying that God can use a natural sign as an instrument to produce a supernatural effect.[132]

sorte de vivisection en y cherchant, d'une part, le sens que les écrivains sacrés lui ont donné, et, d'autre part, ou au delà, le sens que Dieu y aurait déposé à leur insu. Aucun texte ne peut posséder un sens qui, dépassant l'intention de l'auteur instrumental, cesserait pour autant de lui être imputable, et tirerait pour autant origine de l'Auteur principal exclusivement."

[130] Cf. Tuya, "El Sentido Típico," pp. 644-645; Tuya's presentation of this point is the most complete and satisfactory we have encountered.

[131] We cannot apply the notion of principal cause to God and man univocally. This modification involves the whole idea of potential potency in the instrument.

[132] Cf. St. Thomas on the sacraments, *Summa Theologica*, III, q. 77, a. 3, ad 3: "Haec autem virtus instrumentalis conservatur in speciebus sacra-

These principles can be applied to the question in hand, as long as we remember that we are dealing with a divine principal cause and a unique instrumental cause (one that is free and intelligent).[133] Man's proper action of cognition and volition must be operative when God uses him as an instrument in writing the Scriptures. And truly it is: the hagiographer understands and intends the literal sense. Since there is a literal sense of every passage in the Scriptures, man's proper instrumental action is employed in the whole Bible.[134] This assertion answers the demand that the instrument *always* exercise its proper action. But one is unjustified in going further and concluding that any additional sense surpassing the hagiographer's purview is excluded. That might be said only if the fuller sense was taking the place of the literal sense, for then there would be no instrumental action at all. But once we admit the universality of the literal sense and say that the instrument is always acting, there is no reason why God cannot elevate that instrument to produce an additional effect outside the sphere of its proper activity (outside the cognition and intention of the hagiographer). As Tuya remarks: "From the fact that God is using an instrument which is *capable of knowledge,* it does not follow that God can use this intelligent instrument only in as much as he actually knows all that God wanted to express." [135]

* * *

mentalibus divina virtute, sicut et prius erat, et ideo possunt agere ad formam substantialem instrumentaliter, per quem modum aliquid potest agere ultra speciem, non quasi virtute propria, sed virtute principalis agentis." Also q. 79, a. 2, ad 3: "Nihil autem prohibet causam instrumentalem producere potiorem effectum, ut ex supra dictis patet."

[133] We only use the sacraments in comparison to show that an instrument can produce a higher effect. There is a world of difference between man's instrumentality and that of the sacraments. Benoit, *op. cit.*, pp. 286 ff., says that it is only in a broad sense that the word instrument can be used of man at all.

[134] Sutcliffe, *art. cit.*, p. 339: ". . . abstraction made from this plenary sense, every part of the book has a meaning intended both by God and the human author."

[135] Tuya, "Si es posible," p. 395: "Pero de que Dios utilice al hagiógrafo come *instrumento cognoscibile,* no se ve exigencia que Dios no pueda utilizar para esta obra el instrumento *cognoscibile* si no en cuanto es *cognoscente* de todo lo que Dios quiere expresar."

(4) The opponents of the *sensus plenior* now counter with a fourth objection based on the notion of inspiration. That a text be inspired there is required the mutual intention of the two authors; if there is a *sensus plenior* outside the pale of the author's deliberate intention, it is not inspired. And so Bierberg says: "*No single word or sentence of Sacred Scripture considered as inspired has an objective* sensus plenior. . . . When inspiring, therefore, God voluntarily limits the expression of his thought to the character and capacities of the human agent. . . . What God intended, his instruments intended, and vice versa; otherwise there is a lack of proportion between cause and effect."[136] Courtade says the same.[137]

This outlook on inspiration seems almost axiomatic with those who oppose the fuller sense. Yet when we sought for authoritative proof of the idea that inspiration demands that the human author understand and intend fully all that God intends, we could not find any support for it in Church documents, the Fathers, or the great Scholastics. Nor are the authors who advance this idea very generous in supplying us with these references.

True they generally cite a passage from *Providentissimus Deus*;[138] but it is lucid from the context that this encyclical did not have the present problem in mind at all, and the citation reflects no definitive light on the problem. The section in question is as follows:[139]

> "For by supernatural power, He so moved and impelled them to write—He so assisted them when writing—that the things which He ordered, and those only, they, first, rightly understood, then willed faithfully to write down, and finally expressed in apt words and with infallible truth."

The meaning of it is clear when we consider the context. The

[136] Bierberg, *art. cit.*, p. 185.

[137] Courtade, *art. cit.*, pp. 487-489.

[138] *Ibid.*, p. 486.

Bierberg, *art. cit.*, p. 185: "The same conclusion is clear from Pope Leo XIII's classical definition of inspiration."—That it is *not* clear we show above.

[139] *Rome and Scripture*, p. 24.

initial sentence of this portion of the encyclical concerns the extent of inspiration: it says that the canonical books are *wholly and entirely* inspired.[140] All the text in hand means is that God was responsible for every single thing in the Bible, since He moved the authors to put down what He wanted and only what He wanted. He saw to it that they understood exactly what He wanted, willed faithfully to write it down, and expressed it in apt words. The very next sentence of the encyclical reads: "Otherwise it could not be said that He was the author of the entire Scripture." Therefore the words "and those only" have not the least connotation of confining all inspiration to what the human author understood; they simply affirm that the human author intended only what God wanted, and nothing independently of God. With Bierberg we say, "What God intended, the human author intended," but the *vice versa* that he adds *is not in the text, even implicitly.*

With reference to this passage Fr. Bea says: "By this we do not mean to say that God, in certain cases, particularly in the question of prophecies, could not have annexed and would not have desired to annex to the words of the human author a deeper sense, a more ample sense which was not perceived by the human author. . ."[141] Sutcliffe is of the same persuasion: "In those passages where the divine author intended a plenary sense just as in those where there is no plenary sense, the hagiographer correctly conceived, decided to write, and in fact faithfully wrote all and only all that God intended."[142] Marin Sola remarks: "It is evident that to understand the meaning (*recta mente concipere*) is very different from understanding *all* the meaning. Leo XIII says only that the inspired authors understood the *sense* of everything that God inspired—and St. Thomas had already said this before him—but he does not say that they understood *all* the

[140] *Ibid.*, "For all the books which the Church receives as sacred and canonical are written wholly and entirely, with all their parts, at the dictation of the Holy Spirit . . ."

[141] Bea, "L'enciclica," p. 419: "Con ciò non intendiamo dire che Dio, in certi casi, particolarmente quando si tratta di profezie, non abbia potuto e voluto annettere alle parole dell' autore humano un senso più alto, più ampio, non percepito dall' autore humano e notificatoci soltanto da Dio stesso in una fase più avanzata della divina rivelazione."

[142] Sutcliffe, *art. cit.*, p. 339.

sense." [143] Tuya sums it all up admirably: "The Church teaches that the instrument—the hagiographer—could not do a thing in this work unless he received the entire *motio* for his action from the principal cause. However, the Church does not at all positively teach, or even insinuate, that the activity of the principal cause—God—remains restricted in its biblical possibilities by the comprehension or non-comprehension of His intentions by the hagiographer." [144] And we should not forget that if *Providentissimus Deus* is not referring to the problem of a deeper sense here, it may well be referring to it when it says: [145]

> "For the language of the Bible is employed to express, under the inspiration of the Holy Spirit, many things which are beyond the power and scope of the reason of man—that is to say, divine mysteries and all that is related to them. There is sometimes in such passages a fullness and a hidden depth of meaning which the letter hardly expresses and which the laws of interpretation hardly warrant."

If we find no authoritative backing for the notion that inspiration demands the hagiographer's awareness of everything that God intended, we find several good arguments to the contrary: (a) when dealing with the typical sense we quoted several ecclesiastical documents which presupposed the inspiration of that sense. In most cases the human author was not aware of the typical sense. Must we not conclude then that awareness of the full meaning is not necessary for inspiration? Courtade is quite logical:

[143] Marin Sola, *La Evolución homogenea del Dogma Católico* (Madrid: 1952), quoted in Tuya, "El Sentido Típico," p. 632: "Es evidente que entender el sentido (recta mente concipere) es muy diferente de entender *todo* su sentido. León XIII solo dice que los autores inspirados entendieron el sentido de *todas* las cosas que Dios les inspiró, y esto ya lo había dicho antes Santo Tomás; pero non dice que entendieron *todo* su *sentido.*"

[144] Tuya, "Si es posible," p. 388: "La Iglesia enseña que el instrumento—hagiógrafo—no puede hacer nada en esta obra sin la *moción total* del mismo por la causa principal, pero no enseña positivamente ni insinúa que la actividad de la causa principal—Dios—quede coartada en sus posibilidades bíblicas por la comprensión o non comprensión de sus intentos por el hagiógrafo."

[145] *Rome and Scriptures,* p. 14.

in a footnote he denies that the typical sense is inspired (but again without evidence from authority).[146] Muñoz is admirably frank: if he denies the inspiration of the typical sense, he admits that he does not intend to establish his theory on the Scriptures, the Fathers, or ecclesiastical documents, and that the latter do not seem to agree with him.[147] (b) Another argument is the impressive list of theologians [148] who admit that the prophets were not conscious of everything God inspired. Surely we are not to say that these prophecies were not inspired! (c) If we admit, as most do, that a writer did not need to be aware of the fact that he was inspired, why is it so unthinkable that he was unaware of all the implications of what he wrote under inspiration?

A quotation from St. Augustine fits in well here: "Because he was inspired, the human author was at least able to say something: if he had not been inspired, he would not have said anything at all. But because he was an inspired *man*, he did not say all that there was to be said; he said only as much as a man could say." [149]

* * *

(5) A fifth objection is that the *sensus plenior* has no background in either tradition or authoritative teaching. Both Daniélou and de Lubac resent the idea of an innovation in Noematics at this late date.[150] Now with regard to tradition, the *term "sensus plenior"* is admittedly an innovation; the *idea,* however, as conceded even by adversaries of the fuller sense,[151] is very ancient.

[146] Courtade, *art. cit.*, p. 487, n. 1: He reasons that God did not use the human author to give these types their significance. True, but he used the author to give them a *scriptural* significance. We dealt with this problem under the typical sense.

[147] Muñoz, *art. cit.*, pp. 166, 175, Cf. above, c. I. n. 69.

[148] Cf. above, notes 126, 127, this chapter.

[149] St. Augustine, *In Joannis Evangelium,* Tractatus CXXIV (*PL,* 35, 1379-1380): "Quia inspiratus, dixit aliquid; si non inspiratus esset, dixisset nihil. Quia vero homo inspiratus non totum, quod est, dixit; sed quod potuit homo, dixit."

[150] Daniélou, Review of Coppens' *Harmonies,* p. 151.

de Lubac, "Sens spirituel," p. 555.

[151] Courtade, "Les Écritures," p. 481.

Gribomont makes an interesting suggestion about why the *sensus plenior* has only been recently discovered. The ancients were interested in the

It was shown above that the exegesis presented by the N. T. and the Fathers demands a noematical insertion between the literal and typical senses.

With regard to the *sensus plenior* and the authoritative teaching of the Church, it is true that the name is not mentioned in any official documents. Perhaps, however, there is a hint of the idea in the recently quoted words of *Providentissimus Deus.*[152] In *Divino Afflante Spiritu* the reference is even clearer. The Holy Father, after speaking of the literal sense, remarks that in addition God ordained "what was *said* and done" in the Bible to take on a spiritual significance.[153] Thus God intended a spiritual sense of words unknown to the human author. The letter of Fr. Miller, the Secretary of the Biblical Commission (a letter which is an interpretation of the biblical encyclicals), repeats this idea, but does not clearly exclude the human author's consciousness of the spiritual sense of words.[154] The scriptural sense spoken of in

objective aspects of revelation, and so spoke of the typical sense. But the last century naturally drew attention to the subjective aspect, the consciousness of the hagiographer, and so discovered the *sensus plenior.* ("Sens plénier," p. 23.)

[152] Cf. above, p. 136. This passage is quoted with favor by some authors; but Braun (*art. cit.*, pp. 294-295) denies any reference to the *sensus plenior.* There is no allusion, says he, to any sense of which the hagiographer would have been ignorant, a condition which for Braun is essential to the fuller sense.

If we do not make unawareness a part of our definition, the encyclical passage seems very favorable. Tuya ("Si es posible," pp. 373-374) applies it to the *sensus plenior.*

[153] *Rome and Scripture,* p. 93. Italics ours. Braun, (*art. cit.*, p. 297), Tuya ("El Sentido Típico," p. 629), and Leal (*art. cit.*, p. 480), apply this to the *sensus plenior.* Braun thinks it was deliberately so phrased to allow the *sensus plenior.*

Coppens, "Nouvelles Réflexions," p. 16, does not agree on the grounds that the Biblical Commission in 1941 equated spiritual and typical. But in ecclesiastical documents, "spiritual" is too vague a term and has fluctuated too often (cf. c. III, p. 85 above) to argue either pro or con. The important thing is that here it is a sense of words as well as of things.

[154] Athanasius Miller, O. S. B., "Instructio," May 13, 1950. *AAS,* 42 (1950), p. 501: "Spiritalem quoque verborum significationem, dummodo eam a Deo intendi . . . rite constet, debito modo explicare curet.

Braun, *art. cit.*, pp. 298-299, sees in Fr. Miller's cautious phrasing a

these last two authoritative documents is in many aspects identifiable with the *sensus plenior* (for it meets the definition of neither the literal nor the typical sense).

Thus a plausible defense can be offered for the fuller sense against the most serious objections of its adversaries. And it is interesting to observe that the two authors who have written most decidedly against it, Bierberg and Courtade, both concede at the end of their articles that it is not a pure aberration but is valid in some cases. Bierberg says that in mediate revelation (where the prophet was the vehicle of a revelation that he did not fully understand), ". . . the revealed sense is a true and objective *sensus plenior* of the inspired terms—though *not as inspired.*"[155] Courtade too concedes that the "fragile hypothesis" of the *sensus plenior* rests on a fact, the gradual development of revelation in the O. T. Consequently the value of some texts cannot be found in isolation, but rather by giving them their place in the ascending progress of revelation. "Without any doubt the words of Scripture frequently possess a *sensus plenior* which passed beyond the horizon of their human author, if one understands thereby that in the mind of God these words were aimed beyond the end to which the human author destined them, to a more elevated goal which he did not perceive."[156] We cannot admit the restrictions that these two authors place on the idea, but it is encouraging to see that the fuller sense is not completely rejected.

support for his own idea of a *sensus plenior* of which the human author would be unaware.

[155] Bierberg's remarks on the *sensus plenior* distinguish between inspiration and revelation:

(1) Inspiration: "No single word or sentence of Sacred Scripture considered as inspired has an objective *sensus plenior.*" p. 185.

(2) Revelation: (a) Direct—"Direct or immediate revelation contained in Sacred Scripture, therefore, can have no objective *sensus plenior.*" p. 191.

(b) Mediate: "It would seem, then, that only in the case of mediate revelation is there the possibility of an objective *sensus plenior.*" p. 192. This is only *per accidens* and of little practical importance, he observes.

[156] Courtade, "Les Écritures," p. 496: "Sans aucun doute, les paroles de l'Écriture ont fréquemment un sens plénier qui dépassait l'horizon de leur auteur humain, si l'on entend par là que dans la pensée de Dieu elles visaient par delà le but que poursuivait cet auteur un but plus élevé, qu'il n'apercevait pas."

VI. EXAMPLES AND CRITERIA

(1) Examples

After all these long discussions, our patient reader would perhaps ask one more question: when all is said and done, what are some concrete examples of the *sensus plenior?* Truly, it would be useful to list in one place the passages proposed by the more important proponents of the fuller sense, understanding however that there may not be universal agreement on some of the examples offered. In listing these below we should remember that there is a *restricted* possibility for applying the *sensus plenior*—no one maintains that it is applicable to every text of the O. T. or even a majority of texts.

Fr. de Ambroggi cites these passages of the O. T. as susceptible of a *sensus plenior*: [157]

(a) Some of the plural references to God which in their fuller meaning can refer to the Trinity. *E.g.*, Gen. 1:26 and 3:22; Isaias 6:3.

(b) Allusions to the Spirit of God which can refer to the Holy Spirit. *E.g.*, Gen 1:2; and Micheas 2:7.

(c) The Wisdom sections of the Sapiential books which can refer to Christ.

(d) The use of the "word of God" which can refer to Christ. *E.g.*, Isaias 55:10-11; Ps 107:20; Ps 147:15.

(e) Messianic Psalms 8, 62, 69, 98.

Fr. Buzy does not like all of de Ambroggi's examples, and suggests some of his own: [158]

(a) The Protoevangelium (an example common to many authors).[159]

[157] de Ambroggi, 1932 *art.*, pp. 311-312. The Psalm numbers in all these references are according to the Hebrew.

[158] Buzy, *art. cit.*, pp. 391-402.

[159] Perhaps this deserves special consideration in view of Fr. Unger's work, *The First Gospel*, which is dedicated to the thesis that Gen 3:15 by a strict literal sense refers to Christ and Mary. At the outset he distinguishes from the strict, exclusive literal sense another type of

(b) The two lovers in the Canticle of Canticles, Jahweh and Israel, can refer to Christ and his Church. Cf. Ephesians 5:25-33.

(c) The son of man in Daniel's prophecy 7:13-14 can refer to Christ.

(d) In the N. T., the different parables about the Kingdom of God, once having been considered together, give a fuller meaning to any one taken alone. This is true also of the different occasions on which the Parousia is discussed.

(e) The concept of the Son of God as applied to the Jewish kings and then to the priests and then to Jesus takes on a fuller sense.

literal sense which he calls "inclusive" whereby several objects are contained in the same concept but in differing degrees of perfection, so that a text can refer literally to a larger group and then in a more perfect way to a member within that group. On p. 4 he says that this is also called "*the fuller sense* because the words are verified of the more perfect object in a more perfect manner. . . . The Sacred Author intends both the basic and the fuller object." (Here we might add a caution: this is only a fuller sense if the human author was not fully aware of it; otherwise it is strictly literal.)

Of the theory that Gen 3:15 refers to Christ in this inclusive literal sense (fuller sense?), so that it is Messianic in a very indistinct manner, Unger states: "It is difficult to see how this opinion can be reconciled with the emphatic statement of Pius IX that Christ was 'clearly and openly pointed out beforehand.'" (p. 284). He also opposes exegesis of the text as a fuller sense referring to Mary (pp. 288-289). In the body of his work he gives a most complete assemblage of arguments for the literal interpretation of the passage.

To discuss the point with Fr. Unger, one would have to go over one by one his appeals to authority—something far beyond the scope of this work. However, the quality of some of the thirty or more authors who do hold the fuller sense interpretation of the text should make it clear that the question is not one-sided or settled. Since we mentioned his quotation of Pius IX, it is only fair to our reader to point out that Pius IX only said that *the Fathers said* that Christ was clearly pointed out, and the question of the unanimity of the Fathers on this point is highly debatable (all of which, of course, Fr. Unger makes no attempt to hide for he mentions it specifically in the body of his work.)

But independently of a detailed discussion of the use of Gen 3:15 by authorities, we would like to make this observation. The strict literal sense (as distinct from the fuller sense—if Unger is using some other definition, perhaps we may be in accord) requires clear awareness by the

Besides some of these, Ayer offers the following:[160]

(a) The Caiphas prophecy of Jn 11:49-52.

(b) The use of Lev 26:12 ("I will walk among you and will be your God.") in II Cor 6:16—cf. also I Cor 6:19.

(c) The adoption of the Extreme Unction text, Jas 5:14, by the Council of Trent, Session 14, DB 906.

Ternant gives some instances of *theoria*:[161]

(a) The Messianic application of Jacob's oracle (Gen 49:10) and Balaam's oracle (Nm 24:17)—perhaps both were rewritten in Davidic times.

(b) Perhaps some of the Suffering Servant Songs of Deutero-Isaias as applied to Christ.

(c) Royal Psalms 2, 45, 72, 110.

hagiographer. And so whoever was the author of Gen 3:15 would have to be fully conscious that the passage referred to Christ and Mary. On pp. 273-274 Unger seems to say that Adam and Eve were aware of this reference, although perhaps not aware of all that we know about the text with our theological sources. But this point is not so easily settled: (a) First, the necessity of awareness does not deal directly with Adam and Eve. It refers to the author of this passage who came along thousands of years later. What was he conscious of when he composed the passage? If he was not clearly aware of the application to Christ and Mary, it is not a strict literal sense. (b) Secondly, several of the latest works on the Protohistory of Genesis, *e. g.*, the Pirot-Clamer Bible, also R. McKenzie's article ("Before Abraham Was," *CBQ*, 15 (1953), pp. 131-140—a summary of the trends of recent Catholic works), stress now, more than ever before, that much of the imagery and expression of these stories was borrowed from a common Semitic background ("mythology") and purified by the Jews as a vehicle of divine revelation. The religious truths of the revelation, of course, were the peculiar treasure of the Jews. Now, if, for instance, it should be true that the framework of the Adam and Eve story was borrowed, would that not affect the problem of the hagiographer's understanding of what was meant by his text? These are but suggestions; nevertheless they should be considered in judging Unger's work which does not clearly broach them.

[160] Ayer, *op. cit.*, pp. 109-110.

[161] Ternant, *art. cit.*, pp. 478-485. Remember he distinguishes *theoria* from the *sensus plenior*, but only because he defines the fuller sense in terms of the author's unconsciousness.

(d) Texts dealing with the return from the Exile as applied to the Messianic era.

The Höpfl and Gut manual [162] sees Christ using the *sensus plenior* in Lk 24:27, "And beginning then with Moses and with all the Prophets, he interpreted to them in all the Scriptures the things referring to himself." And also Peter employs it in his references to the O. T. in Acts 2:14-36. Sutcliffe [163] mentions the employment of Psalm 8:7, ("Thou has put all things under his feet.") in I Cor 15:26 to refer to Christ's domain. Also he cites the interpretation by Heb 1:5 of II Sam 7:14, "I will be to him a father, and he shall be to me a son."

Among the other authors, Tuya [164] offers the N. T. use of Malachias' sacrifice (1:11), and the interpretation of the Old Law in the Sermon on the Mount. Moriarty and Steinmann suggest that Is 7:14 is an instance of the *sensus plenior*.[165] Laridon picks as an example Jn 19:27, "Woman behold thy son. . . . Behold thy mother," when this is interpreted as a basis for Mary's universal motherhood.[166] Rivera calls the mariological interpretation of

[162] Höpfl and Gut, *op. cit.*, p. 462.

[163] Sutcliffe, *art. cit.*, pp. 333-334.

[164] Tuya, "Si es posible," pp. 371, 375.

[165] Frederick Moriarty, S. J., Review of Coppens' *Harmonies*, *TS*, 11 (1950), p. 301.

Steinmann, *Isaïe*, pp. 88-93.

In connection with Is 7:14 we should like to call to the reader's attention Fr. Cuthbert Lattey's ideas on compenetration, of which he considers this text a prime example. ("The Emmanuel Prophecy," *CBQ*, 8 (1946), pp. 369-376.) He cites several authors for his position, some of whom we have quoted for the *sensus plenior*. As we understand it, the theory of compenetration asserts that certain lines of a passage may refer to a present event, while other lines may deal (exclusively?) with the future. There is a compenetration of the two ideas in the one passage. Such a notion resembles the *sensus plenior* very closely. It would differ from it only if Lattey maintains that certain of the lines have an *exclusive* future application (we are not certain of his position). If these lines actually had a present meaning, but were phrased in hyperbole to *include* a future which the prophet vaguely foresaw, compenetration fuses nicely with the theory of the fuller sense.

[166] V. Laridon, "Ecce Filius tuus, ecce mater tua," *Coll. Brugenses*, 46 (1950), p. 207.

Apocalypse 12 a fuller sense.[167] Van der Ploeg shows how to use the *sensus plenior* in studying exegesis by going through the Epistle to the Hebrews and pointing out all the times it is used.[168]

In the way of more general examples, Fr. Ternant mentions the Septuagint: its translators often apply to objects of a Messianic order texts which originally had in mind the realities of Jewish history.[169] Fr. de Riedmatten says that many places where the Vulgate differs from the Hebrew, it is giving us a *sensus plenior.* In reference to St. Jerome's work he remarks, "It remains incontestable that he has produced a book in which New Testament values lie much closer to the surface than in the original."[170] Finally, Fr. Coppens gives us the most interesting hint of all: the words of Christ narrated in the Gospels represent the fuller meaning and interpretation of the original words of the Master. He says:[171]

> "The words of Jesus . . . have since the beginning been so rich in meaning and possibilities that each one of the four Gospels could refract particular aspects of them. The traditions behind the four Gospels reflect four successive

[167] Cf. Gaetano Perrella, C. M., "Sulla terminologia circa il senso mariologico dell' Apocalisse XII," *DTP*, 45 (1942), pp. 100-103.

[168] Van der Ploeg, "L'exégèse," pp. 199-222.

[169] Ternant, *art. cit.*, p. 381. This concept of the LXX, however, should now be modified by discoveries made in Qumrân, Cave IV. The Hebrew fragments of I Sam found there (Cf. Frank Cross, *Bulletin of the American Schools of Oriental Research,* # 132, Dec. 1953, pp. 15-26.) show a text divergent from the MT and similar to the Hebrew readings which can be reconstructed from the LXX. Thus the LXX would seem to be, not a free translation of the MT, but a faithful translation of another Hebrew text of Samuel.

[170] Henri de Riedmatten, O. P., "Typology in the Scriptures," trans. by K. Pond, *Blackfriars,* 33 (March, 1952), pp. 140-141.

[171] Coppens, "Le problème," p. 18-19. "Les paroles de Jésus . . . ont été dès les origines si riches de sens et de virtualités que chacun des quatre évangiles en a pu réfracter des aspects particuliers. Chacune des quatre traditions évangéliques, reflétant quatre stades successifs de la pensée théologique néo-testamentaire, traduit exactement des nuances authentiques de la pensée du Maître. Les évangélistes en ont développé le sens plénier, le charisme de l'inspiration nous garantissant la fidélité de ce développement au point de départ."

> stages of New Testament theological thought, giving an exact rendition of the authentic nuances in the Master's thought. The Evangelists have developed the *sensus plenior* of these words of Christ; and the charism of inspiration guarantees the fidelity of this development to the original."

If this is true we might look for a *rapprochement* between the theory of the *sensus plenior* and that of the *Formgeschichtliche-schule.*

(2) Criteria

These examples are but a few of the possible uses of the *sensus plenior*. We hope that others will be suggested as more scholars begin to employ this new classification. Yet with even the examples we have, one may well wonder what are the criteria for determining when a *sensus plenior* exists. Basically they seem to be two:

(a) The fuller sense must be a development of what is literally said in the passage. It must be a case of the literal sense being *even more true* in the given case. Any distortion or contradiction of the obvious meaning is not a fuller sense.[172] For instance, the Mass of the Sunday after Christmas applies to Christ's birth a passage from Wis 18:14-15, "For while all things were in quiet silence and the night was in the midst of her course, thy almighty word leapt down from heaven from thy royal throne." The context refers to the destroying angel of the Exodus on his mission of death. To apply such a text to the Nativity [173] is certainly not a development of the literal sense and therefore not a *sensus plenior*.

(b) Besides this resemblance in meaning, *God must have willed*

[172] Tuya, "Si es posible," p. 399, says that the homogeneity of the two senses need not be spontaneously evident. "Y al decir normalmente, no se excluye el caso de descubrirse un *sentido pleno*, en este caso hecho por Dios mismo o por el Magisterio de la Iglesia, entre dos proposiciones que no tengan superficialmente, aunque sí en el fundo, esta íntima vinculación."

[173] The text as used in the Mass has a secondary purpose of connecting the Exodus and the Incarnation, which is perfectly correct.

that the fuller sense be contained in the literal sense. We must have some objective basis for stating that the two are connected in the economy of salvation. This is supplied by the authority of the N. T., the Fathers, the Magisterium, the liturgy, and perhaps even a "majority" of the theologians (obviously these are not all of equal value[174]) when they interpret the O. T. to mean something deeper than its obvious sense.[175] Thus one is not permitted to indiscriminately use the *sensus plenior* as a peg to hang new doctrines upon.[176] We need authority for seeing fuller meanings in the Bible; *e. g.*, the doctrines of the Immaculate Conception and the Assumption *may* be contained in the fuller meaning of Bible texts, but to ascertain this we need the guidance of the Church and the Fathers. Without this authority we may suspect but never be sure. Thus the theological usage of the fuller sense will probably be more postpositive than inventive, *i. e.*, accounting for doctrines which are said to be scriptural, rather than discovering new doctrines.

These two criteria are subject to the control of reason. Does that mean that faith has no role in determining a *sensus plenior*? The relation of faith to the fuller sense is very obscure and offers many difficulties. It seems logical that one who has no faith (the strict theological habit) will not accept a *sensus plenior*, because he will deny the second criterion. On the other hand, in those who are believers there is no question that faith can be helpful in recognizing the fulfillment of a text. Yet it is unlikely that faith is absolutely necessary for such recognition.[177] Otherwise we

[174] de Ambroggi, 1932 art., pp. 309-310.

[175] *Ibid.*, p. 307: "Il senso letterale pieno, si può trovare solo con criteri dogmatici: sotto questo aspetto si può dire un senso dogmatico, che non cessa però di essere letterale."

Coppens, "Nouvelles Réflexions," p. 12: "Il n'appartient pas à l'exégèse scientifique de détecter le sens plénier. S'il est présent quelque part, c'est au Magistère, interprète des intentions de l'Esprit, de le révéler."

[176] Buzy, *art. cit.*, p. 404: "Nous ne la signalons pas comme un instrument de nouvelles découvertes exégetiques dans le futur . . ."

Coppens, *Harmonies*, p. 66: ". . . j'estime pour ma part que la théologie ne peut faire appel qu'avec circonspection à l'usage du sens plénier."

[177] *Ibid.*, pp. 63-64. Coppens disagrees with Laberthonnière's contention that faith is indispensable in the exegesis of the Scriptures and forms almost a separate method of interpretation.

take exegesis out of the domain of human science. Fuller wisely remarks: "Thus one who applies the ordinary rules and principles of interpretation is on the right path to the elucidation of the plenary sense, though the interpreter who is also a believer has an advantage and is in a better condition to grasp the full connection between Old and New Testaments." [178] It might be said that the acceptance of the criteria proposed presupposes faith. The application of the criteria, however, can be the work of human reason,[179] although in many cases faith will enter in.

The criteria dealt with so far concern the *sensus plenior* in general. Within the fuller sense there are several criteria for suspecting whether the author was vaguely conscious of the deeper meaning:

(a) Does the greatness of the things literally spoken of exceed human capacity, so that they can be really fulfilled only in a divine Messias? [180]

(b) Is there an element of brusqueness or strangeness in an otherwise simple narrative? [181]

(c) Is there a great deal of hyperbole in a narrative which otherwise shows little need of it? [182] This must be used with special care in view of the oriental predilection for hyperbole.

(d) In the case of a later redactor (*e. g.*, Chronicles, Esdras), is there a Messianic import superimposed on a text of original non-

[178] Fuller, *art. cit.*, 39 L.

Coppens, *Harmonies*, p. 65: "Ces réserves étant faites, on peut conclure que, *pour être pleinement saisi et d'une manière qui apaise l'esprit*, le sens plénier a besoin de cette lumière surnaturelle que la foi confère aux yeux des croyants."

[179] Coppens, "Nouvelles Réflexions," p. 12: (Continuing n. 175 above) "Mais cette présence une fois signalée, il n'est pas interdit à l'exégèse, même scientifique, de rechercher comment dans un cas particulier le sens plénier, dont le Magistère et la Tradition proclament la présence, s'harmonise dans l'homogénéité avec le sens littéral premier qu'il incombe a l'exégèse scientifique de retrouver."

[180] Vaccari, *art. cit.*, p. 27. Ternant, *art. cit.*, p. 369.

[181] Coppens, *Harmonies*, p. 62.

[182] The criterion of the Antiochenes.

Messianic import?[183] These criteria are not easy to apply—that is why a definition of the *sensus plenior* must allow for vague awareness or no awareness at all: there are a great number of borderline cases where one cannot say. Yet when we have a combination of several of them, we can be reasonably sure that the author was partially aware of the deeper import of his words.[184]

[183] Ternant, *art. cit.*, p. 383.

[184] As this dissertation went to press, there came into our hands a new work on the *sensus plenior*; *El Problema del Sentido Literal Pleno en la Sagrada Escritura* (Santander: Univ. Comillas, 1954), pp. 57, by Severiano Del Páramo, S. J. This is another proof of the interest the question has aroused among the Spanish who are now the most active writers on the subject. (The XII annual Spanish Catholic Biblical meeting in 1951 gave all its evening sessions to the problem; and the topic was resumed in the next two meetings.) This new work is concerned entirely with proving the possibility of the fuller sense, and treats very little of its nature. We might note the following points of interest: (a) The author's definition (cf. Appendix) allows the human author either not to have perceived the fuller sense at all, or to have perceived it vaguely. (b) In proving the *sensus plenior*, he relies heavily on texts from Sts. Peter and Paul about Christ bringing to light things hidden in the O. T. (I Pet 1:10-12; II Cor 3:14-6; Rom 16:25-7; Eph 3:5-6) (c) He mentions on p. 28 a new study by Dr. Turrado claiming that one must posit a *sensus plenior* to understand fully how the N. T. interprets the Old.

CONCLUSION

And so this investigation of the *sensus plenior* draws to a close. It is hoped that the treatment presented has clarified the problem at hand and made our own position clearly understood. At the outset we arrived at a precise definition of the two great senses of Scripture: (a) the literal sense is a sense expressed by the text itself and clearly understood and intended by both authors of Scripture; (b) the typical sense is a sense of things narrated in the text. In the second chapter, by perusing the history of biblical interpretation, we came to the conclusion that much of the exegesis of the past is more-than-literal, and that, while some of it is sheer accommodation, part of it is valid and must be accounted for in any classification of the senses of Scripture.

In the third chapter, from a summarizing of this and related problems, an increasing awareness was pressed upon us that the literal and typical senses do not classify adequately all the valid interpretations of the Bible. There remains a deeper sense of the text itself (therefore not typical) which was not clearly foreseen by the human author (therefore not strictly literal) but was inended by God. This is our *sensus plenior.*

Proceeding to discuss it, we accepted with serious modifications the various subdivisions presented by Canon Coppens, all the while maintaining that these do not exhaust all the aspects of the fuller sense. From a review of the relations of the *sensus plenior* to the strict literal and the typical senses, we concluded that it should form a separate classification, although closer to the literal sense since it flows from the text itself and is a deepening of its literal meaning. A schema for a general classification of the senses of Scripture was suggested.

In face of the serious objections raised against the very possibility of the fuller sense, it was maintained that, on one hand, from all the *a posteriori* evidence available we should posit a *sensus plenior,* and, on the other hand, there is no *a priori* proof that it contradicts in any way the instrumentality of the human author, the doctrine of inspiration, or any document of the Magisterium. *The sensus plenior is, in our opinion, and* salvo meliore judicio, *a fully justified classification for a valid inspired meaning of the Scriptures intended by Almighty God and recognized by interpreters of all time.* Finally, we mentioned some suggested applications of this new sense, and presented rigid criteria to prevent its abuse.

In all this we do not think for a moment that (while we have done our best in the light of the material available) we have more than touched the surface in our treatment. The *sensus plenior* appears to solve many problems—it does not solve them all. It is in no way an exegetical "cure-all." As new authors reflect on the subject—and the number of those who are doing so is encouraging—many more of its possibilities and difficulties will come to light. But already, its very acceptance by so many first-class scholars requires a rethinking of what we formerly considered to be the "literal" interpretation of many O. T. texts and prophecies. (Of course, this does not change the fact that there are certain prophecies which remain truly literal in the strict sense.) The *sensus plenior* allows a much more scientific approach to the limitations of the O. T. authors in their awareness of the future, and enables us to reclassify correctly many of the traditional interpretations of the Bible. The work to be done is immense. God has cast us a challenge: to recognize and evaluate *correctly and fully* all the treasures He has placed in the Bible. The words of Psalm 78 mock us eternally:

> I will open my mouth in parables,
> I will utter hidden things of the olden age . . .
> So that the coming generation, the sons to be born,
> Might know and rise and relate to their sons . . .

FINIS

APPENDIX

In view of the oft repeated statement that everyone defines the *sensus plenior* in a different way, it would seem to be useful to collect in one place the definitions or descriptions of the fuller sense as given by some of the most representative authors. The double asterisk indicates those authors whose general position is unfavorable towards the *sensus plenior*. Full titles are available in the Bibliography which follows immediately.

Aubert, *La Théologie Catholique*, p. 26: . . . c'est-a-dire un sens plus profond qui peut se dégager pour le croyant d'aujourd'hui de la lettre de l'Écriture, bien que les auteurs sacrés n'en aient guère eu conscience au moment même où ils écrivaient.

Ayer, *Compendium Introductionis*, p. 108: Sensus plenior est ille sensus litteralis (latius sumptus), qui includitur quidem in ipsis verbis sacris, sed nonnisi a Deo comprehenditur necnon ab eis qui divinitus dictis aut factis illustrati sunt.

Benoit, *La Prophétie*, pp. 357-358: Les *paroles* mêmes des anciens inspirés ont reçu dans la vaste perspective du plan divin une richesse et une plénitude que n'avaient pas conçues leurs premiers auteurs, mais dont devaient profiter les lecteurs de l'avenir. . . . Ainsi Dieu a commenté sa propre parole par elle-même et éclairé les oracles anciens par le moyen des nouveaux, leur donnant une portée plus profonde qu'on appelle le '*sensus plenior*' ou sens 'plénier.'

** Bierberg, *art. cit.*, p. 187: "This sense is commonly defined as the meaning which is 'drawn from a deeper and fuller explanation of the words,' and which 'God, the primary author, wishes to express beyond the understanding and intention of the sacred writer.'"—Bierberg's quotations are from Höpfl and Gut.

Braun, *art. cit.*, p. 297: Quant aux *dicta*, que seraient-ils sinon certaines paroles inspirées, ayant en commun avec les *facta*: 1. de dépasser la compréhension de l'hagiographe; 2. de répondre à l'intention et à l'ordination de l'auteur principal. Pareille notion est exactement celle du sens plénier.

Coppens, *Harmonies*, p. 36 (preliminary definition): . . . il s'agit d'une signification qui est 'intentionnée' principalement par Dieu et non pas, ou tout au plus d'une manière fort imparfaite, par l'hagiographe, mais qui, par ailleurs, s'appuie sur la lettre des textes et, par conséquent, ne doit pas être acquise par la voie de l'allégorie.

(Final definition), pp. 67-68: L'ensemble des relations virtuelles qui rattachent un texte de l'Ancien Testament à la foi chrétienne et qui se dégagent des rapports qu'il possède avec la doctrine chrétienne ainsi que de sa participation au développement doctrinal et historique qui a conduit l'Ancien Testament au Nouveau.

** Courtade, *art. cit.*, pp. 483-485 (an assembly of his comments): Il est confiné à la lettre: inhérent aux paroles exclusivement et non aux choses. . . . le sens plénier déborde (parfois de beaucoup) la pensée et l'intention de l'écrivain. . . . Or le sens plénier ne se distingue pas adéquatement du sens que l'écrivain avait présent à l'esprit, et qu'il exprimait de son mieux. . . . Il le contient, mais il le prolonge et le complète (He is dependent on Benoit for the latter part.)

de Ambroggi, 1932 art., p. 299: Per senso letterale pieno intendiamo quell' aspetto della verità, che, pur potendo essere compreso direttamente nell'espressione biblica, non era conosciuto dall'agiografo, ma sì da Dio inspiratore che per quelle parole volle significarlo.

Del Páramo, *op. cit.*, p. 19: Se trata, por lo tanto, del mismo sentido literal en cuya expresión verbal se encierra una plenitud, o profundidad, o abundancia o ciertos matices del mismo concepto, que pasaban desapercibidos al autor humano, o los percibía de una manera vaga y confusa, pero que Dios, sabiduría infinita, intentaba dejar allí encerrados en aquellas palabras como un germen que había de germinar y desarrollarse más tarde en un sentido más profundo, claro y completo al calor de posteriores ilustraciones.

de Vaux, review of Coppens' *Harmonies*, p. 281: Le sens plénier est celui que Dieu a en vue lorsqu'il inspire à l'auteur le choix de ces mots; il se conclut des autres textes de la Bible, qui est tout entière l'œuvre du même Dieu, ou de l'économie du salut, qui est conçue et réalisée par le même Dieu. Ce sens plénier est un approfondissement du sens littéral, dans une ligne homogène.

Fernández, *Institutiones Biblicae*, 2nd ed., p. 306 (Same in the 6th ed., p. 381): . . . *Deus per hagiographi verba intendat aliquando sensum abundantiorem, pleniorem illo, quem ipse hagiographus intellexit et exprimere voluit.* Agitur non de duobus sensibus disparatis, sed de senso quodam ampliori, qui potestate vocis contineatur, quique a scriptore sacro non omnino ignoretur.

Fuller, *A Catholic Commentary*, 39d: "This is in effect an extension of the literal sense, for its existence is held by those who maintain that God may imply more in the words of Scripture than the human author is conscious of—a hidden meaning in fact which is revealed only later, whether by more explicit prophecy or by the fulfilment of it in events."

Leal, *art. cit.*, p. 476: Se trata de un verdadero sentido bíblico y divino;

por tanto, que está en la letra de la Sagrada Escritura formando un todo armónico y homogéneo con el literal inmediato y obvio, pero que trasciende el alcance de autor humano, y es sólo visto y querido por Dios, autor principal del libro inspirado.

O'Flynn, *art. cit.*, p. 181: ". . . a fuller or more profound meaning conveyed by God through the words of Scripture, but not known (or, at least, not clearly known) to the sacred writer."

Penna, *La Lettera*, p. 279: . . . *senso letterale pieno*, intendendo segnelare il senso contenuto nell'ambito della lettera, ma compreso solo da Dio senza essere percepito dall' agiografo. Il lettore moderno lo deduce non dal semplice esame del contesto immediato, ma da tutto il complesso della rivelazione divina.

Renié, *Manuel*, 2nd ed., I, p. 189: . . . à côté du sens littéral historique qui ressort du texte en soi, tel que l'a probablement compris l'auteur inspiré, il y a pour certains passages dogmatiques ou prophétiques un sens plus ample et plus profond, qu'on peut appeler le sens *intégral* (*sensus plenior*), également voulu de Dieu, auteur principal. Ce sens est le prolongement du sens historique, mais la Révélation chrétienne seule nous permet de le découvrir.

Simon and Prado, *Praelectiones Biblicae*, I, 6th ed., p. 251 (The *sensus plenior*, also called *supralitteralis*): quatenus veritates refert verbis quidem hagiographi divinitus expressas, sed quas idem hagiographus neque explicite tradere intendit nec, seclusa speciali revelatione, assequi valet.

Sutcliffe, *art. cit.*, p. 334: "It is a true Scriptural sense borne by the words of the Bible, intended by God, but not necessarily known to the human author, who writing under divine inspiration used the same words with a humbler and more restricted signification."

Ternant, *art. cit.*, p. 153: distinct du sens littéral mais le continuant et l'approfondissant dans une ligne homogène, et qui, réalisé lui aussi à l'insu de l'auteur sacré, se deduit de 'la portée fonctionnelle du texte dans l'économie de la Révélation entière.'

Tuya, "Si es posible," p. 372: Entendemos por sensus plenior de la Escritura aquel sentido:

(a) Incluído en la letra del texto,
(b) Intentado por Dios,
(c) Desconocido por el hagiógrafo. Por los menos explícitamente en su plenitud . . .
(d) Y que sólo puede ser descubierto a la luz de la revelación posterior.

BIBLIOGRAPHY

Since the reader already has available an exhaustive bibliography on modern Hermeneutics in the works of Canon Coppens, we shall present here only a list of those works used in this dissertation. (Three works, which we felt should be included, but were unfortunately unavailable for personal use, are marked with a double asterisk.)

Aubert, R., *La Théologie Catholique au milieu du XXe siècle.* Louvain: Casterman, 1954.

Ayer, Ildefonsus, O. F. M. Cap., *Compendium Introductionis Generalis in Universam S. Scripturam.* Rome: Ferrari, 1948, 2nd ed.

Bardy, G., "L'exégèse patristique," *Initiation Biblique.* Paris: Desclée, 1939. Edited by Robert and Tricot, pp. 295-304.

Barsotti, D. Divo, *Il Mistero Cristiano nell'Anno Liturgico.* Florence, 1950.

Bate, H. N., "Some Technical Terms of Greek Exegesis," *The Journal of Theological Studies,* 24 (1923), pp. 59-66.

Bea, A., S. J., "L'Enciclica 'Humani Generis' e gli Studi Biblici," *La Civiltà Cattolica,* 101, v. 4 (1950), pp. 417-430.

———., "Progress in the Interpretation of Sacred Scripture," *Theology Digest,* 1 (Spring, 1953), pp. 67-71. A summary of an article in *Gregorianum,* 33 (1952).

Benoit, Pierre, O. P., *La Prophétie,* French Translation of the *Summa Theologica,* IIa—IIae, qq. 171-178. Paris: Desclée, 1947. Appendice II, pp. 355-359.

Bierberg, Rudolph, "Does Sacred Scripture have a *Sensus Plenior?*", *Catholic Biblical Quarterly,* 10 (1948), pp. 182-195.

Bläser, Peter, M. S. C., "St. Paul's Use of the Old Testament," *Theology Digest,* 2 (1954—Winter), pp. 49-52.

Bonnefoy, Jean-François, O. P., "Origène théoricien de la méthode théologique," *Mélanges offerts au R. P. Ferd. Cavallera.* Toulouse: Institut Catholique, 1948, pp. 87-145.

Bonsirven, Joseph, S. J., "L'exégèse Juive," *Initiation Biblique.* Paris: Desclée, 1939. Edited by Robert and Tricot, pp. 290-295.

———., *Exégèse Rabbinique et Exégèse Paulinienne.* Paris: Beauchesne, 1939.

Bouyer, Louis, "Liturgie et exégèse spirituelle," *Maison-Dieu,* 7 (1946), pp. 27-50.

Braun, F-M., O. P., "Le sens plénier et les encycliques," *Revue Thomiste,* 51 (1951), pp. 294-304.

Brown, Raymond E., "The History and Development of the Theory of a

Sensus Plenior," *The Catholic Biblical Quarterly*, 15 (1953), pp. 141-162.

Brownlee, William H., "Biblical Interpretation among the Sectaries of the Dead Sea Scrolls," *The Biblical Archaeologist*, 14 (1951), n. 3, pp. 54-76.

Bullough, Sebastian, O. P., "Fifty Years of Scripture Studies," *Blackfriars*, 27 (1946), pp. 246-251.

Burghardt, Walter, S. J., "On Early Christian Exegesis," *Theological Studies*, 11 (1950), pp. 78-116.

Buzy, Denis, S. C. J., "Un problème d'herméneutique sacrée: sens plural, plénier et mystique," *L'Année Théologique* (1944), pp. 385-408.

Camelot, Th., O. P., "Clément d'Alexandrie et l'Écriture," *Revue Biblique*, 53 (1946), pp. 242-248.

Cerfaux, Lucien, "Simples réflexions à propos de l'exégèse apostolique," *Problèmes et méthode d'exégèse théologique*, by L. Cerfaux, J. Coppens, and J. Gribomont. Louvain: Desclée de Brouwer, 1950, pp. 33-44.

———., "L'exégèse de l'Ancien Testament par le Nouveau Testament," *L'Ancien Testament et les Chrétiens*. Paris: Cerf, 1951, pp. 132-148.

Ceuppens, F., O. P., "Quid S. Thomas de multiplici sensu litterali in S. Scriptura senserit," *Divus Thomas* (Piacenza), 1930, pp. 164-175.

Charlier, Célestin, "La lecture sapientielle de la Bible," *Maison-Dieu*, 12 (1947), pp. 14-52.

Chenu, M.-D., O. P., "Les deux âges de l'allégorisme scripturaire au moyen âge," *Revue de Théologie Ancienne et Médiévale*, 18 (1951), pp. 19-28.

Chifflot, Th-G., O. P., "Comment lire la Bible," *La Vie Spirituelle* (October, 1949), pp. 232-261.

Claudel, Paul, "Lettres au R. P. Maydieu, Directeur de la *Vie Intellectuelle*," part of "Sur l'exégèse biblique," by Claudel, Massignon and Daniélou, *Dieu Vivant*, 14 (1949), pp. 76-81.

Colunga, Alberto, O. P., "Las audacias exegético-bíblicas de la teología moderna," *La Ciencia Tomista*, 78 (1951), pp. 441-458.

Congar, Yves, O. P., "Que pouvons-nous trouver dans les Écritures?", *La Vie Spirituelle* (October, 1949), pp. 227-231.

Coppens, Joseph, *The Old Testament and the Critics*. Patterson: St. Anthony Guild, 1942.

———., "Miscellanées bibliques," *Ephemerides Theologicae Lovanienses*, 23 (1947), pp. 182-188.

———., *Les Harmonies des Deux Testaments*. Tournai & Paris: Casterman, 1949.

———., "Le problème d'un sens biblique plénier," *Problèmes et Méthode d'Exégèse Théologique*, by L. Cerfaux, J. Coppens, and J. Gribomont. Louvain: Desclée de Brouwer, 1950, pp. 11-19.

———., "Bibliographie," *Problèmes et Méthode d'Exégèse Théologique*, pp. 79-90.

———., "Pour une meilleure intelligence des Saintes Écritures," *Ephemerides Theologicae Lovanienses,* 27 (1951), pp. 500-507.

———., "Nouvelles réflexions sur les divers sens des Saintes Écritures," *Nouvelle Revue Théologique,* 74 (January, 1952), pp. 3-20.

———., ***Vom christlichen Verständnis des Alten Testaments.* Louvain: Folia Lovaniensia, 1952.

Cornely, Rudolph, S. J., *Introductio Generalis.* (Volume I of the *Cursus Sacrae Scripturae*). Paris: Lethielleux, 1885.

Cotter, Anthony C., "The Obscurity of Scripture," *Catholic Biblical Quarterly,* 9 (1947), pp. 453-464.

Courtade, Gaston, S. J., "Le sens de l'histoire dans l'Écriture et la classification usuelle des sens scripturaires," *Recherches de Science Religieuse,* 36 (1949), pp. 136-141.

———., "Les Écritures ont-elles un sens 'plénier'?", *Recherches de Science Religieuse,* 37 (1950), pp. 481-499.

d'Alès, Adhémar, "Julien d'Eclane, exégète," *Recherches de Science Religieuse,* 6 (1916), pp. 311-324.

Daniélou, Jean, S. J., "Traversée de la Mer Rouge et Baptême aux premiers siècles," *Recherches de Science Religieuse,* 33 (1946), pp. 402-430.

———., "Les divers sens de l'Écriture dans la Tradition Chrétienne Primitive," *Ephemerides Theologicae Lovanienses,* 24 (1948), pp. 119-126.

———., *Origène.* Paris: La Table Ronde, 1948.

———., "Exégèse et dogme," part of "Sur l'exégèse biblique," by Claudel, Massignon, and Daniélou, *Dieu Vivant,* 14 (1949), pp. 90-94.

———., *Sacramentum Futuri.* Paris: Beauchesne, 1950.

———., "Qu'est-ce que la typologie?", *L'Ancien Testament et les Chrétiens.* Paris: Cerf, 1951, pp. 199-205.

———., "The Fathers and the Scriptures," *The Eastern Churches Quarterly,* 10 (1953), pp. 265-273.

de Ambroggi, D. P., "Il senso letterale pieno nelle Divine Scritture," *La Scuola Cattolica,* 60 (1932), pp. 296-312.

———., "I Sensi Biblici, Direttive e studi recenti," *La Scuola Cattolica,* 78 (1950), pp. 444-456.

———., "I Sensi Biblici, proposte per chiarire la terminologia," *La Scuola Cattolica,* 80 (1952), pp. 230-239.

Del Páramo, Severiano, S. J., *El Problema del Sentido Literal Pleno en la Sagrada Escritura.* Santander: Univ. of Comillas, 1954.

Delporte, Lucien, "Les principes de la typologie biblique et les éléments figuratifs du Sacrifice de l'Expiation," *Ephemerides Theologicae Lovanienses,* 3 (1926), pp. 307-327.

de Lubac, Henri, S. J., *Catholicism,* trans. by L. C. Sheppard. New York: Longmans, Green, 1950.

———., *Corpus Mysticum.* 2nd ed., Paris: Aubier, 1944.

———., "'Typologie' et 'Allégorisme'," *Recherches de Science Religieuse,* 34 (1947), pp. 180-226.

———., "Sur un vieux distique, la doctrine du quadruple sens," *Mélanges offerts au R. P. Ferdinand Cavallera.* Toulouse: l'Institut Catholique, 1948, pp. 347-366.

———., "Sens spirituel," *Recherches de Science Religieuse,* 36 (1949), pp. 542-576.

———., *Histoire et Esprit.* Paris: Aubier, 1950.

Dentan, Robert C., "Typology—Its Use and Abuse," *Anglican Theological Review,* 34 (1952), pp. 211-217.

de Riedmatten, Henri, O. P., "Typology in the Scriptures," trans. by K. Pond, *Blackfriars,* 33 (March, 1952), pp. 132-141.

De Vine, C. F., C. Ss. R., "The Consequent Sense," *Catholic Biblical Quarterly,* 2 (1940), pp. 145-155.

Devreesse, Robert, "La methode exégètique de Théodore de Mopsueste," *Revue Biblique,* 53 (1946), pp. 207-241.

———., *Essai sur Théodore de Mopsueste.* Biblioteca Apostolica Vaticana: 1948.

Dodd, C. H., *According to the Scriptures.* London: Nisbet, 1952.

Dubarle, A.-M., O. P., "Le sens spirituel de l'Écriture," *Revue des Sciences Philosophiques et Théologiques,* 31 (1947), pp. 41-72.

Dupont-Sommer, A., *The Dead Sea Scrolls,* trans. by E. M. Rowley. Oxford: Blackwell, 1952.

Enchiridion Biblicum. Rome: Arnodo, 1954, 2nd. ed.

Fernández, Andrea, S. J., "Hermeneutica," *Institutiones Biblicae.* 2nd ed. Rome: Pontifical Biblical Institute, 1927, pp. 306-307.

———., *Ibid.,* 6th ed. (1951), pp. 380-385.

———., "Sensus typicus, sensus plenior," *Biblica,* 33 (1952), pp. 526-528.

———., "Sentido plenior, literal, típico, espiritual," *Biblica,* 34 (1953), pp. 299-326.

———., "Nota referente a los sentidos de la S. Escritura," *Biblica,* 35 (1954), pp. 72-79.

Fischer, Balthasar, "Le Christ dans les Psaumes," *Maison-Dieu,* 27 (1951), pp. 86-109. A summary is given in *Theology Digest,* 1 (Winter, 1953), pp. 53-57.

Fuller, R. C., "The Interpretation of Holy Scripture," an article in *A Catholic Commentary on Holy Scripture.* London: Nelson, 1953.

Gelin, Albert, S. S., "Le problème de l'Ancien Testament," *Recherches et Débats,* 13 (February, 1951), pp. 3-13.

———., "Comment le peuple d'Israël lisait l'Ancien Testament," *L'Ancien Testament et les Chrétiens.* Paris: Cerf, 1951, pp. 117-131.

Grant, Robert M., *The Bible in the Church.* New York: Macmillan, 1948.

Gribomont, Jean, O. S. B., "Le lien des deux Testaments selon la théologie de S. Thomas," *Ephemerides Theologicae Lovanienses,* 22 (1946), pp. 70-89.

———., "Sens plénier, sens typique et sens littéral," *Problèmes et Méthode d'Exégèse Théologique*, by L. Cerfaux, J. Coppens, and J. Gribomont. Louvain: Desclée de Brouwer, 1950, pp. 21-31.

Guillet, Jacques, S. J., "Les exégèses d'Alexandrie et d'Antioche, conflit ou malentendu?", *Recherches de Science Religieuse*, 34 (1947), pp. 257-302.

Hamman, A., O. F. M., "Pourquoi faut-il lire l'Ancien Testament? ", *La Vie Spirituelle* (July, 1951), pp. 5-24.

Hartmann, Louis N., C. Ss. R., "St. Jerome as an Exegete," *A Monument to St. Jerome*, edit. by Francis X. Murphy, C. Ss. R. New York: Sheed & Ward, 1952, pp. 35-81.

Hebert, A. G., *The Throne of David*. London: Faber, 1941.

Höpfl, H. and Gut, B., O. S. B., *Introductio Generalis in Sacram Scripturam*. Roma: Arnodo, 1950, 5th ed.

Kehoe, Richard, O. P., "The Spiritual Sense of Scripture," *Blackfriars*, 27 (1946), pp. 246-251.

Kerrigan, Alexander, O. F. M., *St. Cyril of Alexander, Interpreter of the Old Testament*. Rome: P. B. I., 1952.

Lagrange, M. J., O. P., "L'interprétation de la Sainte Écriture par l'Église," *Revue Biblique*, 9 (1900), pp. 135-142.

Laistner, M. L. W., "Antiochene Exegesis in Western Europe during the Middle Ages," *The Harvard Theological Review*, 40 (1947), pp. 19-31.

Laridon, V., "Ecce Filius tuus, ecce mater tua," *Collationes Brugenses*, 46 (1950), pp. 177-182, 205-208.

Lattey, Cuthbert, "The Emmanuel Prophecy: Isaias 7:14," *Catholic Biblical Quarterly*, 8 (1946), pp. 369-376.

Leal, Juan, S. J., "El Sentido 'Plenior' de la Sagrada Escritura," *Razon y Fe*, 144 (1951), pp. 474-482.

Lecler, Joseph, "Littéralisme biblique et typologie au XVIe siècle," *Recherches de Science Religieuse*, 51 (1953), pp. 76-95.

Lewis, C. S., *The Allegory of Love*. Oxford: Univ. Press, 1936.

Mariès, L., "Extraits du Commentaire de Diodore de Tarse sur les Psaumes," *Recherches de Science Religieuse*, 9 (1919), pp. 79-101.

———., *Etudes préliminaires à l'édition de Diodore de Tarse sur les Psaumes*. Paris: 1933.

Marsh, H. G., "The Use of Μυστήριον in the Writings of Clement of Alexandria," *The Journal of Theological Studies*, 37 (1936), pp. 64-80.

McCasland, S. Vernon, "The Unity of the Scriptures," *Journal of Biblical Literature*, 73 (1954), pp. 1-10.

McKenzie, John L., S. J., "A Chapter in the History of Spiritual Exegesis: de Lubac's *Histoire et Esprit*," *Theological Studies*, 12 (1951), pp. 364-381.

Miller, Athanasius, O. S. B., "Zur Typologie des Alten Testaments," *Antonianum*, 25 (1950), pp. 425-434.

Mondésert, Claude, "Le symbolisme chez Clément d'Alexandrie," *Recherches de Science Religieuse*, 26 (1936), pp. 158-180.

———., *Clément d'Alexandrie.* Paris: Aubier, 1944.

Moriarty, Frederick L., S. J., "Bulletin of the Old Testament," *Theological Studies,* 12 (1951), pp. 320-342.

Muñoz Iglesias, Salvador, "El llamado sentido típico no es estrictamente sentido bíblico viejo-testamentario," *Estudios Bíblicos,* 12 (1953), pp. 159-183.

Murphy, Roland E., O. Carm., *A Study of Psalm 72 (71).* Washington: C. U. A. Dissertation, 1948.

Newman, John H., "Holy Scripture in its Relation to the Catholic Creed," *Discussions and Arguments.* London: Longmans, Green, 1911.

———., *The Arians of the Fourth Century.* London: Burns, Oates, 5th ed.

O'Flynn, John A., "The Senses of Scripture," *Irish Theological Quarterly,* 21 (1954), pp. 181-184.

———., "Newman and the Scriptures," *Irish Theological Quarterly,* 21 (1954), pp. 264-269.

Ogara, Florentinus, S. J., "De typica apud Chrysostomum prophetia," *Gregorianum,* 24 (1943), pp. 62-77.

Patrizi, Franciscus X., *Institutio de Interpretatione Bibliorum.* 2nd ed. Rome: 1876.

Penna, Angelo, *Principi e Carattere dell' Esegesi di S. Gerolamo.* Rome: P. B. I., 1950.

———., *La Lettera di Dio, presupposti di esegesi biblica.* Brescia: Morcelliana, 1952.

Perrella, Gaetano, C. M., "Sulla terminologia circa il senso mariologico dell' Apocalisse XII," *Divus Thomas* (Piacenza), 45 (1942), pp. 96-103.

———., "Il pensiero di S. Agostino e S. Tommaso circa il numero del senso letterale nella S. Scrittura," *Biblica,* 26 (1945), pp. 277-302.

Pesch, Christianus, S. J., *De Inspiratione Sacrae Scripturae.* Freiburg: Herder, 1925.

Pirot, L., "L'exégèse catholique," *Initiation Biblique.* Paris: Desclée, 1939. Edited by Robert and Tricot, pp. 324-335.

Pontet, Maurice, *L'Exégèse de S. Augustin Prédicateur.* Paris: Aubier, 1944.

Prat, Fernand, S. J., "Les historiens sacrés et leurs sources," *Études,* 86 (1901), pp. 474-500.

Renié, J., S. M., *Manuel d'Écriture Sainte.* Lyon: Vitte, 1935, 2nd ed., Vol. I.

Rivera, A., S. J., "'Inimicitias ponam . . .'—'Signum magnum aparuit' (Gen. 3, 15; Apc. 12, 1)," *Verbum Domini,* 21 (1941), pp. 183-189.

Rome and the Study of Scripture. St. Meinrad: Grail, 1946, 4th ed.

Russel, Ralph, O. S. B., "'Humani Generis' and the 'Spiritual' Sense of Scripture," *The Downside Review,* 1950-51, pp. 1-15.

Samain, Pierre, "Note sur le sens spirituel de l'Écriture," *Revue Diocésaine de Tournai,* 3 (1948), pp. 429-433.

** Schildenberger, Johannes, *Von Geheimnis des Gotteswortes.* Heidelberg: 1950.

Schoder, Raymond V., S. J., "The Rebirth of Scriptural Theology," *American Ecclesiastical Review,* 117 (1947), pp. 81-101.

Seisdedos, Francisco A., "La 'theoria' antioquena," *Estudios Bíblicos,* 11 (1952), pp. 31-67. A paper read in the Biblical Meeting (Spanish) of 1941.

Seynaeve, Jaak, W. F., *Cardinal Newman's Doctrine on Holy Scripture.* Louvain Dissertation: 1953, Series II, Tome 45.

Simon, H. and Prado, J., C. Ss. R., *Praelectiones Biblicae.* Turin: Marietti, 1938. Vol. I, "Propaedeutica," 3rd ed.

———., *Ibid.,* 6th ed. (1949).

Smalley, Beryl, *The Study of the Bible in the Middle Ages.* New York: Philosophical Library, 1952.

Spicq, C., O. P., *Esquisse d'une histoire de l'Exégèse Latine au Moyen Age.* Paris: Vrin, 1944.

———., "L'avènement de la théologie biblique," *Revue des Sciences Philosophiques et Théologiques,* 34 (1951), pp. 561-574.

———., *L'Épitre aux Hébreux.* 2 vols. Paris: Gabalda, 1952-53.

Steinmann, Jean, "Entretien de Pascal et du Père Richard Simon sur les sens de l'Écriture," *La Vie Intellectuelle* (March, 1949), pp. 239-253.

———., *Le prophète Isaïe.* Paris: Cerf, 1950.

Sutcliffe, Edmund F., S. J., "The Plenary Sense as a Principle of Interpretation," *Biblica,* 34 (1953), pp. 333-343.

Synave, P., "La doctrine de S. Thomas d'Aquin sur le sens littéral des Écritures," *Revue Biblique* (1926), pp. 40-65.

Ternant, P., "La θεωρία d'Antioche dans le cadre des sens de l'Écriture," *Biblica,* 34 (1953), pp. 135-158, 354-383, 456-486.

Tuya, Manuel de, O. P., "¿El sentido 'típico' es Sentido Bíblico?", *La Ciencia Tomista,* 78 (1951), pp. 571-574.

———., "Si es posible y en qué medida un *sensus plenior* a la luz del concepto teológico de inspiración," *La Ciencia Tomista,* 79 (1952), pp. 369-418.

———., "El sentido típico del Antiguo Testamento es 'verdadera y estrictamente' sentido de la Biblia," *La Ciencia Tomista,* 80 (1953), pp. 625-661.

Unger, Dominic J., *The First-Gospel, Genesis 3:15.* St. Bonaventure, New York: Franciscan Institute, 1954.

Vaccari, S., S. J., La θεωρία nella scuola esegetica di Antiochia," *Biblica,* 1 (1920), pp. 3-36.

Van der Ploeg, J., O. P., "L'exégèse de l'Ancien Testament dans l'Épître aux Hébreux," *Revue Biblique,* 54 (1947), pp. 187-228.

———., "The Place of Holy Scripture in the Theology of St. Thomas," *The Thomist,* 10 (1947), pp. 398-422.

Venard, L., "Utilisation de l'Ancien Testament dans le Nouveau," *Initia-*

tion Biblique. Paris: Desclée, 1939. Edited by Robert and Tricot, pp. 286-290.

———., " Citations de l'Ancien Testament dans le Nouveau Testament," *Supplément au Dictionaire de la Bible,* II, cols. 23-51.

La Vie Intellectuelle, "Autour de l'exégèse biblique, " (December, 1949), pp. 502-514.

Vincent, A., " L'exégèse moderne et contemporaine de l'Ancient Testament," *Initiation Biblique.* Paris: Desclée, 1939. Edited by Robert and Tricot, pp. 304-317.

** Vischer, W., *Das Christuszeugnis des Alten Testaments.* 1936-46.

Wright, G. Ernest, " Exegesis and Eisegesis in the Interpretation of the Scripture," *The Expository Times,* 48 (1936-37), pp. 353-357.

Zarb, S. M., O. P., " Utrum S. Thomas unitatem an vero pluralitatem sensus litteralis in Sacra Scriptura docuerit," *Divus Thomas* (Piacenza), (1930), pp. 337-359.

BOOK REVIEWS

Burghardt, Walter J., S. J., Reviews of de Lubac's introductions to *Homélies sur la Génèse* and *Homélies sur l'Exode* of Origen, " Sources Chrétiennes," *Theological Studies,* 9 (1948), pp. 262-266, 278-282.

Chadwick, H., Review of Daniélou's *Origène. The Journal of Theological Studies,* 50 (1949), pp. 219-221.

Congar, Yves, O. P., Review of Vischer's *L'Ancien Testament, témoin du Christ, La Vie Intellectuelle* (October, 1949), pp. 335-343.

Daniélou, Jean, S. J., Review of Coppens' *Les Harmonies des Deux Testaments, Dieu Vivant,* 16 (1950), pp. 149-153.

———., Review of Vischer's *L'Ancien Testament, témoin du Christ, Dieu Vivant,* 15 (1950), 139-141.

de Gandillac, Maurice, Review of Daniélou's *Origène, Dieu Vivant,* 14 (1949), pp. 145-149.

de Vaux, R., O. P., Review of Coppens' *Les Harmonies des Deux Testaments,* " Bulletin," *Revue Biblique,* 57 (1950), pp. 280-281.

———., " Bulletin," *Revue Biblique,* 58 (1951), p. 453.

Lampe, G. W. H., Review of Devreesse's *Essai sur Théodore de Mopsueste, The Journal of Theological Studies,* 50 (1949), pp. 224-227.

McKenzie, John, S. J., Review of Devreesse's *Essai sur Théodore de Mopsueste,* "A New Study of Theodore of Mopsuestia," *Theological Studies,* 10 (1949), pp. 394-408.

———., Review of Daniélou's *Origène, Theological Studies,* 10 (1949), pp. 446-448.

Moriarty, Frederick L., S. J., Review of Coppens' *Les Harmonies des Deux Testaments, Theological Studies,* 11 (1950), pp. 298-301.

Prümm, K., S. J., Review of Coppens' *Les Harmonies des Deux Testaments, Biblica,* 31 (1950), pp. 512-517.

Weisengoff, John P., Review of *Problèmes et Méthode d'Exégèse Théologique* by Cerfaux, Coppens, and Gribomont, *Catholic Biblical Quarterly,* 14 (January, 1952), pp. 83-85.